THREE ARK ROYALS
1938 – 1999

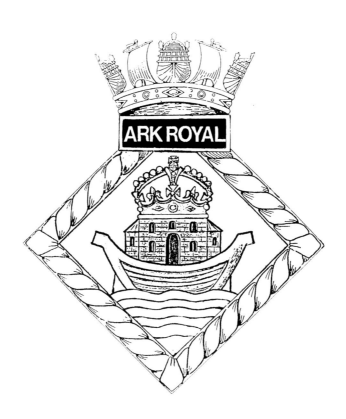

Neil McCart

FOREWORD BY
REAR-ADMIRAL T. W. LOUGHRAN CB

To All Those Who Have Served In HMS *Ark Royal*
between 1938 and 1998

Front Cover: A magnificent watercolour painting of HMS *Ark Royal* 1955-1979 by artist Brian Conroy, Greatham, Hampshire.

Back Cover: Watercolour paintings of the two *Ark Royals* 1938 and 1985 by artist Brian Conroy.

Cover Design by Louise McCart
© Neil McCart/FAN PUBLICATIONS 1999
ISBN: 1 901225 02 X

Typesetting By: Highlight Type Bureau Ltd,
Clifton House, 2 Clifton Villas,
Bradford, West Yorkshire BD8 7BY

Printing By: The Amadeus Press Ltd,
517 Leeds Road,Huddersfield,
West Yorkshire HD2 1YJ

Published By FAN PUBLICATIONS
17 Wymans Lane, Cheltenham, GL51 9QA, England. Fax & Tel 01242 580290

Contents

Foreword
by Rear-Admiral T. W. Loughran CB

Having served in the carriers *Centaur* and *Victorious*, both featured in earlier books in this series, it gives me a special pleasure to contribute to this further volume on the three most recent *Ark Royals*. Within these pages you will find details of the particular threads which have linked the three ships: the Silver Bell donated by the survivors of the 'Wartime' *Ark* which records the Battle Honours and the names of the commanding officers of all three ships; Her Majesty Queen Elizabeth The Queen Mother, who has proved to be an inspirational 'Lady Sponsor'; and the history of innovative aviation development from the angled deck of the 'Old' *Ark* to the STOVL ramp of the present ship.

The *Ark Royals* have rarely been out of the news, accounting perhaps for the extraordinary place this best known of all ships' names occupies in the hearts of the British public. In the relatively short life of the World War II ship, she was a symbol of defiance to the Axis powers who regularly made false claims of damage against her, along with premature reports of her sinking – 'Where is the *Ark Royal?*' was their propaganda cry. In answer, she was everywhere with her squadrons of Swordfish, Skua and later Fulmar aircraft, including memorable attacks on the *Scharnhorst* at Trondheim, the *Bismarck* in the Atlantic, and finally supporting the Malta convoys. It was here that she was ultimately lost to submarine attack.

The second ship, in which I flew, came equipped with the facilities to operate her new generation of high-performance jet aircraft, but she had different battles to fight. The post-war years led to the abandonment of the fixed-wing carrier programme with the possible demise of the embarked capability in the Fleet Air Arm. Those who operated the ship from the mid-60s until the end of 1978 were charged with keeping this expertise alive, not only from the organic Air Superiority and Power Projection aspect, but also to sustain the Royal Navy as a balanced maritime capability with the appropriate experience throughout the fleet. They did not fail us.

However, breathing new life into the fixed-wing Fleet Air Arm fell to other ships: HMS *Hermes*, earlier converted to a commando carrier, and to HMS *Invincible*, the first of the new 'through deck cruisers/ASW carriers'. The Falklands Campaign finally killed off any suggestion that these ships with their Sea Harriers were anything but the new (if novel) platforms to deliver the traditional carrier roles to the fleet. The three ships of the new class, *Invincible, Illustrious* and *Ark Royal* (public opinion had pressured the Ships Names Committee into continuing the *Ark* name), faced a lengthy campaign which was eventually to meet with success in ending the Cold War. The removal of the stalemate balance of terror, however, left a far less stable world to which these versatile ships with their unusual air groups have proved singularly well adapted. They have played their part in the UN enforcement of World Order, (for which the former Republic of Yugoslavia theatre has proved the most significant for the present *Ark*), while providing the evident capability to support the political and diplomatic efforts in the Gulf. Meanwhile STOVL has come of age in the shape of the Sea Harrier FA2.

At the time of writing, HMS *Ark Royal*, with her first ten years of operations behind her, prepares for the refit which will equip her for the 21st century. She will undoubtedly play her part in the transition to the new generation of bigger carriers, the value of which as platforms for Power Projection by all arms of the Services has now been recognized.

Terry Loughran CB

Rear-Admiral

Part One

HMS *Ark Royal*
1938-1941

Chapter One

Building and Launching

By 1935 Adolf Hitler had been Chancellor of Germany for two years, and in March that year Paul Joseph Goebbels, the Minister of Propaganda, announced the establishment of a German Military Air Force and the raising of a 36-division army totalling half a million men. Both were contrary to conditions laid down in the Treaty of Versailles, but all German governments since the early 1920s had been either surreptitiously or openly breaking conditions of the treaty and, apart from the French occupation of parts of the Ruhr in 1921 and 1923, there was little that the Allied powers were willing, or able, to do about it. 1935 was also the year in which the people of the Saar region voted overwhelmingly to be reunited with Germany, Italian troops invaded Ethiopia, and Stanley Baldwin succeeded Ramsay MacDonald as the Prime Minister of Great Britain. As far as the Royal Navy was concerned it was the year in which Admiral of the Fleet Lord Jellicoe, a naval hero of the Great War, died, and on 18 June an Anglo-German Naval Agreement was signed. It limited Germany's fleet to 35 per cent of Britain's surface fleet and to 45 per cent of its submarines. However, it deeply upset the French for, not only was it negotiated without any reference to Britain's wartime ally, but it was looked upon as signalling Britain's approval of violations of the Treaty of Versailles and, more importantly, Britain's approval of German rearmament. There is no doubt that Versailles was dead, but it was really an admission by the British Government that there was nothing the Allies could do to stop Germany rearming.

Another significant event for the Royal Navy in 1935 was the laying of the keel for the most important warship since the end of the Great War when, on Monday 16 September, at the Birkenhead shipyard of Cammell Laird & Co, 12-year-old Wendy Johnson, the daughter of the company's managing director, gave the signal which caused a shipyard crane to lower a large rectangular steel plate at the yard's main slipway. It was the first keel plate for Yard Number 1012, which was to become the Royal Navy's

The launch of the third *Ark Royal* at Birkenhead on Tuesday 13 April 1937. A good crowd of shipyard workers has gathered at the head of the slipway.
(C. H. G. Heath)

The *Ark Royal* in the River Mersey in May 1938 following her builder's trials. During the trials it was realized that smoke emissions would hamper flying operations and it was decided to heighten her funnel. In the background is the Liver Building and Princes Pier.
(A. Hernandez)

H.M.S. 'ARK ROYAL.'

third and, perhaps, most famous, *Ark Royal*.

The planning of this new aircraft carrier had started in 1931, when it was agreed that the new ship would have to be able to steam at speeds of between 27 and 30 knots, have an endurance to match that of the latest battleships and be capable of operating about 70 aircraft. It was even agreed that the vessel would have a substantial island superstructure, as it had been shown that such a structure was no impediment to flying operations as had been previously thought. It was also decided that the new ship would have two hangars to increase its aircraft carrying capacity and although this would give the carrier a higher freeboard, the flight deck could be kept drier in inclement weather. As well as its impressive height the new carrier's overall length of 800 feet included an enormous overhang aft which was intended to give the most favourable airflows for aircraft as they landed. Earlier aircraft carriers had only two aircraft lifts, one at either end of the flight deck, but this carrier would have three and it was expected that this arrangement would improve the speed and ease of handling aircraft. Both hangars were 60 feet wide with 16 feet of clear headroom. The upper hangar was 564 feet long while the lower hangar was 452 feet long and together they gave a combined deck space of 60,960 square feet, which was 7,790 square feet more than that in HMS *Courageous*. Her armament consisted of 16 single 4.7-inch guns in groups of two, two eight-barrel pom-poms fore and abaft the island and eight quadruple .5-inch machine-guns. She was to be a three-screw ship, powered by three sets of geared turbines which developed 102,000 SHP with steam provided by six Admiralty Three Drum boilers in three boiler rooms. The uptakes from the three boiler rooms were grouped into a single funnel which was in the vessel's island superstructure. Although the hangars themselves were not armoured, the ship was fitted with side armour which rose to the lower

hangar deck abreast the island and it was intended to protect the ship against 6-inch shellfire. The flight deck itself was armoured to give protection against 500lb bombs. As far as the accommodation was concerned all the Chiefs' and Petty Officers' messes had their own pantries, with hot and cold water laid on, electric hot cupboards for keeping meals warm, and even electric toasters. In the broadside mess decks the stools and benches were covered with sponge-rubber cushions, and the decks of all the living spaces were covered with a rubber composition for ease of cleaning and comfort. However, in the Royal Navy bunks were not yet available for ratings, who still slept in the traditional hammocks.

The launch date for the new aircraft carrier was set for Tuesday 13 April 1937 and, as always at Birkenhead, it was an event which brought the whole town to a standstill. The ceremony was to be performed by Lady Maude Hoare, the wife of the First Lord of the Admiralty, Sir Samuel Hoare. The immense possibilities of air power and communications were clearly foreseen by Hoare, but he is probably best remembered today for the ill-fated Hoare-Laval plan when Hoare, as Foreign Secretary, and French Prime Minister, Pierre Laval, agreed to a partition of Abyssinia in an attempt to appease Italy's Benito Mussolini. However, after the plan was leaked to the press the reaction was so violent that it led to Hoare's resignation, but in June 1936 he was taken back into Stanley Baldwin's government as First Lord of the Admiralty.

Sir Samuel and his wife travelled up to Liverpool from London on Monday 12 April 1937, and the following day they embarked on the Admiralty yacht *Enchantress* at Princes Landing Stage for what must have been a very stylish, but expensive, crossing of the Mersey to Birkenhead where the yacht berthed alongside the shipbuilder's yard. After passing through the firm's offices, where they were

A very smart new carrier off Southsea in January 1939.

(Fleet Air Arm Museum)

welcomed by the chairman of Cammell Laird & Co, they crossed the shipyard to inspect a guard of honour provided by HMS *Eaglet*. They then mounted a special platform which had been built for the launching ceremony. A short religious service was held and then at midday Lady Maude Hoare stepped forward to perform the ceremony. 'We have come here today,' she declared, 'to launch this great ship and to wish her Godspeed. No words of mine can be adequate to express our feelings of pride and thankfulness in the magnificent achievement. I name this ship *Ark Royal*. May God guide her and keep all who sail in her.' She then took a bottle of wine, which was suspended from a bollard high above, and flung it against the steel plates of the ship's stem. However, because the bottle had been covered in an anti-splinter material, it rebounded unbroken. After managing to retrieve the bottle, Lady Hoare had to make three more attempts before it finally smashed and the wine flowed down the bows of the ship. Then, slowly but surely, the *Ark Royal* began to move down the slipway, and to the cheers of the onlookers she entered the water and slowly swung upstream on the tide. Quickly the tugs drew in the cables which had been thrown out from the vessel and by the time the official visitors had assembled at the shipyard's moulding room for lunch the *Ark Royal* had been brought safely to her moorings in the fitting-out basin. At the luncheon the chairman of Cammell Laird proposed the toast of '*Ark Royal*' and he presented the vessel's sponsor with a diamond bracelet. Sir Samuel Hoare, after proposing

the toast of 'The Builders' and the '*Ark Royal*', told the guests that the vessel was the most up-to-date aircraft carrier in the world and that she was the first of several carriers which would be built to the same design, embodying significant improvements over previous vessels. However, it seems he envisaged the *Ark Royal's* future role in time of war as acting as an escort for vital food convoys, and it was apparent that the Admiralty did not fully appreciate the full potential of air power at sea.

On Saturday 30 April 1938, 12 months after her launching, the *Ark Royal* left her fitting-out basin at Birkenhead and was towed by tugs downriver to the Gladstone Dock on the Liverpool shore of the Mersey, where she went into dry dock. The sight of the new aircraft carrier in the river caused a great deal of interest, and sightseers crowded the river banks or viewed the new ship while crossing the river by ferry. As well as having her underwater hull scraped and repainted, the remaining two of her three propellers were fitted (the centre propeller having already been fitted before she was launched), and on Saturday 14 May she left the graving dock to put to sea for her builder's trials. At this stage it was thought that she would be handed over to the Admiralty and commissioned in July 1938, but during her trials off Arran it was realized that smoke emissions would seriously hamper flying operations and it was decided to raise the height of the funnel. It was also decided to fit stiffening plates to the after part of the hull in order to counteract what was

The *Ark Royal* entering Grand Harbour, Malta, on 19 January 1939. Her flight deck is manned by both RN and RAF personnel, and it can be seen that the paintwork forward has taken a battering from rough seas.

(*M. Cassar*)

thought to be excessive vibration, but despite this she made 31.7 knots over the Arran measured mile. Following her trials she returned to her fitting-out basin at Birkenhead where work on the modifications was started and her last items of equipment were fitted.

It was in November 1938 that the great bulk of her ship's company joined and Ron Skinner, who arrived on board on Saturday 12 November, having travelled up by train from Portsmouth Dockyard, remembers going into the upper hangar to find it full of parked cars which belonged to the officers who had been standing by the ship at Liverpool. They had been loaded on board for the passage to Portsmouth. Ron recalls that soon after he joined, the ship sailed for several days of trials which were successfully completed and finally, with the ship at anchor in Liverpool Bay eight miles from the Mersey Bar Light Vessel, she was accepted from the builders by her new commanding officer, Captain A. J. Power MVO RN, at 5.16pm on Wednesday 16 November 1938. She was also commissioned into the Royal Navy and the White Ensign replaced the Red Ensign at her masthead. Just over an hour later, at 6.25pm, she weighed anchor and steamed a few miles inshore before anchoring three miles from the Mersey Bar Light Vessel, which was now shrouded in fog. At just after 10pm that evening the tugs *Maycock* and *Flying Breeze* berthed alongside to disembark the Admiralty trials party and the remaining workmen from Cammell Laird & Co. After spending the night at anchor in Liverpool Bay, at 7am on Thursday 17 November the *Ark Royal* weighed anchor and set course down the Irish Sea for the Channel and then Portsmouth.

At 4.20am on Friday 18 November she passed the Eddystone Light, at 1.27pm she was off the Needles and two and a half hours later she anchored at Spithead for the first time. Next morning, at 9.25am, she weighed anchor and steamed up harbour to secure starboard side alongside Middle Slip Jetty at 10.22am. The Navy's latest aircraft carrier was ready to start her operational service.

The *Ark Royal* had joined the fleet less than two months after the Munich Agreement and at that time the settlement and dismembering of Czechoslovakia was not yet the symbol of capitulation which it would eventually become, and there was a great deal of hope that the agreement really would mean 'peace for our time'. This then was the atmosphere of optimism on board the *Ark Royal* when, on Tuesday 22 November 1938, she hoisted the flag of Rear-Admiral G. C. Royle, the Rear-Admiral commanding aircraft carriers, and took the place of HMS *Courageous* as the flagship. Four days later she went into dry dock where she remained until mid-December. During that time she was visited by the C-in-C Home Fleet, Admiral Sir Charles Forbes, and by her sponsor, Lady Maude Hoare, who visited the ship on Friday 9 December. On Wednesday 14 December the carrier was moved out of

D Lock to Pitch House Jetty, and while she was there the south coast was hit by heavy snowstorms which meant that the ship's company had the task of clearing the flight deck of snow. With most of the ship's company on leave it was a quiet Christmas alongside in Portsmouth Dockyard, and on Friday 30 December 94 ratings joined the ship from the naval barracks to make up the full complement. On New Year's Day 1939 the first christenings took place in the ship's chapel when Margaret Walley and Richard Cobbet were baptized, and over the next nine days the personnel of 800, 810, 814, 820 and 821 Skua and Swordfish Squadrons joined the ship. The *Ark Royal* slipped her berth in Portsmouth Harbour at 3.10pm on Tuesday 10 January 1939, to anchor out at Spithead for the remainder of the day and overnight, and at 7.43am the next morning she left to steam round the Isle of Wight where, south of St Catherine's Point, she safely landed on the aircraft of all five squadrons. On Thursday 12 January, in company with the destroyer *Wren*, she carried out flying exercises in the Channel, during which she used her hydraulic accelerators for the first time, before setting course for Gibraltar and the warmer waters of the Mediterranean to complete her work-up. During the passage the *Ark Royal* was forced to stop when contaminated feed water was found in one of her boilers, but she was soon under way again and on the morning of Monday 16 January she anchored in Gibraltar Bay. Later that morning she weighed anchor and set course for Malta, again in company with the *Wren*. Next day, Tuesday 17 January, she suffered her first flying accident at 2.21pm when a Swordfish crashed on landing after its undercarriage collapsed. Four men who were on the flight deck were injured, but the aircrew were unharmed. During the afternoon of Thursday 19 January the carrier arrived in Malta's Grand Harbour, where she remained moored in Bighi Bay for four days.

The *Ark Royal's* work-up began in earnest on Monday 23 January when, with the ever-faithful HMS *Wren*, she slipped her moorings in Grand Harbour and set course for Alexandria. During the passage the weather was too rough to allow flying, but at just after 6am on Thursday 26 January she rendezvoused with the *Glorious* off Alexandria and the two carriers spent the day operating their aircraft before anchoring in Aboukir Bay that afternoon. Next day the *Ark Royal* weighed anchor and steamed into Alexandria's Outer Harbour, where the ship's company were introduced to the dubious delights of the Egyptian city. On the morning of Monday 30 January the *Ark Royal* and *Glorious* sailed from Alexandria to carry out flying exercises off the coast, but that night, at just before midnight, two aircraft from the *Glorious* were lost, and the *Ark Royal*, which was about 15 miles away, steamed to the scene to assist with the search for the missing aircrew. Both ships combed the area until well after daylight on 31 January, but sadly the body of only one officer, Lt

The first flying accident when a Swordfish's undercarriage collapsed on landing, but fortunately the crew clambered out unhurt.

(F. George)

Another view of the *Ark Royal* as she moors in Bighi Bay, Grand Harbour, for her first visit. *(F. George)*

11

A very smart *Ark Royal* at Alexandria in early 1939, during the last months of peace.

(Fleet Air Arm Museum)

During the afternoon of Friday 24 March 1939 the *Ark Royal* returned to Portsmouth from the Mediterranean. Here she passes the Round Tower at Old Portsmouth. *(Maritime Photo Library)*

Newcombe, was recovered by the *Glorious*. At 9.20am Vice-Admiral Royle transferred to the *Glorious* for the funeral of Lt Newcombe, and at just before midnight both carriers anchored off Alexandria. The first two weeks of February were spent carrying out flying exercises off the Egyptian coast, with weekends spent in Alexandria Harbour. On one of these breaks 80 members of the ship's company took the opportunity to make a 48-hour excursion to Cairo and the Pyramids, before both aircraft carriers finally departed on the morning of Thursday 16 February and set course for Valletta. After further exercises off Malta, and a four-day stopover in Grand Harbour, on the morning of Thursday 23 February both *Ark Royal* and *Glorious*, together with HMS *Wren*, left Malta to steam west once again for Gibraltar. The end of February 1939 saw both carriers taking part in combined fleet exercises in the Atlantic Ocean off the coast of Morocco, in company with the battleships *Nelson, Ramillies* and *Warspite*. This was followed by a three-day break alongside at Gibraltar,

but on the morning of Monday 6 March the *Ark Royal* sailed once again for 'Exercise 2Q' with the battleship *Barham*, the cruiser *Shropshire*, the *Glorious* and the submarine HMS *Clyde*. Four days later the *Ark Royal* was back alongside 43 berth of Gibraltar's main wharf where, over the following three days, Vice-Admiral Royle carried out an inspection of the whole ship. He was obviously very satisfied with his flagship for after a few days of relaxation the carrier sailed on the afternoon of Friday 17 March to return to home waters.

On the morning of Saturday 18 March 1939, 'Flying Stations' was piped at 8.55am and flying operations carried on all through the morning until noon when they were stood down. During the next 40 minutes the aircraft were struck down into the hangars where refuelling and maintenance was being carried out. Suddenly, at 12.39pm, the fire alarms sounded as fire broke out in the upper hangar and quickly swept through the Swordfish aircraft. The ship went to General Fire Stations and Captain Power turned the *Ark Royal* into the wind and brought her to a stop. By 1pm the fire was under control and an hour later the ship was able to get under way again. At the time of the accident the carrier had been steaming north-west in a position Lat 38° - 34' N/Long 09° - 36'W, off the coast of Portugal south of Lisbon, and it appears that an electrical fault in an aircraft radio had ignited aviation fuel, with the end result that eight Swordfish aircraft were destroyed or damaged beyond repair. The rest of the day was spent cleaning up and jettisoning the burnt-out and damaged aircraft as the *Ark Royal* continued to steam north. Fortunately, what could easily have turned out to be a disaster was averted by the fast and efficient action of the carrier's fire parties. In the early hours of Tuesday 21 March the *Ark Royal* rendezvoused with the battleship *Nelson* and the battlecruiser *Repulse* to take part in 'Exercise KC', which involved trade protection in the Western Approaches. The exercise was concluded during the afternoon of 23 March and after flying all serviceable aircraft off to RAF Eastleigh and to Worthy Down, *Ark Royal* steamed into Portsmouth Harbour to secure alongside South Railway Jetty at 2.50pm. The first phase of her work-up had been completed.

During the five weeks spent alongside in Portsmouth leave was taken and repairs to the fire damaged upper hangar were carried out. By the end of March 1939, with Germany having occupied the dismembered parts of what had been Czechoslovakia, the euphoria over Munich had given way to grim realization that the threat of war was drawing ever closer. On 25 March, for the first time, Adolf Hitler talked of the 'Polish problem' which, he said, might have to be settled by military means. Germany's quarrel with Poland was essentially about the city of Danzig which, prior to the Treaty of Versailles, had been part of Germany and since the population of the city were German they desperately wanted to be reunited with that country. However, far from contemplating another Munich Britain was, for the first time in her history, forging a political and military alliance with an east European country - Poland - on account of, it could be said, 'a quarrel in a faraway country between people of whom we know nothing.' On 31 March 1939 Britain and France offered total and unqualified support to Poland, 'in the event of any action which clearly threatens Polish independence, and which the Polish Government accordingly considers it vital to resist with their national forces.' Not only were Britain and France unable, either militarily or geographically, to give any effective aid if Poland were to be attacked by either Germany or Russia (in the event it was by both), but the Poles themselves, unlike the Czechs in 1938, had not even developed their army very efficiently. Even more dangerously, it gave Adolf Hitler a real impetus to reach an agreement with the Soviet Union. However, the new alliance was a political fact and while he was in Britain,

Colonel Joseph Beck, the Polish Foreign Minister, visited the *Ark Royal* at Portsmouth. During his stay British Government officials were hoping to persuade him to compromise over Danzig, but whatever his thoughts were as he toured the aircraft carrier he would have known that with their guarantee to Poland, and by their dealings with Czechoslovakia just six months previously, Britain and France were committed to resistance, and in circumstances far less favourable than those prevailing in October 1938.

It was at 9.45am on Saturday 29 April 1939 that the *Ark Royal* left Portsmouth Harbour for the Channel, to embark the Skua and Swordfish aircraft of 803, 810, 820 and 821 Squadrons for deck landing practice, and during the whole of May she operated out of Portland for the second phase of her work-up. At 5.32pm on Tuesday 2 May, while flying off the Swordfish of 821 Squadron in Lyme Bay, one of the aircraft crashed into the sea on take-off, but fortunately the three crew members were rescued safely by the destroyer HMS *Boreas*, which was carrying out planeguard duties. On Saturday 6 May, the *Ark Royal* left Portland Harbour early and soon afterwards the Fifth Sea Lord landed on board by Swordfish. The ships of the Home Fleet then rehearsed a steam past and royal escort for an event which was to take place later that afternoon. Earlier in the year, in an attempt to cement relations with the USA and in particular to help President Roosevelt to revise his country's Neutrality Act, it had been arranged that King George VI and Queen Elizabeth would make a state visit to Canada and the USA, and to carry them and their party of 69 from Portsmouth to Quebec the Government had chartered the Canadian Pacific Line's transatlantic liner *Empress of Australia*. Ironically the 22,000-ton liner had started her life in December 1913 as the Hamburg Amerika Line's passenger ship, *Tirpitz*, but in 1919, as a result of the Treaty of Versailles, she had been handed over to the British Government and was then purchased by the Canadian Pacific Line who renamed her *Empress of Australia*. Escorted by the battlecruiser *Repulse* and the cruisers *Southampton* and *Glasgow*, the *Empress of Australia* left the Solent during the afternoon of Saturday 6 May and by 5.15pm she was off Weymouth and within sight of the Home Fleet. The *Ark Royal* fired a 21-gun salute, the ship's company cheered ship and a few minutes later the Skua and Swordfish aircraft from the carrier's squadrons executed a fly-past over the liner as she steamed westward. By 8.30pm all the aircraft had landed safely back on the *Ark Royal,* while the carrier, together with other vessels of the Home Fleet, continued to escort the liner until dusk when they handed over the duty to the *Repulse* and the two cruisers, and the *Ark Royal* returned to Portland.

On Wednesday 10 May the carrier, together with HMS *Boreas*, made another early start for Lyme Bay where she again carried out flying exercises. That afternoon a Swordfish crashed on deck while landing and was destroyed by the resulting fire. Fortunately, however, there were no casualties and the burnt-out airframe was ditched in Lyme Bay. During the weekend of Saturday and Sunday 20/21 May the *Ark* was opened to visitors in Portland Harbour and she proved to be a very popular attraction. After the weekend she once again made daily forays from Portland to carry out flying exercises in the local areas of Weymouth and Lyme Bays. During this period she operated with the battleships *Rodney*, *Royal Sovereign* and *Royal Oak*, and on Tuesday 30 May she embarked the First Lord of the Admiralty, the Earl of Stanhope, and the C-in-C Home Fleet, Admiral Sir Charles Forbes, who were given a four-hour flying display by the Swordfish and the Skuas. The end of May 1939 saw the *Ark Royal* moored to B1 buoy in Portland Harbour, after completing her flying operations with HMS *Boreas*. On the political scene the Soviet Government had made it clear that its foreign policy was not rigid and that it was not committed to an alliance with Britain and France, which gave fresh encouragement to Germany.

On Friday 2 June the *Ark Royal* left Portland at just after 6am and after flying off her aircraft to their respective airfields, she embarked the pilot off the Nab Tower at 12.45pm and just under an hour later she was secured alongside South Railway Jetty in Portsmouth Harbour for a short maintenance period. At 10.45am on Wednesday 7 June 1939, the lower deck was cleared and all hands were mustered on the flight deck for a memorial service for the 99 men who had been lost in the tragedy of the submarine HMS *Thetis*, which had sunk during her builder's trials in Liverpool Bay six days earlier. In the full glare of the world's press, with the stern of the boat visible above the water, frustratingly unsuccessful rescue attempts had been made to recover her ship's company and the trials party, before they suffocated and died. Memorial services for the men were held throughout the ships of the Home Fleet. It was at 5pm on Thursday 8 June that the *Ark Royal* put to sea once again and, after anchoring in Sandown Bay for the night, she started her accelerator trials in the vicinity of the Nab Tower. These commenced with the launch of an unmanned, damaged aircraft and they continued for two days before the carrier returned to South Railway Jetty for a break of five days before the final day of trials which took place on Thursday 15 June. After anchoring at Spithead that evening, she then carried out flying exercises in the Channel before joining HMS *Repulse* and units of the 2nd Battle Squadron at anchor in Weymouth Bay. On the morning of Thursday 22 June the ships weighed anchor and steamed along the coast to Torbay where they anchored for a four-day visit to Torquay, during which the Mayor of the town visited the *Ark Royal* and the aircraft carrier was opened to the public. It was to be the ship's last ceremonial peacetime visit because in Europe political events were continuing to deteriorate as the continent drifted towards its second catastrophic war of the 20th century.

The *Ark Royal* alongside South Railway Jetty, Portsmouth, in March 1939. Semaphore Tower and the masts and rigging of HMS *Victory* can be seen in the background. *(Maritime Photo Library)*

Chapter Two

War And The *Admiral Graf Spee*

Following her visit to Torquay with the 2nd Battle Squadron, the *Ark Royal* remained in the area carrying out flying exercises until the morning of Wednesday 28 June 1939, when she left her Torbay anchorage and set course for Portsmouth. During the afternoon her aircraft flew off to their bases and at 12.30pm the following day she secured alongside Pitch House Jetty. Eleven days later the carrier moved into D Lock dry dock for routine maintenance, remaining there for 14 days before shifting to South Railway Jetty on 25 July. Later that same day Vice-Admiral Royle lowered his flag and left the ship, his place being taken by Vice-Admiral L. V. Wells who hoisted his flag in the *Ark Royal* on the following day. Although Admiral Wells had entered the Royal Navy in 1901, before manned flight had become a reality, he had commanded the aircraft carrier HMS *Eagle* from 1933 to 1935. He was, in fact, one of the few Flag Officers with any real experience of naval aviation.

At 11.30am on Saturday 29 July 1939 the *Ark Royal* slipped her moorings and left Portsmouth to embark the Skuas of 800 and 803 Squadrons and the Swordfish of 810, 818 and 821 Squadrons, before anchoring in Sandown Bay for the night. Next day, at just after 11am, she weighed anchor and steamed east up Channel for the North Sea. That evening, at just after 10pm, she was off Dungeness as she entered the Strait of Dover, and on the last day of July she was operating her aircraft in the North Sea, off the coast of North Yorkshire. During the morning of Tuesday 1 August, when she was off the Firth of Forth, one of her Swordfish crashed into the sea after suffering an engine failure, but fortunately the aircrew were rescued safely by HMS *Boreas*. That same afternoon the carrier anchored at Rosyth, below the Forth Bridge, and next morning she put to sea for flying exercises in the area. That afternoon, at just after 2pm, Skua L2932 crashed on take-off and caught fire which caused it to sink rapidly. Despite a thorough search of the area there was no trace of its aircrew, and Sub-Lt C. E. Watts RN and Ldg Airman W. H. Norman became the first fatalities in an aviation accident from the carrier. That evening the *Ark Royal* anchored off Rosyth and next day she put to sea for exercises with the Swordfish of 821 Squadron, before anchoring in Kirkcaldy Bay for the night. On Friday 4 August she was at sea once again and at 1.30pm the ship was stopped close to the scene of the accident two days earlier, and a memorial service was held for the lost aircrew. That evening, at just before 7pm, she secured to

A1 buoy at Rosyth, for a Bank Holiday weekend break. On Sunday 6 August, Ceremonial Divisions were held on the flight deck, with Admiral Wells inspecting the ship's company. On the holiday Monday the ship was opened to visitors for just over four hours, but on Tuesday 8 August the *Ark Royal* put to sea once more with the destroyers *Foxhound* and *Fearless* to carry out flying exercises, and they remained in the Rosyth area for three days before setting course for Scapa Flow on Friday 11 August. That evening, at just before 10pm, they were off Girdle Ness and the city of Aberdeen and at 9.30am on Saturday 12 August the *Ark Royal* arrived at the famous wartime anchorage to join Admiral Forbes who was flying his flag in the battleship *Nelson*, her sister ship *Rodney*, the battleships *Royal Oak* and *Royal Sovereign* and the battlecruisers *Hood* and *Repulse*. Three days later the whole fleet sailed for 'Exercise K', with the *Ark Royal* providing the air strike force for the fleet. Although the Home Fleet returned to Scapa Flow on 18 August, for the *Ark Royal* it was just long enough to refuel before she put to sea once again with the battleships *Nelson* and *Rodney*. This time 'Exercise KD' as it was code-named, took the carrier north into the Norwegian Sea, to the area off the coast at Trondheim. During the exercise the *Ark Royal* flew continuous anti-submarine and fighter patrols, although during the afternoon of Sunday 20 August the ship stopped for 15 minutes whilst fire parties on board successfully extinguished a fire in the lower hangar. Next day the *Ark Royal* moored at Invergordon and the aircraft of 803 and 820 Squadrons were catapulted off to nearby Evanton for night-flying exercises. Leave was granted to the rest of the ship's company, but three days later, at 12.45pm on Thursday 24 August, it was all brought to an abrupt end when a signal was received ordering the *Ark Royal* and the two battleships to raise steam immediately and to 'proceed with all dispatch' for their war station at Scapa Flow. That afternoon the two squadrons returned from Evanton and now that all leave was cancelled, patrols were out scouring the streets of Invergordon for any liberty men who were already ashore. It was 5pm before the *Ark Royal* and the other units were able to proceed to sea, and as they steamed north 'Action Stations' was exercised, this time with the grim sense of reality behind it.

On 23 August 1939, in a move which electrified the world, Russia and Germany signed a non-aggression pact, which left the way open for a German invasion of Poland without the threat of a possible war on two fronts. Secretly

An obsolete Hawker Osprey flies over the *Ark's* flight deck. *(Fleet Air Arm Museum)*

armies on the Polish frontier and, in turn, Poland started calling up its military reservists. On Friday 25 August, as the *Ark Royal* and units of the Home Fleet arrived back at Scapa Flow, Britain and Poland signed a formal alliance which was an unambiguous declaration of Britain's intention to fight if Poland were invaded. However, by implication all the assurances were related to an invasion by Germany, and there was nothing mentioned about action if Russia invaded Poland. Even so, it was also clear that the British Government still hoped for a compromise over Danzig, as a memorandum from the Foreign Office drafted proposals which would give the citizens of Danzig the right to determine their own political allegiance which, in effect, meant handing the city to Germany. However, it was all too late, for not only was the Polish Government refusing to negotiate, but Hitler had set 25 August as the date for the German invasion of Poland. Although he hesitated for a few days, the offensive finally began in the early hours of Friday 1 September 1939 when 52 German Divisions, totalling 1,500,000 men, slammed into Poland from Silesia, East Prussia and Slovakia, against a Polish Army just a third of its size.

Meanwhile, the *Ark Royal*, together with Admiral Forbes in HMS *Nelson* and other heavy units of the battle fleet, had left Scapa Flow and steamed into the Norwegian Sea between Iceland and the Shetlands. On Friday 1 September one of the carrier's Swordfish was on a reconnaissance flight over the Norwegian coast in poor visibility when it had to make a forced landing in a Norwegian fjord. As the crew paddled ashore in their dinghy they were somewhat downcast at the thought of being interned in Norway, but fortunately they landed close to an air base and the Norwegians managed to get them on a ship to England, where they arrived just a few hours before war was declared. The *Ark Royal* was in the same area on Sunday 3 September, in a position Lat 58° - 17'N/Long 19° - 09'W, when war was declared against Germany. At shortly after 11am, Lt Charles Coke RN (later CO HMS *Victorious*), the Flag Lieutenant, received a

Russia and Germany had agreed to carve up Poland, with Russia getting the eastern part of the country, which prior to 1914 had formed part of the Russian Empire, while Germany would recover East Prussia which had been taken away by the Treaty of Versailles. That same day Hitler made it clear to Chamberlain that Germany was fully prepared to go to war with Britain if attacked by her. Next day President Roosevelt cabled Hitler personally, appealing to him to avoid war and to resolve Germany's differences with Poland by negotiation. France also urged Poland to refrain from military action if Danzig declared itself under German rule. It was all to no avail as Germany massed her

Swordfish ranged on the *Ark's* flight deck during flying operations.   *(C. L. Asher)*

Blackburn Skuas flying off to search for the German pocket battleship *Admiral Graf Spee* in the Atlantic Ocean. The weather is obviously hot and many members of the ship's company are wearing old-fashioned pith helmets to protect them from the sun. The battlecruiser *Renown* and another escort ship are in the background.   *(F. George)*

The 9,521-ton German liner *Watussi* scuttles herself after being caught off the Cape of Good Hope during the search for the *Admiral Graf Spee*.   *(F. George)*

very short signal marked 'Urgent Priority', which he took to Admiral Wells. It read: 'General from C-in-C Home Fleet Total Germany'. Soon afterwards Captain Power announced over the ship's tannoy, 'I have just received the signal to commence hostilities against Germany.' The news came as no surprise to anyone and flying continued while the *Ark Royal* and the battlefleet continued their patrol. On the morning of Wednesday 6 September the *Ark Royal* anchored in Scapa Flow to refuel, but within 24 hours she was at sea again in company with the battlefleet for a patrol lasting for three days before she returned to Scapa for refuelling. Once again, within 24 hours she was at sea again, this time with a destroyer screen which included HM Ships *Eskimo*, *Faulknor*, *Firedrake* and *Foxhound*. On the morning of Thursday 14 September she received a signal that the SS *Fanad Head*, a 5,000-ton cargo ship, had been stopped and boarded by a U-boat in a position Lat 56° - 43'N/Long 15° - 21'W, which was some 200 miles south-west of the *Ark Royal's* position. The carrier immediately set course for the scene of the incident which was, in fact, being carried out by OLt O. H. Lemp in *U30*, which had sunk the *Athenia* just a few hours after the outbreak of war. Lemp's boarding party had just left the *Fanad Head* and the submarine was trying to sink the merchantman by gunfire, whilst the crew looked on from the ship's boats, when they were surprised by three Skuas from the *Ark Royal*. The U-boat rapidly torpedoed the cargo ship before diving, and as it disappeared beneath the waves, the Skuas came in too low and two of them were seriously damaged by the blast from their own bombs and were forced to land in the sea nearby. The third Skua remained in the vicinity and shortly afterwards *U30* surfaced, whereupon the aircrew attacked the submarine with machine-guns, forcing it to dive once again. Then, with his fuel running low, the Skua was forced to return to the *Ark Royal* which, meanwhile, had launched six Swordfish to continue the action. However, in the interval before their arrival Lemp had surfaced once again and taken prisoner the surviving aircrews from the two Skuas before submerging to fire another torpedo into the *Fanad Head*. It was at this moment that the Swordfish arrived on the scene and immediately dropped their bombs on *U30*, whose outline could be seen beneath the surface, but although the explosions were very close to the submarine, she suffered only superficial damage to her bows and torpedo tubes. In the event Lemp was able to call at Reykjavik to land an injured crew member, after which he returned to Germany with the crews of the two Skuas, who were the first Royal Naval personnel to be taken as prisoners of war in the Second World War. As for the *Fanad Head*, her back was broken and she soon sank.

Meanwhile, at 2.40pm, as the *Ark Royal* steamed towards the scene, KLt G. Glattes commanding *U39* found himself in the track of the carrier and her escorts and he was able to manoeuvre into a position within 900 yards of her and fire a salvo of torpedoes. The carrier had just flown off a number of Skuas, and it was just as she was resuming her course that Ldg Signalman J. E. Hall, who was on watch on the bridge, raised the alarm and reported a torpedo approaching the ship on the port bow. Fortunately, Lt Rudd, the Officer of the Watch, reacted swiftly by immediately putting the helm over to turn bows on in order to present the smallest target. In the event two torpedoes passed harmlessly by the port side, with one of them exploding in the carrier's wake. At the same time the four escorting destroyers moved in to attack and, whilst the *Ark Royal* steamed out of danger, they quickly established asdic contact with the U-boat and blew her to the surface with well-placed depth charges. As she broke the surface they opened fire, but ceased when they saw that the crew were abandoning the vessel. In the event all her crew of 43 officers and men were taken prisoner by HMS *Faulknor*. The *U39* was the first submarine to be sunk during the Second World War and it was an excellent example of the potency of asdic-fitted destroyers working together as a team.

The *Ark Royal* spent two more days at sea before anchoring in Loch Ewe at 7.30am on Sunday 17 September, and two and a half hours later the new First Lord of the Admiralty, Mr Winston Churchill, went aboard to pay a brief visit to the carrier. Naturally, he was very interested in hearing about the activities of 14 September, and before he left he signed the wardroom visitors' book. That same afternoon, after having refuelled, the *Ark Royal* and her destroyer screen left Loch Ewe to carry out a further patrol, but next day came news of the sinking of the aircraft carrier *Courageous* while carrying out an anti-submarine patrol in the South-West Approaches, with the loss of 518 men, including her commanding officer. This tragedy, together with the close escape which the *Ark Royal* had had herself just four days previously, led to her recall back to Loch Ewe where she remained for 48 hours, with recreational leave being granted. It was at 7.20pm on Wednesday 20 September that the *Ark Royal* left Loch Ewe and returned to Scapa Flow, where she arrived the following morning. Meanwhile, in the North Sea the submarine HMS *Spearfish* was on patrol in the Heligoland Bight as part of the Admiralty's intelligence-gathering operations, to watch the movements of the German heavy units in the German naval base at Wilhelmshaven. On 24 September, after the War Cabinet in London had lifted the rules against sinking merchant ships without warning, the submarine HMS *Sunfish* sank a large German freighter, and HMS *Trident* sank an 8,000-ton oil tanker. However, that evening the submarine HMS *Spearfish* came under attack herself and although she was not destroyed, she was seriously damaged, being unable to dive again after surfacing. Next morning, on receiving her distress signals, units of the Home Fleet, including the battleships *Rodney* and *Nelson*, the battlecruisers *Hood* and *Repulse*, the *Ark Royal* and a destroyer screen, left Scapa Flow to escort the damaged submarine on her voyage home. On the following day, when the fleet was in a position Lat 57° - 36'N/Long 02° - 53'E, about 180 miles east of Aberdeen, the *Ark Royal* was on station astern of the *Rodney* when she was attacked by a Dornier 18 flying boat. At 11am two of the carrier's Swordfish had reported three of the Dorniers shadowing the fleet, about ten miles to the south-east. The ships immediately went to 'Action Stations' and nine Skuas were launched from the *Ark Royal*. Because the flying boats kept low in the air they were very difficult to detect, and when they were spotted two managed to escape. The third Dornier was attacked and brought down by Lt B. S. McEwen and PO B. M. Seymour, with its crew being rescued by the destroyer HMS *Somali*. The crew of the Skua had the distinction of being the first to destroy a German aircraft during the Second World War. Unfortunately, the shadowers had reported the fleet's position and at 2.19pm that afternoon five twin-engined Heinkel IIIs, which had approached under the cover of clouds, attacked the British force. Under fierce anti-aircraft fire four of them jettisoned their bombs and made off, but the fifth aircraft dived at the *Ark Royal* and released his 2,000lb bomb before roaring away in a climbing turn. One officer on the carrier's bridge described the missile as looking like an Austin Seven motor car, and as Captain Power ordered the helm hard over to starboard and the *Ark Royal* was turning, the bomb exploded in the sea, just 30 yards from the port bow. The massive explosion caused a wall of water to rise as high as the flight deck, and then it cascaded over the forward end and lifted the ship's bow out of the water. The vessel took a 5° list to starboard, righted herself within moments, and then turned back on her course. The only damage caused was to some crockery in the wardroom pantry. The Heinkel, which was flown by Lt A. Francke, then flew back over the carrier's flight deck and sprayed the ship with machine-gun bullets, before breaking off the action in the face of a fierce barrage of anti-aircraft fire. With smoke from the anti-aircraft guns and the soot and smoke belching from the carrier's funnel, together with the explosion itself, it is no wonder that Lt Francke thought he had hit the *Ark Royal* and he reported his attack on the carrier and his belief that his bomb had hit the ship. He did not, however, claim to have sunk the *Ark Royal*, but at 5.30pm the next day, Wednesday 27 September, which was 16 hours after the aircraft carrier had anchored safely at Scapa Flow, Hamburg Radio broadcast an important communication to its listeners. It went: 'Where is the *Ark Royal*? She was hit in a German attack on September 26 at 3pm. Where is the *Ark Royal*? Britons ask your Admiralty.' The notorious William Joyce - 'Lord Haw Haw' - took up the theme in his radio broadcasts, and on 11 October the newspaper *Völkischer Beobachter* published a lurid drawing

of an aircraft carrier being torn apart by a huge explosion under the headline, 'Schwerpunkt des Angriffs: Der Flugzeugträger' (Point of Main Effort in the Attack – The Aircraft Carrier). It was the start of a propaganda campaign which made the *Ark Royal* a household name the world over. On Sunday 1 October, in an attempt to quash the enemy account, the US Naval Attaché visited the *Ark Royal* at Scapa Flow, but despite his report which was made public, rumour about the carrier's demise continued. However, for the time being the *Ark Royal* was safe and destined for much warmer waters than those in Scapa Flow and the North Sea.

Almost as soon as the American visitor had left the ship the *Ark Royal* left Scapa Flow and steamed south to Loch Ewe where she anchored the following morning, and in the evening, together with the battlecruiser *Renown* and a destroyer screen which included HM Ships *Hardy*, *Hasty*, *Hereward* and *Hostile*, she sailed once again, bound for Sierra Leone. In late August 1939 the German pocket battleship, *Admiral Graf Spee*, had left Wilhelmshaven to sail through the Iceland-Faroes Gap and then south to the Atlantic trade routes between the River Plate and Britain. Her mission was to seriously disrupt this important trade route, but it was not until 30 September that, disguised as her sister *Admiral Scheer*, she sank the 5,000-ton tramp steamer *Clement* off the Brazilian coast. Prior to this she had transmitted a radio report, and it was in response to the knowledge that a German heavy unit was loose in the Atlantic that the *Renown* and *Ark Royal* were being sent south, code-named Force K. The German pocket battleships or, more accurately, heavy armoured cruisers, were ideal for commerce raiding and on a cruiser's displacement of 11,750 tons, they carried a battleship's main armament of six 11-inch guns which could fire a 670lb shell 30,000 yards. Their diesel engines developed 54,000 SHP, which gave them a speed of 26 knots and at 15 knots they had a radius of action of 10,000 miles. Their secondary armament consisted of eight 5.9-inch guns, six 4.1-inch anti-aircraft guns and eight 21-inch torpedo tubes. They carried an Arado 196A catapult floatplane with a range of 665 miles, and by any standards they were formidable warships which, had they been commissioned in large numbers, would have been a real threat to the convoy system. Also at sea in late August 1939 was the *Admiral Graf Spee's* supply ship, the *Altmark*, keeping well clear of main shipping lanes. After sinking the *Clement*, the *Admiral Graf Spee* set course for the coast of West Africa before heading south-east and past the Cape of Good Hope into the Indian Ocean. The *Ark Royal* and the *Renown* would have a long and fruitless search for the enemy ships which was to last for the remainder of the year.

As Force K steamed south they ran into heavy seas and it was not until Friday 6 October that conditions moderated and reconnaissance patrols could be flown throughout each

On 17 December 1939, during her search for the *Admiral Graf Spee,* the *Ark Royal* put into Rio de Janeiro to refuel. The visit, in the glare of the world's media, left no doubts that the carrier was still very much afloat and undamaged.

(Imperial War Museum HU69907)

day from dawn to dusk. By the morning of Saturday 7 October Force K was in mid-Atlantic, in a position Lat 40° - 04'N/Long 35° - 17'W, and the weather was distinctly warmer as the ships continued to steam south. At 10.37am on Tuesday 10 October, according to the *Ark Royal's* log, a motor vessel was sighted and 45 minutes later it was stopped by Force K. However, obviously all was in order for 13 minutes later, at 11.35am, the vessel was allowed to proceed. Two days later, at 7.22am on Thursday 12 October, Force K anchored at Freetown in Sierra Leone. This visit to the West African port lasted for just over 59 hours, and although leave was granted, it was restricted to three hours each day between 3pm and 6pm. It was at 7pm on Saturday 14 October that the six ships of Force K weighed anchor and put to sea to continue their search. Once again they steamed south and in the early hours of Wednesday 18 October they crossed the equator for the first time, but needless to say, this was not the time for holding the traditional ceremony. On Saturday 21 October, after reaching a position 30° south of the equator, Force K retraced its course and steamed north arriving at Freetown

on the morning of Monday 23 October where leave was granted, but again restricted to three hours a day. Next day the Governor of Sierra Leone visited the ship, and at 4pm on Wednesday 25 October the lower deck was cleared and a rather belated 'Crossing the Line' ceremony was held on the flight deck. This was, in fact, the first time that such a ceremony had been held on board a ship which was securely at anchor in a port. Three days later, at 5.11pm on Saturday 28 October, the *Ark Royal* steamed south to search for the German raider, which was believed to be off the coast of West Africa.

In fact at that time the *Admiral Graf Spee* was in the South Atlantic, midway between Cape Town and Montevideo, and having refuelled from the *Altmark* she was heading for the Indian Ocean with her course set to pass well south of the Cape of Good Hope. The last merchant ship which she had sunk was the MV *Trevanion*, some six days earlier in a position Lat 19° - 14'S/Long 04° - 02'E, and although Force K steamed as far south as Lat 07° -54'S/Long 10° - 06'W, they never came anywhere near the German ship. In fact, on 6 November when Force K had anchored at Freetown once again, she was in the southern Indian Ocean searching for more hapless victims. During the *Ark Royal's* eight days at anchor in the West African port, the ship's company were entertained on board by the West African Police Band, which Beat Retreat. On Tuesday 14 November the *Ark Royal* and Force K left for another Atlantic Ocean patrol, but two days later they were back in Freetown for another 48 hours at anchor. Meanwhile, on 15 November, the *Admiral Graf Spee* had captured the small 706-ton oil tanker, the MV *Africa Shell*, in the Mozambique Channel, ten and a half miles off Cape Zavora. The tanker had been unable to send out a distress call, but as the German pocket battleship had picked up warnings that her presence in the Indian Ocean was known to the British, her captain set course once again for the South Atlantic. At 9.30pm on Saturday 18 November the *Ark Royal* and *Renown* and four destroyers sailed from Freetown to steam south again. By Saturday 25 November Force K was in a position Lat 23° - 41'S/Long 03° - 30'E, but at that time the *Admiral Graf Spee* was well south-east of Cape Town, having rendezvoused with the *Altmark* to carry out an overhaul to her main engines. At 8am that morning two Swordfish from the carrier crashed into the sea with the loss of two crew members. Although the starboard seaboat was away within three minutes of the accident, it was only able to recover two survivors and the body of Ldg Airman Shaylor, who was buried at sea later that day. By Thursday 30 November Force K was in a position Lat 37° - 42'S/Long 20° - 08'E, south of the Cape of Good Hope, although by this time the *Admiral Graf Spee* had steamed north-west towards the coast of South America, and on 25 November the German warship and Force K passed each other, but just outside the range of the *Ark Royal's* air patrols. On Friday 1 December Force K rendezvoused with the cruisers *Sussex* and *Shropshire*, which had been detached from the Mediterranean to operate off the Cape of Good Hope. Next day, at about 10.30am, a signal was received from a South African reconnaissance aircraft reporting a suspicious ship close to Force K's position, which turned out to be the 9,521-ton Woermann Line's SS *Watussi*. The German liner had left the port of Beira on 24 November, and at her maximum speed of 13 knots she was hoping to avoid the Royal Navy's patrols to return safely to Germany. Unfortunately for her, her presence coincided with the *Admiral Graf Spee's* foray into the Mozambique Channel, and with the Royal Navy and the South African Defence Forces concentrating their searches for the German pocket battleship in the area off the Cape of Good Hope, it was inevitable that the *Watussi* would be caught. Eight days after leaving Beira, at 10.16am on Saturday 2 December, when she was about 90 miles south of Cape Agulhas and making good progress towards the vast, and relatively safe, expanse of the South Atlantic, her crew sighted a JU86 airliner, but the fact that it was a

German aircraft gave them no comfort for it was actually a reconnaissance aircraft of the South African Air Force. The JU86 circled the *Watussi*, fired a machine-gun burst across her bow and dropped a bomb close alongside her, in an attempt to persuade her master to steer towards Cape Town. However, when the aircraft left the scene the *Watussi* resumed her original course, but it was not long before Swordfish aircraft from the *Ark Royal* were maintaining a standing patrol over her. At about 3.25pm, when the *Watussi* was some 60 miles from the South African coast, she was seen to stop and begin lowering her boats. The Swordfish attempted to dissuade her crew from scuttling by firing their machine-guns, but it was not long before smoke was seen belching from her after hatch and she was ablaze from stem to stern. It was 6.15pm before the *Ark Royal* and Force K, together with the two cruisers, arrived on the scene, and the blazing derelict was by then listing heavily to starboard, with her guard rails under water. Once the survivors, among them women and children, had been taken aboard the *Sussex*, all that was left was for the gunners from the *Ark Royal* and *Renown* to finish off the unfortunate passenger liner, and by 6.43pm she had been dispatched. That same evening, as Force K steamed towards Cape Town, a signal was received stating that the 10,440-ton Blue Star Line cargo ship, *Doric Star*, had been sunk by a German pocket battleship in a position Lat 19° - 15'S/Long 05° - 05'E, about 1,200 miles to the north of Force K's position, which was approximately three days' steaming away. It was clear therefore that full fuel tanks were needed, and at 7.45am on Sunday 3 December the *Ark Royal* secured alongside A berth in Cape Town's New Docks. As fuelling hoses were connected, ten hours' leave was granted to the ship's company and by 1.30pm the city was full of sailors.

At 7.20am on Monday 4 December, after a stay of less than 24 hours, during which time the fuel and additional stores had been embarked, the *Ark Royal* and *Renown* put to sea once again, and by that time news had come in of another sinking by the German pocket battleship. This time the victim was the 7,983-ton steamship *Tairoa*, and she was in a position close to that of the *Doric Star* which had been sunk 24 hours earlier. Three days later, on Thursday 7 December, Force K was in the vicinity of the two sinkings, but that same day the 3,895-ton cargo ship, SS *Streonshalk* was sunk by the *Admiral Graf Spee* in a position Lat 25° - 00'S/Long 27° - 50'W, east of Rio de Janeiro. Documents captured on the cargo vessel provided the information that a convoy of four merchant ships, escorted by only one armed merchant cruiser, would be sailing from Montevideo within days. As it transpired, Commodore Harwood's cruiser *Ajax* was in the River Plate area, and he would soon be joined by the *Exeter* which was steaming up from the Falkland Islands, and by the *Achilles* which was heading south from Rio de Janeiro. At 5.35pm

On the morning of Monday 29 January 1940 the *Ark Royal* rendezvoused with the heroic cruiser HMS *Exeter* which had been damaged in the Battle of the River Plate. The *Ark's* squadrons performed a fly-past over the cruiser which was cheered by the whole of Force K. *(F. George)*

on Friday 8 December, with Force K in mid-South Atlantic, there was a fatal accident when a Skua from the *Ark Royal* crashed into the sea, killing the pilot, Sub-Lt P. T. Bethall RN, although the other crew member, Ldg Airman Taylours was rescued.

It was at 5.25am on Wednesday 13 December that the *Admiral Graf Spee* sighted the three British cruisers east of the River Plate Estuary and 25 minutes later the German warship opened fire, thus initiating the Battle of the River Plate. As Commodore Harwood had planned, the German vessel was forced to split her fire, although at first she did concentrate on the *Exeter*, allowing the *Ajax* and *Achilles* to close to the maximum range of their 6-inch guns and open rapid fire. Unfortunately, this was not before the *Exeter* had been seriously damaged, and as well as putting the cruiser's B turret out of action, the blast from the shell swept across the bridge killing everyone except Captain Bell, her commanding officer, and two others. Soon afterwards *Exeter's* A turret was knocked out, and by 6.30am she was down by the bows with a 7° list, but fortunately for her the *Admiral Graf Spee* then turned its attention to the other

two cruisers, and there followed a very spirited action during which the *Ajax* and *Achilles* inflicted severe damage on the pocket battleship. Perhaps the most significant damage, from the British point of view, was the destruction of the oil purification plant, and by 9am it was clear that the pocket battleship was in no condition for the long Atlantic voyage back to Germany. Although the action continued for the rest of the day, the enemy ship was now heading westwards for Montevideo, with the *Ajax* and *Achilles* shadowing her. The final rounds of the battle were fired at 8.48pm when, just 50 miles from the coast of Uruguay, the *Admiral Graf Spee* fired three 11-inch salvoes at the *Achilles*, to which the cruiser replied with five salvoes. Between 9.30pm and 9.45pm the German ship fired for the last time, but the two shadowers were well out of range, and at shortly before midnight the pocket battleship anchored off the neutral port of Montevideo well within Uruguay's territorial waters. Commodore Harwood had won the initial battle, but now every effort had to be made to stop the *Admiral Graf Spee* from escaping.

Initially the British and French response to the *Admiral*

Graf Spee was that, in accordance with international law, she should leave the neutral port within 24 hours, while the German Ambassador to Uruguay wanted the vessel to be able to remain there for up to 15 days in order to repair the damage. The Uruguayan Government was prepared to grant 72 hours and gave until 8pm on Sunday 17 December for their unwelcome guest to leave. However, as the *Ark Royal* and the *Renown* would not arrive in the area until Tuesday 19 December at the earliest, there then followed a series of high profile press releases from the British to the effect that the cruiser *Cumberland*, the *Renown* and the *Ark Royal* were already in the area off the River Plate, when in fact only the first of the three had joined Harwood's force during the evening of 14 December. By the morning of Friday 15 December the *Ark Royal* and *Renown* were still 400 miles south-west of Pernambuco (Recife), and it was clear that they would have to refuel en route to the River Plate. Eventually, at 6.36am on Sunday 17 December, the *Ark Royal* anchored off Rio de Janeiro and then an hour later she proceeded slowly into the harbour to secure alongside at just before 9am. Inevitably the visit was highly publicized throughout the world, although it was 17 days before the British censors allowed British newspapers to report the event, but since there were no such restrictions on the media in Brazil, the news that the two British capital ships were still 1,200 miles away quickly reached the *Admiral Graf Spee*, whose captain, nevertheless, had already decided on his future course of action.

Meanwhile, in Rio de Janeiro, the visit of the *Ark Royal*, *Renown*, and the cruiser *Neptune*, which had joined Force K off Pernambuco, albeit just for fuel, was causing great interest. In view of repeated German announcements that the aircraft carrier had been sunk, press photographers were happy to take shots of the *Ark Royal's* brass nameplate near her stern. At just before noon the British Ambassador to Brazil boarded the *Ark Royal* to confer with Vice-Admiral Wells and to update him on the situation in and around Montevideo. At 5.50pm, just over ten hours after her arrival, the *Ark Royal*, together with the *Renown* and *Neptune*, left Rio de Janeiro and set course for Montevideo at maximum speed. Meanwhile, at 5.30pm, just 20 minutes before they had slipped their moorings, at Montevideo the *Admiral Graf Spee* weighed anchor and slowly moved out towards the open sea. For most of that day the German merchant ship *Tacoma* had been alongside her and valuables had been removed, including the ship's bell, which was a clear sign that something was afoot. Ashore speculation and rumour were rife, but it was generally thought that she was heading out to fight the British force, which now consisted of the cruisers *Ajax* and *Achilles*, and the Kent-class vessel *Cumberland*, with 8-inch armament, and thousands of people were lining the shores hoping to watch the spectacle. The *Admiral Graf Spee*

cleared the breakwater and, with her battle ensigns flying, she moved slowly towards the swept channel. At about 8.15pm, when she was approximately six miles south-west of Montevideo and about a mile outside territorial waters, she suddenly altered course to the west and anchored in shallow water. Boats began to pass between the pocket battleship and the *Tacoma* as her ship's company were evacuated then, at 8.54pm, there was a massive explosion which was quickly followed by several more as the *Admiral Graf Spee* was torn apart by scuttling charges. A great pall of black smoke rose high into the air over the scene as the once-proud warship settled in the water and began to sink, the first news of these dramatic events being relayed from the *Ajax's* Fairey Seafox which was monitoring the situation. It was a dramatic finale to the Battle of the River Plate, and later that evening Kapitän Langsdorff, her commanding officer, taking full responsibility for the scuttling of his ship, committed suicide. It transpired that on the morning of 13 December, when he had first sighted the British squadron, he mistook them for a single cruiser and two destroyers, and by the time he realized his error it was too late. In the action which followed, his ship incurred serious damage and he had decided to seek shelter in a neutral port in order to effect repairs, before breaking through the British blockade and returning to Germany. However, once in harbour it was clear that repairs would take at least two weeks, and with the skilful British propaganda magnifying the strength of the naval force outside the harbour, he came to the conclusion that his position was hopeless. In fact, even without the propaganda, an attempt by the *Admiral Graf Spee* to escape would almost certainly have failed for, had she managed to evade the three waiting cruisers, on Monday 18 December the *Ark Royal's* Swordfish would have been within range, and soon after that the *Renown* would also have been on the scene.

Although the *Ark Royal* took no direct part in the battle, her very presence in the area obviously had its effect on Kapitän Langsdorff, but now it was all over she and the *Renown* were ordered to search for the *Altmark* which was known to be at large in the Atlantic. They were unable to locate her and after a fruitless search lasting ten days, during which the Swordfish crews were flying from dawn to dusk, Force K returned to Freetown at 9am on Wednesday 27 December and that afternoon, at 3pm, leave was piped for the first time since her call at Cape Town 24 days previously. As Christmas Day had been spent in mid-Atlantic, just south of the equator, with reconnaissance patrols being flown continuously, Thursday 28 December was set aside as 'Christmas Jollification Day' and, despite the sweltering tropical heat and humidity, a full Christmas dinner was served and a fancy dress parade was held on the flight deck. Two burly able seamen sang 'Alone Among The Swordfish' to the popular tune of 'Underneath The Arches'

Flying off Skuas with HMS *Renown* in the Atlantic, early 1940.   *(Fleet Air Arm Museum)*

and four members of the ship's company, heavily disguised as Wren officers, gave a Noel Coward impersonation, which must have mystified any local people who were privy to the proceedings. New Year's Day 1940 was also spent at Freetown and on the following day work resumed, with ammunition being embarked from lighters.

At 9.30pm on Wednesday 3 January 1940, the *Ark Royal* weighed anchor and left Freetown to steam 700 miles up the coast of West Africa for a three-day visit to the city of Dakar in the French colony of Senegal, where she arrived on the morning of Friday 5 January. After the stifling heat of Sierra Leone, Dakar was a relative haven with a cooler climate and a thriving city, which proved very popular with liberty men. When the visit ended on the morning of Monday 8 January the *Ark Royal* set out to rendezvous with the *Renown* the next day, after which the two ships steamed south to within 300 miles of the Brazilian coast, east of Pernambuco where, at 10.55am on Monday 15 January, they were joined by the cruiser HMS *Ajax*. As the cruiser neared the two ships, the *Ark Royal's* lower deck was cleared, the flight deck was manned, and the little cruiser was cheered as she steamed past looking very spick and span after her part in the recent battle with the *Admiral Graf Spee*. Four days later the force anchored at Freetown, and on Monday 22 January the *Ajax*, together with the destroyers *Hasty* and *Hero*, left Freetown to return to the UK. It was two days later, at 5.30pm on Wednesday 24 January, that the *Ark Royal, Renown*, and the destroyers *Dainty* and *Diamond*, left Freetown to embark upon another search for the *Altmark*. Once again they steamed to the south-west, and at 11.45am on Monday 29 January, in a

position Lat 17° - 00'S/Long 24° - 52'W, the three cruisers, *Dorsetshire, Shropshire*, and the heroic *Exeter*, hove into sight on the horizon. As the first two joined the battlecruiser, destroyers and aircraft carrier, the *Ark Royal's* squadrons made a ceremonial fly-past over the *Exeter*, then at 4.32pm, the whole of Force K, augmented by the two additional cruisers, steamed past up *Exeter's* starboard side and cheered ship, after which she took station astern of the *Ark Royal*. On Saturday 3 February Force K anchored at Freetown once again, but at 5.33pm on Tuesday 6 February the *Renown* and *Ark Royal* left the port to return home.

The passage to Spithead took nine days and finally, at 9.27am on Thursday 15 February, the *Ark Royal* anchored in the Solent. Soon afterwards all the aircraft were flown off to their shore stations and at 3.25pm the carrier weighed anchor to steam up harbour and secure alongside South Railway Jetty just under an hour later. That afternoon, as the ship's company set off to their homes on long leave, deammunitioning began, and on the morning of Saturday 17 February the ship was shifted into D Lock where she was docked down. On board, Commander R. M. T. Taylor RN assumed the duties of Executive Officer, in place of Commander J. A. S. Eccles, who was leaving on his promotion to Captain.

A few days earlier, as the *Ark Royal* was arriving at Spithead, the destroyer HMS *Cossack*, commanded by Captain P. Vian RN, had run alongside the *Altmark* in Jossingfjord, Norway, and armed boarding parties had released the prisoners whose ships had fallen victim to the *Admiral Graf Spee*. It was the final act in the hunt for the pocket battleship's supply vessel.

Chapter Three

Norway And Force H

On Friday 1 March 1940, as Adolf Hitler issued a formal directive to his military for the invasion of Denmark and Norway, the *Ark Royal* was refloated in Portsmouth's D Lock and eight days later she was moved back to South Railway Jetty to prepare for sea. It was 5.15pm on Saturday 16 March when the carrier slipped her moorings and steamed out to anchor at Spithead for the night. Next morning, at 8am, she weighed anchor and departed for her trials and during the afternoon, off the Isle of Wight, she met HMS *Pegasus*, the ship which was formerly the second *Ark Royal*; it appears to have been the only occasion on which the two vessels met at sea. The *Ark Royal* spent five days off Portland undergoing trials, during which time she embarked the Skuas of 800 and 801 Squadrons and the Swordfish of 810 and 820 Squadrons. Thursday 21 March was spent at anchor off Portland, but next morning at 11am she weighed anchor and with the destroyers *Active*, *Bulldog* and *Voyager*, she set course for the Mediterranean. Apart from one hour when she stopped south of Sardinia for repairs to her starboard engine manoeuvring valve, the passage to Malta was made without a break and she arrived in Grand Harbour during the morning of Thursday 28 March, where she secured to No 13 buoy in Bighi Bay. The following day she received a visit from the C-in-C Mediterranean, Admiral Sir Andrew Cunningham, and on the morning of Sunday 31 March she left Malta with HMS *Glorious* to make the passage to Alexandria. The two carriers secured to buoys in Alexandria Harbour during the afternoon of Tuesday 2 April and after six days in the port they put to sea for exercises, during which Vice-Admiral Wells and his staff transferred from the *Glorious* by air. Next afternoon the two ships were ordered back into Alexandria Harbour, for the military situation in Europe had deteriorated and the 'Phoney War' was clearly over.

On 9 April 1940, in a swift series of land, sea and air strikes, Germany invaded Denmark and Norway, claiming it possessed proof that Britain and France were intending to occupy parts of Scandinavia. This was, in fact, quite true as the Allies had for some time been wanting to occupy the Swedish iron ore fields and the strategic port of Narvik, through which Germany's iron ore travelled. In early March Britain and France had formally requested Swedish and Norwegian approval to send troops to Finland through their countries, and although this request had been rejected, London and Paris were primarily interested in occupying the Swedish iron ore fields.

On the morning of Wednesday 10 April, the day after the German invasion of Denmark and Norway, Captain C. S. Holland RN joined the ship as the CO designate to Captain Power and soon afterwards *Ark Royal* and *Glorious*, together with the destroyers *Bulldog* and *Westcott*, left Alexandria for a high-speed passage to Gibraltar where they arrived during the early evening of Saturday 13 April. By that time, in what was called the Second Battle of Narvik, ten British warships, led by the elderly battleship *Warspite*, had sunk seven German destroyers which, from the Allied point of view, was the only ray of light during the whole campaign. Meanwhile back in Gibraltar all naval leave was cancelled from 2pm on Sunday 14 April, and liberty men who were ashore were recalled to their ships. That evening, to everyone's surprise, Vice-Admiral Wells transferred his flag to the *Glorious* which sailed for Scapa Flow at 10pm, but the *Ark Royal* remained firmly alongside 43/44 berths. Next day, apart from dressing ship to celebrate the 'Victory at Narvik Fjord', she remained inactive at Gibraltar and on the morning of Tuesday 16 April she left harbour to carry out flying exercises which lasted all day. Then suddenly, during the late afternoon there came an urgent signal ordering the carrier to return to Gibraltar, refuel and then make a fast passage north to Greenock. In the event she left Gibraltar at 9.40pm on 16 April with the *Bulldog* and *Westcott*, and just 74 hours later she was secured to a buoy in the Firth of Clyde, off Greenock, where she joined the *Glorious*. By Monday 22 April both the carriers were at sea again, bound for Scapa Flow, where they arrived the next morning and, having refuelled, they were at sea again by midday bound for Norway, with the *Ark Royal* once again flying the flag of Vice-Admiral Wells.

Initially the duty of the *Ark Royal* was to protect troop convoys and provide air support for the Army which had landed at Namsos with the intention of advancing on Trondheim. However, the Fleet Air Arm's Swordfish and Skua aircraft were totally outclassed by the German Messerschmitt 110, and even the Heinkel III bomber was almost 50mph faster than the Swordfish. The disparity was equally as great with armament, as the long years of neglecting the Fleet Air Arm had left the British pilots facing a first-class enemy in machines which were obsolete. By Wednesday 24 April, a cold raw day with occasional snowstorms and a complete contrast to the eastern Mediterranean, the *Ark Royal* was north-west of Trondheim and in the late afternoon a force of 12 Skuas was launched, while RAF Gladiators took off from the

HMS *Ark Royal* in the Mediterranean, 1940.

(Fleet Air Arm Museum)

The *Ark* carries out a jackstay transfer with one of her escorts.

(Fleet Air Arm Museum)

Glorious. The latter aircraft were to be land-based and were destined for a landing ground on a frozen lake, but the Skuas were on operations to disrupt enemy lines of communication around Trondheim. They actually found German JU88s attacking an Allied roadblock, but the bombers, with their superior speed, evaded the fighters. The force returned to *Ark Royal* at between 8pm and 8.45pm, having been airborne for almost four hours, and although two of the aircraft were forced to land in the sea through lack of fuel, their crews were rescued safely. Next morning, with weather conditions having improved, the first sorties of Swordfish and Skuas were flown at just after 3am, which was when the sun rose in those latitudes. The aircraft had been ordered to attack enemy shipping at Trondheim and an enemy airfield near the port. In the event the attack on Trondheim Harbour had some success, with three ships suffering direct hits and a Heinkel bomber being shot down, but once again the superior speed of the German bombers had allowed others to escape. The sortie on the enemy airfield was less successful and altogether ten Fleet

Air Arm aircraft were lost, five of them as a result of enemy action. Each night the carrier task force withdrew seawards to avoid retaliation which everyone was expecting, and by mid-morning on 26 April they had returned to a position about 80 miles off the coast to continue operations.

Meanwhile, the RAF Gladiators which had been delivered by the *Glorious* were soon destroyed by far superior German aircraft, and by Saturday 27 April only three of the original 18 were left and they had run out of fuel, leaving the Army dependant on the Fleet Air Arm for its air support. To make matters worse, the naval pilots were not trained for this combat role, there was no radio communication between the ground forces and the naval aircraft, and of course they were outnumbered by the German aircraft, and outclassed by them in speed and armament. During the course of 26 April three enemy bombers were shot down, for the loss of the same number of naval aircraft, and several Skuas were damaged. One of these had been flown by PO Haddon, who managed to shoot down a Heinkel after it had damaged his aircraft and wounded him. That day the Luftwaffe made a heavy attack on Andalsnes, but because of a lack of communication, the *Ark Royal's* fighters arrived on the scene after the raid was over. Between 4am and 9.30am next morning, Saturday 27 April, there were a number of submarine alerts and at 9.20am enemy aircraft were spotted shadowing the force. Once again the enemy's superior speed enabled the shadowers to escape British fighters which were sent up, but during the day the *Ark Royal's* aircraft kept up their patrols in support of the Army. In one incident the CO of 801 Squadron, Captain R. T. Partridge RM, shot down a Heinkel III which, in its turn, shot down his aircraft. Both planes managed to make forced landings very close to each other, and when Captain Partridge and his observer found shelter for the night in a nearby unoccupied house, by a strange twist of fate they ended up sharing it with the German aircrew from the Heinkel III. Fortunately the British pair eventually made it back home. During the day four German aircraft were shot down for the loss of two Skuas and one Swordfish. Although the hard-pressed Fleet Air Arm aircrews were holding their own, a decision had already been made to evacuate Allied troops from Namsos and Andalsnes. It was the beginning of the end of the Allied intervention in Norway.

At 3am on Sunday 28 April the first sortie of 12 Swordfish, escorted by Skuas, was flown off the *Ark Royal* to attack Vaernes airfield near Trondheim in an attempt to disrupt enemy air activity in anticipation of the forthcoming withdrawal of Allied troops on 1 May. There is no doubt that this early raid was a success with some enemy aircraft being destroyed on the ground, and the Skuas shooting down five Heinkels for the loss of one fighter. In addition they also damaged some flying boats in Trondheim Harbour, and all the Swordfish returned safely even though most had been hit by anti-aircraft fire. At just after midday three Junkers 88 bombers were seen approaching the *Ark Royal* and the whole force opened up a formidable AA barrage. One of the bombers turned back and one was shot down, but not before it had dropped its bombs between the *Ark Royal* and HMS *Sheffield*, but fortunately none of them found their target. During the day more enemy bombers were reported in the vicinity and a formation of JU88s was broken up by aircraft from the *Glorious*. On Tuesday 30 April the carriers provided air cover for the first of two evacuation convoys of French ships which were to withdraw Allied forces from Andalsnes, and it was none too soon for German units advancing north from Oslo had linked up with their forces fighting around Trondheim. At dawn on Wednesday 1 May fighters from both the *Ark Royal* and the *Glorious* were launched to provide fighter cover for one such operation, and not long afterwards HMS *Curlew*, which was one of the few Royal Navy ships to be fitted with radar to provide early warning of enemy attacks, was detached from the force which left

the rest of the vessels having to rely solely on their lookouts. Suddenly, at 8am, without any warning, as the *Ark Royal* was steaming on a steady course, there was a terrific explosion 40 yards from her starboard quarter, followed by a second one further off. A JU88 had approached the force unseen and having dived at the carrier directly out of the sun, it had dropped its bombs and, despite a heavy AA barrage, had managed to escape unscathed. Fortunately the pilot's judgement had not been good and the carrier, which had literally been a sitting target, escaped. Later that day, at 3.25pm, another high-level bombing attack erupted, but again there were no hits and this was followed by a three-hour respite. However, at 6.24pm a group formation of 12 Junkers 87s (Stukas), and five twin-engined Heinkel III bombers, was reported to be heading for the force and within minutes there was a great confusion of AA barrage and bombs exploding on both sides of the *Ark Royal*, with huge columns of water rising to masthead height. Although one bomb fell only ten yards from the carrier, it failed to explode and the only casualty was one Heinkel III which was shot down by one of the airborne Skuas. That evening, at 8pm, Captain C. S. Holland assumed command of the *Ark Royal,* which had fortunately come through the onslaught unharmed again, along with the rest of the force, and at 11.15am on Friday 3 May the carrier anchored in Scapa Flow. That afternoon Captain Power left the ship, and at 4pm on Saturday 4 May the *Ark Royal* weighed anchor and put to sea, this time bound for the area off Narvik.

After the withdrawal of Allied troops from central and southern Norway, the British and French forces could concentrate their efforts on the northern Norwegian port of Narvik, although, unknown to the Allies, Hitler had already issued orders for the invasion of Holland, Belgium and France, but as the German Army prepared for its massive offensive in the West, the last acts were being played out in what had been a catalogue of blunders and lost opportunities in Norway. At 5.45pm on Monday 6 May the first of the *Ark Royal's* fighter patrols were launched to support the Army around Narvik. However, by 8 May the patrols were again encountering fierce opposition, and two days later the campaign in Norway became more of a sideshow as 136 divisions of the German Army advanced into Belgium, Holland and France where, facing them, were half that number of Allied troops, including just ten divisions of the British Expeditionary Force (BEF). Nevertheless, on 12/13 May British and French landings went ahead at Narvik under the cover of a naval bombardment, and during that time the Skuas and Swordfish were in the air over the town of Narvik bombing railway lines and generally supporting the army operations. Unfortunately, the main battles in the low countries were going very badly for the Allies, with Holland capitulating on 14 May and the German Army breaking through the

HMS *Ark Royal* with HMS *Renown* and the cruiser *Glasgow* in the Mediterranean.   *(Fleet Air Arm Museum)*

Allied Namur-Sedan lines in massive strength. For three days the German divisions poured through the gap, cutting off the small BEF and the French 7th Army from the main body of the French 1st and 2nd Armies, consisting of 65 divisions. By 23 May the BEF and the two French Armies in Belgium had been pushed back into two small perimeters around Dunkirk and Calais and it was only the unwarranted caution of the German commanders which prevented their complete destruction. The sheer magnitude of the disasters which had befallen the British and French Armies pushed Norway even further into the sidelines, whence the Allies now wished to withdraw as quickly as possible. However, the aircrews from the *Ark Royal* had had some success in shooting down enemy bombers, and on Friday 24 May the carrier anchored once again in Scapa Flow to refuel, before steaming south to Greenock to embark stores and ammunition. During the early morning of Thursday 30 May the *Ark Royal* sailed in company with the *Glorious* for Scapa Flow, from where she would depart at 8.06am on the last day of May for northern Norway for the last time, to cover the final withdrawal of Allied troops. Although the Allies had captured Narvik on 28 May, further south the Belgian Army had capitulated and the

shattered BEF was being evacuated from Dunkirk. The final evacuation of Allied troops from Norway took place between Tuesday 4 and Saturday 8 June and as the Norwegian Government had sued for peace it was clear to the Germans that the Allied effort in Norway would soon collapse, and so the two battlecruisers *Scharnhorst* and *Gneisenau*, together with the cruiser *Hipper*, were sent into the Norwegian Sea to prey on Allied shipping; their success was to be beyond their own expectations. At just after midnight on Saturday 8 June, HMS *Glorious* embarked RAF Gladiators and Hurricanes, before being detached from the main force at 2.58am with the destroyers *Acasta* and *Ardent*, to return independently to Scapa Flow. She had been at sea since Friday 31 May when, with the *Ark Royal*, she had left Scapa Flow and according to the Admiralty, she was low on fuel. The wisdom of sending an aircraft carrier virtually unescorted across the Norwegian Sea must be open to question, and the fact that during the passage no fighter patrols were flown by the *Glorious* compounded the folly. During the morning of 8 June the German force caught and sank an oil tanker and its armed trawler escort, but they left the hospital ship *Atlantis* to proceed unharmed. That afternoon, at 4pm, the German force sighted the *Glorious* with the two destroyers, and at 4.30pm they opened fire on her. She sank at 5.40pm, despite the efforts of the *Acasta* and *Ardent* to protect her, before they too were sunk. In his history of the Second World War, Sir Winston Churchill remarked of the *Glorious'* shortage of fuel, 'This explanation is not convincing. The *Glorious* presumably had enough fuel to steam at the speed of the convoy. All should have been kept together.' Lost with the three ships were 1,515 officers and men with only 43 survivors, 40 from the *Glorious* and three from the two destroyers. Fortunately, the *Ark Royal* did remain with the troop convoy and the Germans did not search for her, but instead set course south-east for Trondheim. However, German bombers were also on the lookout for the convoy from Narvik, and at 10.56pm on Sunday 9 June the *Ark Royal* was attacked by seven Heinkel IIIs, one of which was shot down by fighters. Next day at 2.40pm, HM Ships *Rodney* and *Renown*, which had been sent out to hunt for the German battlecruiser force, were sighted by the convoy. That night, at just after midnight, came the news that Italy had declared war on the Allies, and on the morning of Wednesday 12 June the *Ark Royal* left the convoy and with the *Rodney*, *Renown* and a destroyer screen, steamed towards the Norwegian coast to launch an attack on the German warships *Scharnhorst*, *Gneisenau* and *Hipper* which were reported to be at Trondheim. In fact, only the *Scharnhorst* was in port and the latter two were at sea again, but at seven minutes past midnight on the morning of Thursday 13 June, 15 Skuas were flown off to attack shipping at Trondheim. There then followed a wait of over three hours before, at 3.25am, the seven surviving Skuas landed back on board. The plan had called for the RAF to make a synchronized attack on a nearby Luftwaffe base, and since this had not materialized, the 15 Skuas went straight into a force of Me 109s and 110s. In the event one bomb hit the *Scharnhorst*, but failed to explode, so the operation turned out to be a very expensive failure. On top of this, at 4.24am, whilst the force was still hoping for the return of at least some of the eight overdue aircraft, the destroyers *Antelope* and *Electra* collided in thick fog. Soon afterwards the *Ark Royal* set course for Scapa Flow, leaving the *Rodney* and *Renown* to escort the damaged destroyers, and she anchored safely in B3 berth at 4.25pm on Friday 14 June, the day on which German troops marched into Paris. On the following day Verdun, the French town on the River Meuse with its 12th-century cathedral which had been defended so valiantly in the war of 1914-18, was captured by the German Army as French troops pulled out of the Maginot Line.

By now a large part of the BEF had been rescued from the port of Dunkirk, although virtually all their equipment had been lost, and a new government had been formed with Winston Churchill as the Prime Minister. From France came the bad news that the French Army was in full retreat and that the British 51st Highland Division was trapped at St Valery. Finally, on Friday 21 June 1940, France surrendered to Germany and there were to be no more land campaigns in Western Europe for five years.

The *Ark Royal* remained at the anchorage in Scapa Flow for only three days before, at 3.30pm on Monday 17 June, she weighed anchor and set course for Gibraltar, with the destroyers *Escapade*, *Faulknor* and *Fearless*. It was no coincidence that her day of departure was also the day upon which the French Government, headed by Philippe Petain, sued for peace, for plans had been laid for the most distasteful action in which the Royal Navy has ever taken part. At 3.35pm on Tuesday 18 June, the *Ark Royal* joined the battlecruiser HMS *Hood*, and together the two ships steamed to Gibraltar where they arrived during the morning of Sunday 23 June. Faced with imminent invasion, one of the most difficult problems facing the British Government was the future of the powerful French Navy. Concerns over this question had been agitating ministers since 11 June. France had agreed to armistice terms which provided for her fleet to go to metropolitan French ports, there to be demilitarized under Axis control. This opened up the possibility of their being seized by the Germans which, when joined with the Italian Fleet, would give them an overwhelming superiority over the British, particularly in view of the Royal Navy's worldwide commitments. The alternative was to rely on the promises of the French naval commander, Admiral Francois Darlan, never to let the ships fall into German hands which seemed to the British Government a very dangerous gamble, although many British naval and political leaders were prepared to accept this. When they met on 27 June, the War Cabinet in London had considered the problem so urgent that they had set 3 July as the day on which all French naval vessels should be seized or disarmed, and 'Operation Catapult' had been initiated under the command of Vice-Admiral Sir James Somerville. A specially constituted Force H was already forming up at Gibraltar and both the *Ark Royal* and the *Hood* were included in this.

The largest concentration of French warships lay at the naval base of Mers-el-Kebir, three miles west of the Algerian port city of Oran. Present at that time were four heavy units of the French Fleet, the battlecruisers *Dunkerque* and *Strasbourg*, and the battleships *Bretagne* and *Provence*, both of which dated from 1915, as well as the seaplane tender *Commandant Teste* and the destroyers *Volta*, *Mogador*, *Terrible*, *Lynx* and *Kersaint*. Admiral Somerville was ordered to present the French naval officers at Mers-el-Kebir with four choices, which were:-

1. To bring their ships to British harbours to 'fight with us'.
2. To steam their ships to British ports and hand them over to British crews.
3. To demilitarize their ships to British satisfaction.

4. To scuttle their ships.

If none of these choices was accepted then Admiral Somerville was ordered to endeavour to destroy the ships at Mers-el-Kebir and particularly the *Dunkerque* and *Strasbourg*, using 'all means' at his disposal. In order to carry out these orders, maximum naval strength was concentrated at Gibraltar, and at 1.30pm on Monday 24 June Captain Holland, who was to play a vital role in the negotiations with the French, left for Casablanca by air to talk to officials at the French naval base in Morocco, where the uncompleted battleship *Jean Bart* lay after her escape from St Nazaire. Before his departure he had handed over to his Executive Officer, Commander Taylor, who would command the *Ark Royal* for most of the ensuing days until the evening of 4 July. Captain Holland was the ideal person to negotiate with the French naval officers for, until September 1939, he had served as the Naval Attaché at the British Embassy in Paris and as the Royal Navy's Liaison Officer to Admiral Darlan. He was on friendly terms with a number of senior French naval officers, including Admiral Marcel Gensoul at Oran. Within hours of Captain Holland leaving the ship, news reached the Admiralty that the battleship *Richelieu*, which had escaped from Brest to Dakar, had left the West African port and was heading north, and so during the evening of Tuesday 25 June steam was raised and the *Ark Royal* was prepared for sea. Next day, at 10.33am, together with the *Hood* and four destroyers, she put to sea and steamed into the Atlantic, but in the event the cruiser *Dorsetshire* rendezvoused with the French battleship and persuaded her to turn back, and by 9.45pm the *Ark Royal* was back alongside in Gibraltar. Two days later the *Ark Royal* and the *Hood* put to sea again and made an eight-hour, wide diversionary sweep into the Atlantic, returning at 1.50pm to the colony. At 5.50pm on the last day of June, the cruiser HMS *Arethusa*, flying the flag of Vice-Admiral Sir James Somerville, arrived at Gibraltar and within an hour he had transferred his flag to the *Hood*. Monday 1 July passed quietly for the ship's company of the *Ark Royal*, although they remained 'Under Sailing Orders' while diplomatic activity continued ashore in an effort to solve the problem of the French Fleet. Next day, with only 36 hours left for Admiral Somerville to resolve the crisis before his deadline, the battleship *Valiant* arrived at Gibraltar and at 2pm Captain Holland, who had returned from Morocco, joined the destroyer *Foxhound*. Two hours later, at 3.55pm, the *Ark Royal* and the rest of Force H, *Hood*, *Valiant*, *Resolution*, the cruisers *Arethusa* and *Enterprise* and 11 destroyers, set sail and after steaming west into the Atlantic, they turned round after dark and set course for Mers-el-Kebir where Admiral Somerville had to carry out what the First Sea Lord described as, '...one of the most disagreeable and difficult tasks that a British Admiral has ever been faced with.'

At 4.30am on Wednesday 3 July, with Force H off Mers-el-Kebir, all the ships went to Action Stations, and at just after 7am the *Foxhound* steamed up to the anti-submarine boom at the harbour mouth bearing Captain Holland who fully expected to be able to meet Admiral Gensoul, as Admiral Somerville had signalled beforehand: 'I am sending Captain Holland to confer with you. The Royal Navy hopes that the proposals made will allow the valiant and glorious French Navy to range itself at our side. In this case your ships will remain in your hands and no one need have any fear for the future. The British Fleet is lying off Oran to welcome you.' However, on 24 June Admiral Gensoul had received orders from the French Admiralty to scuttle his ships to prevent them from falling into enemy hands, or those of a foreign power, and he maintained that doing anything other than this would have broken the armistice agreement with Germany, which would have been disastrous for France. Writing in 1968 Admiral Gensoul declared, 'The honour of the flag forbade me to submit to an ultimatum presented at gunpoint, even from former allies.' Captain Holland's formal message which was delivered to the Admiral set out the British Government's four options, but ended thus: 'Finally, failing the above, I have the orders of His Majesty's Government to use whatever force may be necessary to prevent your ships from falling into German or Italian hands.' With Admiral Gensoul refusing to speak directly to Captain Holland, who had to conduct his negotiations through a Flag Lieutenant in a motor boat in the middle of the harbour in the scorching sun, it was clear that the situation had reached an impasse, but the French ships were raising steam and preparing to leave harbour. By mid-morning a message had been delivered to Captain Holland which made it clear that the French Fleet would defend itself, and at 11am he returned to the *Foxhound*, which rendezvoused with the *Hood*, to pass on the disappointing results of his efforts. At just before 1pm the French Admiralty signalled to all French warships in the Western Mediterranean to close Oran; it was apparent that Admiral Somerville was running out of time.

During the morning the *Ark Royal* had been cruising about ten miles off Cape Falcon and reconnaissance patrols had been flying continuously, but at just before 1pm Admiral Somerville ordered the carrier's Swordfish to lay mines outside the harbour and six minutes later five planes were launched, armed with magnetic mines, and escorted by six Skuas. That afternoon, with zero hour having been postponed until 3pm, Captain Holland was finally able to meet Admiral Gensoul, but the best concession he could get was that numbers of the crews on the French ships would be reduced, and if they were threatened by the enemy they would sail for Martinique or the USA. This was well short of the British demands and the fruitless negotiations continued until almost 4.30pm, when Captain Holland returned to the *Foxhound*. Meanwhile, at 3.26pm two more

Swordfish, also armed with magnetic mines, took off to drop them in the harbour entrance, and Admiral Somerville once again put back the deadline by another two hours. But finally, at 5.45pm, the *Hood, Resolution* and *Valiant* opened fire on the French ships with their main armament in a heavy and concentrated bombardment which lasted for just over ten minutes, and during the one-sided action the *Ark Royal's* aircraft flew overhead plotting the fall of shot. Soon after the firing commenced the *Strasbourg* and five of the destroyers, in a magnificent feat of seamanship, managed to put to sea and steam eastward at full power, and at 6pm three Skuas and six Swordfish armed with bombs set off in pursuit. However, they failed to hit the battlecruiser and on their return to the carrier two Swordfish force-landed in the sea. Admiral Somerville was determined not to let the capital ship escape and at 7.52pm a further six Swordfish, this time armed with torpedoes, were launched, in the first attack by naval torpedo aircraft on a capital ship at sea during the Second World War. Instead of making an immediate attack, the aircraft shadowed the *Strasbourg* until after sunset when they flew in low from the landward side and dropped their torpedoes at 1,000 yards' range. Once again the battlecruiser emerged unscathed and during their return to the *Ark Royal* two Swordfish were forced to ditch into the sea, with their crews being rescued by the destroyer *Wrestler*. Towards the end of the action French fighter aircraft intervened and shot down a Skua, and a small force of bombers attacked the fleet, but no damage was caused. Altogether two Swordfish and a Skua were lost, and at 6pm on Thursday 4 July Force H returned to Gibraltar.

It had been a very sad day for the Royal Navy, and aerial reconnaissance over Mers-el-Kebir showed that the *Dunkerque*, although beached, was not seriously damaged. At 7.36pm on Friday 5 July the *Ark Royal* and Force H left Gibraltar, once again bound for Mers-el-Kebir, and early next morning, at 5.15am, when they were still some 100 miles off the port, Swordfish of 810 and 820 Squadrons, armed with torpedoes and escorted by Skuas of 800 and 803 Squadrons, were flown off to carry out torpedo attacks on the French battlecruiser. The first wave achieved complete surprise and four of the six torpedoes hit their target. The subsequent waves met heavy anti-aircraft fire, but all the aircraft dropped their torpedoes and returned to the *Ark Royal*. It was in the late afternoon of Saturday 6 July that Force H returned to Gibraltar and Admiral Somerville visited the *Ark Royal* that evening. In February 1942, when the *Dunkerque* was seaworthy again, she was moved to Toulon where, nine months later, with the *Strasbourg*, she was scuttled when Germany broke the terms of the 1940 armistice and marched into the unoccupied areas of France. As it transpired, the French assurances that their fleet would not fall into German hands were honoured.

On the morning of Monday 8 July 1940, the *Ark Royal* put to sea again with Force H, which now included the cruiser *Delhi*. This was the start of the war in the Mediterranean and the situation, with the French Fleet having been lost, and the powerful Italian Fleet having joined the Axis cause, was very different from that which had prevailed earlier in the year when the *Ark Royal* and the *Glorious* were carrying out flying exercises off Alexandria.

Now the lines of communication between Gibraltar and the Eastern Mediterranean were virtually severed and the island of Malta, lying just 60 miles south of Sicily, lay under siege which meant that its magnificent Grand Harbour was no longer a safe anchorage for units of the Mediterranean Fleet. For three years the main naval bases in that theatre of war would be Gibraltar and Alexandria, and only the former had adequate repair facilities.

On 7 July 1940 two convoys carrying evacuees and stores for Alexandria had left Malta and the Mediterranean Fleet, including the aircraft carrier HMS *Eagle*, sailed west from the Egyptian base to provide cover for the vulnerable merchant ships. Force H was to sail east into the Western Basin of the Mediterranean, well within range of Italian aircraft based at Sardinia, to provide a diversion for the convoy as it steamed south-east. Admiral Somerville was moving his fleet to a point south-east of Majorca in order that the *Ark Royal's* aircraft could launch a strike against Italian bases at Cagliari in southern Sardinia. The passage passed quietly until the afternoon of Tuesday 9 July, when a reconnaissance plane was seen to be shadowing the force. Soon after this, at 3.45pm, came the first attack by Italian high-level bombers, with bombs falling uncomfortably close to the British ships. The next raid, which started at 5.25pm, lasted for almost half an hour and it was followed at 6.26pm by a third one. During this final high-level bombing attack a number of heavy bombs fell very close to the *Ark Royal*, with resulting explosions shaking the whole ship. There is no doubt that the accuracy of the high-level bombing was good and in addition, Italian aircraft were flying at too high an altitude for the Skuas to intercept them, although one was shot down, and Lt Smeeton of 800 Squadron shot down a shadowing aircraft. However, in view of the efficiency of the Italian Air Force, the planned attacks on Cagliari were cancelled and Force H was ordered to return to Gibraltar. They arrived off the colony on the morning of Thursday 11 July, when the destroyer HMS *Escort* was torpedoed, but fortunately, by 9am the *Ark Royal* was safely secured in 43 berth on the South Mole. Two days later it was the Italians' turn to make radio broadcasts alleging that the *Ark* had been seriously damaged, and for good measure they added that the *Hood* was also a casualty. Once again, as in 1939, the bombing had been so close that the enemy pilots probably thought they had hit the two ships. Nevertheless, the officers and men of the *Ark Royal* could now take a welcome 12-day break in Gibraltar when all outstanding maintenance tasks could be completed, and they could enjoy some relaxation on the Rock and in the neighbourhoods of La Linea and Algeciras. While the carrier was in the colony there was an air raid, during which some bombs landed close to the dockyard.

The interlude came to an end on the evening of Tuesday 23 July when, with the cruiser *Enterprise* and a destroyer screen, the *Ark Royal* slipped her moorings and put to sea, this time steaming west into the Atlantic before heading north off the coast of Portugal. It had been planned that the carrier's aircraft would make a raid on shipping in the occupied port of Bordeaux, but at midday on Thursday 25 July news was received from RAF reconnaissance aircraft that there was no sign of shipping in the port and the operation was called off. Two days later, at 12.45pm on Saturday 27 July, the carrier was alongside at Gibraltar once again, this time for a four-day stay, during which the evening of 29 July was enlivened by an inter-ship boxing tournament between the *Ark Royal* and the *Hood*. Force H put to sea again at 8am on Wednesday 31 July, and after rendezvousing with the elderly aircraft carrier *Argus* they set course eastwards as part of 'Operation Hurry'. Initially, after the entry of Italy into the war and the surrender of France, the Chiefs of Staff had decided that the island of Malta was indefensible, for although there were four military air bases on the island there were just three fighters and five battalions of infantry. Serious consideration was given in London to abandoning the Eastern Mediterranean and Malta as well. However, the Royal Navy was not at all happy with this thinking, as it had always regarded the island as the keystone of its Mediterranean Fleet, and it was decided that Malta must be held. So began the great struggle to keep the island supplied and to build it up as a striking base. It was estimated that at least two convoys a month, each carrying 40,000 tons of stores, was a minimum requirement, and eight crated fighters were found in a hangar at Kalafrana, the naval air station near Marsaxlokk. These were outdated Gloster Gladiators which had been left behind by HMS *Glorious* earlier in the year before she left the Mediterranean for the Norwegian campaign. They were quickly assembled and four of them were handed over to the RAF for the defence of Malta, with others being earmarked for HMS *Eagle*. The first four aircraft were quickly in action against the Italian Air Force and after one was shot down the three remaining machines were nicknamed 'Faith', 'Hope' and 'Charity', but fortunately they were soon to be reinforced by Hurricane fighters. On 24 July the elderly carrier *Argus* had left Britain carrying 12 Hurricanes and after she had rendezvoused with Force H off Gibraltar Bay the force steamed east towards Alboran Island, which was sighted at 4.30pm on 31 July. That evening enemy aircraft were seen to be shadowing the ships, and as they escaped untouched it was clear that bombing raids could be expected on the next day. By 8am on 1 August Force H was in a position Lat 37° - 33'N/Long 01° - 45'E, about 100 miles south-west of Ibiza, but it was just before 6pm in the evening when three waves of Italian high-level bombers flew over the force and dropped their missiles, some of which fell close to the *Ark Royal*, in an onslaught lasting more than ten minutes.

Meanwhile, in the Eastern Mediterranean, Admiral Cunningham's fleet, which included two battleships and

In early July 1940, in order to divert attention from two convoys which were carrying evacuees from Malta to Alexandria, Force H steamed west to attack Italian bases at Cagliari. However, in view of the efficiency of the Italian Air Force, the attack was called off. In this photograph, taken from the *Ark,* the stern of the *Resolution* can be seen as bombs explode in the sea round the *Hood,* almost obscuring her from view.
(*C. L. Asher*)

HMS *Eagle*, had put to sea to steam west between Crete and Libya to draw enemy surface vessels to the north. During the night of 1/2 August the *Ark Royal, Hood, Enterprise* and four destroyers parted company with the *Argus* and steamed north to a position about 60 miles south-west of Cape Teulada, Sardinia, where, at 2.30am, 11 Swordfish armed with bombs and mines were launched to attack Cagliari Harbour. Sadly, one of the aircraft slewed to starboard as it was taking off and after hitting the forward pom-pom mounting, it crashed into the sea, with the loss of Lt J. R. Robins and his crew. At about the same time, but further south, the RAF Hurricanes flew off the *Argus* and set course for Malta, guided by two of the *Ark Royal's* Skuas. In the event the attack on Cagliari by the Swordfish was a success, although one machine, flown by Lt G. R. Humphries, had made a forced landing on the Italian airfield which was being attacked. At Just before 9.30pm on Saturday 3 August the *Ark Royal* and the remainder of Force H arrived safely back at Gibraltar. As for the defences

at Malta, they had received a very welcome reinforcement of Hurricane fighters. There was to be no respite yet though, and at 7.45pm on Sunday 4 August the *Ark Royal* was at sea once again with the *Hood, Valiant, Arethusa* and a destroyer screen. This time, however, the force steamed into the Atlantic where, during the following afternoon, the two capital ships and the *Arethusa* set course for home while the *Ark Royal* turned round and returned to Gibraltar where she arrived during the morning of Thursday 8 August. This time she remained alongside 43 berth for eight days, during which time essential maintenance was carried out, and on one quiet Sunday afternoon the ship's anti-aircraft gunners opened fire on an Italian reconnaissance plane which was flying over the colony. The carrier left Gibraltar again on Friday 16 August with the battlecruiser *Renown*, the cruiser *Enterprise* and a destroyer screen, to carry out exercises in the Atlantic, but four days later they were once again alongside in Gibraltar dockyard. Five days later, at 6.40am on Sunday 25 August, again with *Renown* and *Enterprise*, the *Ark Royal* sailed into the Atlantic, this time to meet the brand new fleet carrier *Illustrious* which had left Scapa Flow three days earlier to join the Mediterranean Fleet at Alexandria. The two carriers rendezvoused at 8am on 27 August and with the *Ark* in station astern of the *Illustrious*, the force set course for Gibraltar where they arrived on the morning of 29 August.

Next day came the more difficult task for Force H of escorting the new carrier through the Sicilian Narrows. The fleet sailed for the central Mediterranean at 9am on Friday 30 August, and in order to divert enemy attention from the eastbound force, the *Ark Royal's* Swordfish were to execute two bombing attacks on Cagliari. During Saturday 31 August enemy reconnaissance planes were in evidence again, although one was shot down by the *Ark's* Skuas. On the same day, in poor visibility, enemy bombers failed to find the force and at 3.42am on the morning of Sunday 1 September the first sortie took off for 'Operation Smash' on Cagliari airfield. That night the *Illustrious* and her force had started to steam through the narrows, and at 3.45am on Monday 2 September a second sortie of nine Swordfish flew off to bomb another airfield in Sardinia and the power station at Cagliari. Unfortunately, weather conditions were poor and few of the bombers found their targets, but just over four hours later all the Swordfish were back on board. Next day, at just before 1pm, the *Ark Royal* was back in Gibraltar, and on Thursday 5 September the *Illustrious* arrived safely at Alexandria.

Yet again the *Ark Royal* faced a demanding schedule, and despite the fact that she was in need of dockyard maintenance, the carrier had been earmarked for another important operation, this time off the coast of West Africa. At home the beleaguered British Government was considering ways of assisting General de Gaulle and his Free French Forces to win over the French African colonies to his cause, and although capturing Casablanca and Morocco was out of the question, it was decided to carry out 'Operation Menace', the seizure of the Vichy-controlled port of Dakar, where the *Ark Royal* had made a courtesy call only eight months previously. The carrier was to provide the main air strikes for the operation, and she left Gibraltar at 5.30pm on Friday 6 September, in company with the *Barham*, *Resolution* and a destroyer screen, setting course for the coast of West Africa. By 14 September the carrier was within flying range of Dakar and a Skua was sent to photograph the harbour. Next day, after further reconnaissance, the *Ark Royal* and the remainder of the invasion convoy set course for Freetown where they would wait for the operation to begin, and they arrived there during the late afternoon of 16 September. It was generally thought that the invasion would be unopposed and over the next three days two Free French Caudron Luciolles biplanes and 23 French naval personnel, who were to act as liaison officers, were embarked. However,

problems arose with the ship's main engines and her engineers spent most of the five days at anchor repairing one of the main valves to the port turbines. Fortunately, this work was completed by 9am on Saturday 21 September, when the *Ark Royal*, together with the *Barham* (flagship Admiral Cunningham), the *Resolution*, the cruisers *Cumberland* and *Dragon* and a destroyer screen, were able to sail for Dakar. At 5.35am on 23 September the two Luciolles aircraft were flown off to a local airfield where the pilots were promptly arrested. That day, to the surprise of the attacking forces, the Vichy authorities not only refused to transfer their loyalty to de Gaulle, but they also opened fire on the invading force, damaging the *Resolution*, the *Cumberland* and two destroyers, with the battleship *Richelieu* firing her 15-inch guns at the British force. Next day, at 6am, six Skuas armed with 500lb bombs were flown off to attack the troublesome French battleship. Although all the aircraft returned safely they did not hit the *Richelieu* which, once again, was firing its devastating salvoes at the British fleet. That afternoon, at just before 2pm, nine Swordfish and six Skuas were flown off on a second strike, but once again no hits were scored on the French battleship and three Swordfish were shot down by French fighters. One of the planes came down in the sea and the crew were rescued by HMS *Escapade*. On Wednesday 25 September, although the *Richelieu* was damaged, it was apparent that to continue with the invasion would cause very heavy casualties and as it was unlikely to succeed it was called off at noon and the British force, with a badly damaged *Resolution*, limped back to Freetown, where the *Ark Royal* anchored at 2.40pm on Saturday 28 September. The invasion of Dakar had proved to be a complete and humiliating failure, during which the *Ark Royal* had lost nine aircraft. On board everyone welcomed the news that the carrier would now return to the UK for a refit, and early on Monday 30 September she left Freetown and set course for Liverpool. It was during the afternoon of Tuesday 8 October that the *Ark Royal* steamed up the River Mersey, and by 5.10pm she was high and dry in the Gladstone Graving Dock just off Bootle's Crosby Road.

During the 21 days that the *Ark Royal* spent in dry dock all the ship's company were able to take some leave, and although they had only been away from home for just over four months, the situation in Britain was very different now. The blitz on London was at its height and during the previous month 6,954 civilians had been killed and 10,615 injured as a result of the bombing. Just a few weeks before the carrier's arrival in Liverpool, invasion scares were at their height and massive air raids had been launched against the cities of Southampton, Bristol, Cardiff, Manchester and Liverpool itself. However, such interruptions did not stop the occasional ceremonial visits and on Friday 11 October the First Lord of the Admiralty visited the ship and addressed those members of the ship's

Blackburn Skuas ranged for take-off in the Mediterranean, 1940. *(Fleet Air Arm Museum)*

The *Ark Royal, Argus* (with Hurricanes on deck), and the *Rodney* at sea in the Mediterranean in mid-November 1940.
(Imperial War Museum A9543)

company who were on board. However, during the last week of October, with the refit almost completed, all efforts were directed towards cleaning up and getting everything shipshape once again, and at 9am on Tuesday 29 October the carrier was manoeuvred out of dry dock. Just two and a half hours later she was disembarking the pilot off the Mersey Bar Lightship, before setting course for the Firth of Clyde. During her 24 hours in the Clyde she re-embarked her squadrons, with 808 Squadron of Fairey Fulmars replacing 803 Squadron's outdated Skuas. The Fleet Air Arm had desperately wanted a new aircraft to replace its antiquated biplanes, but the thinking of the 1930s dictated that even with a high-performance fighter a crew of two was desirable to cope with the growing sophistication of navigational aids. Inevitably this imposed an extra size and weight penalty, but before the arrival of the Sea Hurricane and Seafire the Fairey Fulmar was the best aircraft available. The first prototypes, flown in January 1937, were designed as light bombers, but after modifications were made in 1938 the Fulmar became a fleet fighter. The first production aircraft flew in January 1940 and a few weeks later it went to Boscombe Down and then to HMS *Illustrious* for trials. Pilots found the Fulmar, with its maximum speed of 247mph and its eight .303-inch machine-guns in the wings, a great improvement on the Skua, and the only criticism was its slow rate of climb. However, when the original concept was evolved it was considered very unlikely that carrier-borne aircraft would be matched against much superior land-based aircraft. Unfortunately, on the last day of October, as the Fulmars were landing on, one of them crashed into the sea, but the aircrew were rescued by the destroyer *Duncan* and they rejoined the carrier, minus their aircraft, an hour later. That same afternoon the *Ark Royal* left the Clyde, and with a screen of six destroyers, set course for Gibraltar.

After a very rough passage through severe south-westerly gales and heavy seas, the carrier arrived in Gibraltar and rejoined Force H at just before 3pm on Wednesday 6 November 1940. Soon after her arrival she hoisted the flag of Vice-Admiral Sir James Somerville, who embarked with his staff. Once again the *Ark Royal* had arrived to a much altered and very uncertain strategic situation, with Gibraltar under a real threat of an overland attack from Spain and the Battle of the Atlantic under way. The fall of France had provided bases for the U-boats on the western seaboard of that country, and packs of submarines were making concerted and highly successful attacks on convoys. In the Eastern Mediterranean Italy had invaded Greece which, initially, eased the threat on Malta, but which would lead to further disasters for the British Army. Soon after her arrival in Gibraltar the *Ark Royal* and Force H were on the offensive once again, and at 6.20pm on Thursday 7 November, in company with the battleship *Barham*, the cruisers *Berwick*, *Glasgow* and *Sheffield*, and a destroyer screen, they left Gibraltar and set course east for hostile waters. Meanwhile, in the Eastern Mediterranean, Admiral Cunningham's force, which included four battleships and the *Illustrious*, had left Alexandria to escort five vital cargo ships to Malta. At 4.30am on the morning of Saturday 9 November, having closed the island of Sardinia, nine Swordfish were flown off to bomb the airfield and seaplane base at Cagliari. This time they encountered heavy anti-aircraft fire, but after hitting hangars, a power station and a number of seaplanes, all returned safely. However, at 10am as the force was retiring, an enemy reconnaissance plane was sighted and shot down, but not before it had reported the carrier's position, and at 11.20am a high-level bombing attack developed on the fleet. This time, however, the Fulmars of 808 Squadron went into action and they were able to intercept the enemy and break up some of their formations, but even so, the bombing was accurate and there were a number of near misses. During the operation the *Barham* and some of the escorting destroyers passed safely through the narrows and joined Admiral Cunningham's fleet in the Eastern Mediterranean, whilst at 9am on Monday 11 November the *Ark Royal* returned safely to Gibraltar where, on the following day, she was joined by the *Renown* which had returned from a fruitless search of the Atlantic for the pocket battleship *Admiral Scheer*. Meanwhile, on the same day that the *Ark Royal* returned to Gibraltar, 21 Swordfish from the *Illustrious* launched their devastating attack on the Italian naval base at Taranto, badly damaging three battleships and two cruisers.

The ships of Force H began their next mission at 4am on Friday 15 November, when the *Ark Royal*, *Renown* and *Sheffield* put to sea to escort the *Argus* east to a position Lat 37° - 23'N/Long 06° - 36'E where, at 6.10am the next day, the elderly carrier flew off 12 Hurricanes for Malta. By the morning of 19 November Force H and the *Argus* were back at Gibraltar. As always it was not long before the *Ark Royal* was at sea once again and this time it was to take part in an operation to escort vital merchant ships through the narrows en route to Malta, and to rendezvous with the elderly battleship *Ramillies* which was steaming west from Alexandria to join them. In addition the cruisers *Manchester* and *Southampton* would steam east, each of them carrying 700 RAF personnel for deployment in Egypt. The two cruisers arrived at Gibraltar on 21 November, whilst the merchant ships and their escort passed through the Strait of Gibraltar during the night of 24 November, and at 7am on Monday 25 November the *Ark Royal*, *Renown*, *Manchester*, *Sheffield* and *Southampton* left Gibraltar to join them as they steamed eastward. Next day, at 10.30am, with the force in a position Lat 37° - 02'N/Long 01° - 10'E, a Fulmar crashed astern of the *Ark Royal*, but otherwise it was a quiet day. At 8am on Wednesday 27 November, the fleet was in a position 150 miles south-south-west of Sardinia, and 50 miles north of the African coast, with the *Ramillies* and her escorts steering a converging course from the east. At about this time a patrolling Swordfish sighted four enemy cruisers and six destroyers, but due to a communications error it was almost 10am before the sighting report reached Admiral Somerville in the *Renown*, and then it came in as eight cruisers and six destroyers. Initially it was thought that the sighting referred to the *Ramillies*, but by 10.30am it was realized that a strong enemy force, including battleships, was at sea. Admiral Somerville decided to join forces with the *Ramillies* and at 11.30am, after the rendezvous, he altered course to the north-east in order to close the Italian warships, which included the battleships *Vittorio Veneto* and *Cesare*, in order to close the range. At just after midday the enemy ships were in sight and at 12.25pm the *Renown* opened fire at extreme range. Meanwhile, on the *Ark Royal* 11 Swordfish armed with torpedoes had taken off at 11.30am and although one hit was recorded on the destroyer *Lancieri*, the Italian force was not handicapped and they all escaped to the north-east. With his ships coming dangerously close to enemy air and submarine bases at Cagliari, Admiral Somerville broke off the engagement and set course back to the convoy. A second strike by the *Ark Royal's* Swordfish failed to do any more damage to the Italian ships, but at just after 2pm enemy bombers attacked the British force. Fortunately they did not hit anything, but at 4.40pm four waves of Italian bombers attacked the *Ark Royal* and they came very close to hitting the carrier, with bombs straddling the ship and bursting just yards from her. The enormous splashes drenched the flight deck with water, and light bulbs and crockery were broken, but the carrier herself steamed out of the melee unscathed and with her anti-aircraft guns blazing. That evening the *Ramillies* joined Force H and after leaving the convoy, they all turned round and made for Gibraltar which they reached during the afternoon of Friday 29 November.

The first week of December provided a welcome respite for the *Ark Royal's* ship's company, while the carrier remained alongside and essential maintenance was undertaken, and during the afternoon of Friday 6 December she was host to a number of VIPs when the Governor of the nearby Spanish town of Algeciras, the Governor of Gibraltar, the Flag Officer North Atlantic, Admiral Sir Dudley North, and Vice-Admiral Sir James Somerville paid a visit. It was on the morning of Monday 9 December that the *Ark Royal* went to sea again, for two days of exercises off the colony. During the flying training on 10 December a Fulmar crashed into the sea, with the crew being safely rescued by HMS *Firedrake*, but on the next day at 9.40am, soon after the start of flying operations, two Swordfish were in collision and tragically the crew of one of them were killed, with only one body

being recovered. The pilot, Lt S. G. J. Appleby and the TAG, Ldg Airman L. D. Clark, went down with the plane and the body of the observer, Sub-Lt J. W. A. Grant, was recovered from the sea. That same afternoon, at 1.30pm, the *Ark Royal* returned to Gibraltar where the funeral of Sub-Lt Grant took place the next morning, and there was a memorial service for the other two members of the aircrew. Two days later, at 10.30am on Saturday 14 December, the carrier left Gibraltar with the *Renown* to search the area around the Azores where it was believed the German heavy cruiser *Admiral Hipper* might be, having slipped through the blockade of the Denmark Strait. In the event, the enemy cruiser had left Brunsbuttel on 30 November, and having travelled up the Norwegian coast undetected, she passed through the Strait on 6/7 December. Following this she had been searching for British shipping in the western half of the Atlantic, and so Force H's sweep around the Azores came to nothing and on Thursday 19 December they returned to Gibraltar. After refuelling, the *Ark Royal*, together with the *Renown*, *Malaya*, and the *Sheffield*, left the colony at 5.25pm the following day to escort two fast merchantmen, *Clan Fraser* and *Clan Forbes*, to Malta. Three days later, during the late afternoon of Monday 23 December, the heavy units parted company with the two cargo vessels and turned round to set course back to Gibraltar, leaving *Sheffield* to continue the escort. It was at just after midday on Christmas Eve that the *Ark Royal* arrived back in the colony, but there was to be no holiday for her ship's company for that same day, 700 miles west of Cape Finisterre, the *Admiral Hipper* encountered the 20-ship troop convoy WS5A which was bound for the Middle East. The convoy was being escorted by the cruisers *Berwick*, *Bonaventure* and *Dunedin*, together with the carriers *Argus* and *Furious* which were carrying aircraft reinforcements to Takoradi, on the Gold Coast (Ghana), from where they would be flown to Egypt. After shadowing the convoy for a time the *Admiral Hipper* launched an attack and damaged the 14,000-ton *Empire Trooper*. There then followed a running gun duel between the *Berwick* and the German cruiser during which both ships suffered damage, as a result of which the *Admiral Hipper* broke off the action and headed for the port of Brest. Meanwhile, at 2pm on Christmas Day, the *Ark Royal* and Force H left Gibraltar to head into the Atlantic and the area around the Azores again to search for the German vessel. Despite strong winds and heavy seas the carrier managed to fly reconnaissance patrols, but yet again they were to no avail for on 27 December the *Admiral Hipper* reached her destination at Brest. Three days later Force H arrived back in Gibraltar where the New Year of 1941 was celebrated, while the *Ark's* engineers had the task of repairing defective boilers.

On Tuesday 7 January 1941 the *Ark Royal* and Force H put to sea again to escort four merchantmen on their voyage through to Malta. In addition the carrier was transporting five Swordfish aircraft of 821 Squadron, which were launched in the early hours of Thursday 9 January, and although their flight path took them close to enemy airfields in Sicily they all arrived safely at Malta. Later that day, at just before 2pm, a high-level bombing attack developed, but the enemy aircraft were intercepted and largely broken up by the *Ark Royal's* Fulmars. Although the return passage to Gibraltar passed uneventfully for Force H and they arrived back in the colony during the evening of Saturday 11 January, the situation for Admiral Cunningham's force which had taken over the convoy escort was not so good, with the destroyer *Gallant* having hit a mine, while the aircraft carrier *Illustrious* was severely damaged in a dive-bombing attack by German aircraft. In Gibraltar the *Ark Royal* was to remain alongside for 16 days, her longest time in harbour since October 1940, and the opportunity was taken to carry out essential maintenance. During the afternoon of Tuesday 28 January the carrier put to sea once again and performed deck landing practice in company with the *Renown,* just east of Gibraltar. Just over 24 hours later she was back alongside 43 berth of Gibraltar's South Mole, to prepare for her next important offensive operation, an attack on the hydro-electric power station and dam at Lake Tirso on the island of Sardinia. The *Ark Royal, Renown, Malaya, Sheffield* and destroyers left Gibraltar at 12.30pm on Friday 31 January and steamed east into the central Mediterranean. Two days later, early on the morning of Sunday 2 February, eight Swordfish all armed with torpedoes were flown off in very poor weather conditions with strong winds, heavy rain and thick cloud, to attack their target. One of the aircraft became detached from the flight and eventually it returned to the ship, whilst the remaining planes, after a very difficult flight and in the face of heavy anti-aircraft fire, did reach the target and dropped their missiles. One of the Swordfish was shot down, with the aircrew being taken prisoner, but the remainder returned safely to the *Ark Royal* and with weather conditions deteriorating still further, Admiral Somerville cancelled his proposed attack on the port of Genoa and Force H returned to Gibraltar during the evening of Tuesday 4 February. Two days later, at 3.25pm, Force H sailed in more favourable weather to implement the attack on Genoa. By the early hours of Saturday 8 February the force was north of Cape Formentor on the north-east tip of Majorca, and during the course of that day a Spanish commercial aircraft flew over, followed by two Vichy French planes. It was clear to Admiral Somerville that the element of surprise had almost certainly been lost and he ordered Force H to alter course to the south-east to make it appear that they intended another attack on Sardinia. Fortunately the day passed quietly, although that afternoon a Fulmar crashed on deck whilst landing. At 7pm Force H again changed course to the north-east and at about the same time three Italian

battleships, escorted by seven destroyers, left La Spezia to make straight for the Strait of Bonifacio where they were to rendezvous with a cruiser force from Naples in a search for Force H. At just after 5am on the morning of Sunday 9 February, with the *Ark Royal* having been detached from the main force, and right in the centre of the Ligurian Sea, 16 of her Swordfish took off, armed with bombs and mines. Their targets were the port of Leghorn (Livorno), the airfield and railway junction at Pisa and the naval base at La Spezia. The attack on Leghorn was a success, but one aircraft was lost and its crew, Midshipmen N. G. Attenborough and S. W. Foote, and Ldg Airman G. W. Halifax, were buried with full military honours by the Italian Navy. Mines were dropped in the harbour entrance at La Spezia and while the strike force was in action, the *Renown, Malaya* and *Sheffield* closed the Italian coast off Genoa and commenced bombarding the port. At 9am, when the aircraft had returned and Force H had regrouped, Admiral Somerville turned round and set course for Gibraltar, which was the most dangerous part of the whole operation. The *Ark Royal* maintained a constant patrol of six Fulmars over the force, but apart from two high-level bombers who dropped their explosives about 1,000 yards astern of the carrier, no further air attacks developed. Fortunately Admiral Somerville avoided the Italian surface fleet, although at one stage the two forces were only 30 miles apart, and by dark on 9 February Force H was in the Gulf of Lyon. At 5.30am on the morning of Tuesday 11 February they passed the Alboran Islands and finally, at 5.20pm, the *Ark Royal* secured alongside 43 berth at Gibraltar.

Meanwhile, in the much colder waters of the Denmark Strait and the North Atlantic, the German battlecruisers *Scharnhorst* and *Gneisenau* were at large, and the cruiser *Admiral Hipper* was once more at sea and searching for convoys on the Atlantic between Britain and Sierra Leone. On 9 February, while Force H was still in the Ligurian Sea, she had intercepted an unescorted convoy of 16 ships which were en route to the UK and had sunk seven of them. This meant that there would be no respite for the *Ark Royal* and Force H, and just 24 hours after arriving in Gibraltar from the attacks on the Italian ports, they were at sea again with a destroyer screen and heading for the mid-Atlantic to track down the German raider. However, the *Admiral Hipper* was suffering engine problems and she had returned to Brest for a period in dry dock. Back on the North Atlantic, at 8.50am on Monday 17 February, the *Ark Royal* and Force H rendezvoused with convoy WS6 in a position Lat 47° - 01'N/Long 31° - 24'W. The convoy was being escorted by the cruiser HMS *Birmingham* and the armed merchant cruiser HMS *Cathay*, an ex-P&O liner which was armed with a few, very ancient, 6-inch guns. The convoy consisted mainly of fast passenger liners which had been converted to troop transports, and they were

On 27 November 1940, when the *Ark Royal* was south-west of Sardinia escorting an eastbound convoy, she was attacked by Italian bombers. Here she is seen steaming hard through the enormous columns of water thrown up by the bomb explosions. *(Imperial War Museum A2325)*

carrying reinforcements for the garrison at Singapore in response to a very aggressive Japanese foreign policy in the Far East. As the convoy steamed south, the *Ark Royal* flew air reconnaissance patrols continuously from dawn to dusk, and fortunately there were no alarms. On Friday 21 February, in a position Lat 31° - 07'N/Long 30° - 06'W, the convoy escort duties were taken over by HMS *Malaya* and Force H set course for Gibraltar, which they reached during the afternoon of Tuesday 25 February. The *Ark Royal's* ship's company were then able to enjoy a six-day break in the colony's small town before, at 1.15pm on Monday 3 March, Vice-Admiral Sir James Somerville hoisted his flag in the carrier and she put to sea for just over 24 hours of flying exercises west of Gibraltar before she returned to 43 berth and secured alongside. Suddenly, on Saturday 8 March, the battleship HMS *Malaya,* which was escorting a convoy off the coast of West Africa, reported a sighting of the *Scharnhorst* and *Gneisenau* some 350 miles north-east of the Cape Verde Islands and by 9.15pm that evening the *Ark Royal, Renown,* the cruiser *Arethusa* and two destroyers were at sea again and steaming south-west for the Canary Islands. Next day a report was received that the enemy ships had sunk a lone merchantman close to the position where the *Malaya* had

sighted them, but reconnaissance flights failed to find any trace of them. At 5pm on Monday 10 March Force H rendezvoused with the convoy SL67, which was steaming slowly towards home. Four days later, when the convoy was in a position Lat 33° - 45'N/Long 21° - 39'W, one of the *Ark Royal's* Swordfish failed to return from a reconnaissance flight with the loss of its aircrew, Sub-Lts D. M. Ferguson and J. K. M. Watt. Three days later, in the early hours of Monday 17 March, it was thought that the German warships were close by and a striking force of Swordfish aircraft was ranged, but it turned out to be a false alarm. On Wednesday 19 March the *Ark Royal* and Force H handed over responsibility for convoy SL67 to the cruiser *Kenya,* and they set course for Gibraltar. No sooner had they altered course than a signal was received ordering Force H to steam north to search for the German oil tanker *Antarktis,* which had sailed from Vigo to support the German warships. That evening the reconnaissance aircraft sighted another tanker, SS *Bianca,* steaming for Bordeaux and it was known that this vessel had been captured by the enemy raiders. Next morning, as a result of the reconnaissance searches carried out by the *Ark Royal's* aircraft, the *Renown* intercepted the *Bianca* whereupon the German boarding party quickly scuttled her, and another ship which had been captured by the enemy warships, the SS *Casimiro,* scuttled herself. However, events soon took a more dramatic turn when a Fulmar from the *Ark Royal* finally sighted the *Scharnhorst* and *Gneisenau,* which were about 145 miles from the carrier. Unfortunately, a radio defect prevented the pilot from relaying a message to Force H and it was not until 6.17pm that Admiral Somerville learned that the two enemy warships were just 145 miles away. With darkness falling it was far too dangerous to send out a strike force at such a range and another Fulmar was flown off in the hope that it could pinpoint the enemy's position. Unfortunately, with the weather conditions deteriorating and with the remaining vestiges of daylight fast disappearing, the search proved fruitless and it had to be abandoned until the following day. Next morning the searches were resumed, but still without any sighting, and at 4.30pm there was tragedy when a Swordfish armed with depth charges crashed into the sea over the bows as it was accelerated off. The aircraft literally broke into two parts and the depth charges exploded under the ship, killing the aircrew, Sub-Lt P. E. Opdall, Sub-Lt C. R. Hearn and Ldg Airman B. C. Biggs, and causing some minor damage to the carrier. That evening an RAF Hudson spotted the enemy warships making for Brest, and as the *Ark Royal* was too far away to fly off another strike, she and the *Renown* altered course for Gibraltar, where they arrived on the morning of Tuesday 25 March. With the German battlecruisers and the *Admiral Hipper* still at large, the *Ark Royal* and *Renown* stayed alongside just long enough to refuel and after only 13 hours in Gibraltar they put to sea again to patrol the area west of the Bay of Biscay and Cape Finisterre, between Lisbon and Ushant, in atrocious weather conditions. Despite severe storms, reconnaissance flights were flown throughout the hours of daylight, but by the end of the month it was evident that the *Scharnhorst* and *Gneisenau* were not about to leave Brest, and the *Renown* and *Ark Royal* returned to Gibraltar at 9am on Tuesday 1 April.

After only 24 hours in Gibraltar, the *Ark Royal, Renown, Sheffield* and the destroyers put to sea again at 2.12am on Wednesday 2 April and set course for the central Mediterranean. During the hours that the carrier had spent in Gibraltar, 12 Hurricanes, which had been delivered to the colony by the *Argus,* were embarked along with their pilots, and Force H was bound for a point some 420 miles west of Malta where the aircraft would be flown off. The passage was uneventful and at 6.20am on 3 April the Hurricanes departed for their long flight through hostile airspace. Two hours later an enemy shadowing plane was spotted, but by then Force H was steaming hard for Gibraltar where they arrived during the morning of Friday 4 April. Later that day the *Ark Royal* slipped her moorings again and once at sea the remaining outdated Skuas of 800 Squadron were flown off, to be relieved by the Fulmars of

807 Squadron which had arrived in Gibraltar aboard the *Furious.* She had also embarked four more Swordfish aircraft of 825 Squadron which were fitted with ASV radar equipment, and on the following day, with the *Furious,* the *Ark Royal* returned to Gibraltar. However, no sooner was she alongside than a signal was received to the effect that the *Scharnhorst* and the *Gneisenau* were preparing to leave Brest, and so at 7pm that evening, with the *Renown, Sheffield, Furious* and the destroyers, she left to steam north into the Atlantic. Within 24 hours of them sailing it was realized that the German ships were, in fact, still alongside and the opportunity was taken to send the *Ark Royal* back to Gibraltar for three hours in order to complete her fuelling, and after embarking 160 tons of FFO she returned to the Atlantic for ten days to keep up a patrol off Cape Finisterre, during which time continual reconnaissance patrols were flown in very rough weather conditions. Despite the constant heaving and rolling of the flight deck there was only one flying accident when, during the afternoon of Tuesday 8 April, a Swordfish crashed while landing, but fortunately with no casualties. At 2.15pm on Wednesday 16 April the *Ark Royal* returned to Gibraltar's South Mole, and three-quarters of an hour later Captain L. E. H. Maund RN joined the ship. Three days later, at 6.30pm on Saturday 19 April, Captain Holland disembarked to fly home to the UK and Captain Maund took over the command of the aircraft carrier. He was to be the *Ark Royal's* last commanding officer.

Four days after Captain Maund took command of the aircraft carrier, the elderly HMS *Argus* arrived in Gibraltar loaded with 23 RAF Hurricanes and their personnel, and most of 23 April was spent loading the aircraft onto the *Ark Royal* where the Fleet Air Arm engineers were employed assembling them and making them airworthy. Then, at 10.40pm she sailed with the rest of Force H, bound for the central Mediterranean. Although the force was in the flying-off position by Saturday 26 April, bad weather over Malta delayed the operation for 24 hours and the 23 Hurricanes were finally launched on the morning of Sunday 27 April. Next day, at just after 5am, as Force H was approaching Gibraltar, six Swordfish were flown off and one of them crashed into the sea after veering off course and hitting the island superstructure, with the loss of one crew member, Ldg Airman D. R. Evans. At 6pm that evening the *Ark Royal* berthed at Gibraltar once again, this time for a seven-day break.

The *Ark Royal's* next operational foray into the central Mediterranean began on Monday 5 May when, at just after 9am, she left Gibraltar in company with the *Renown,* the cruisers *Fiji, Naiad,* and *Sheffield,* and the destroyers of Force H. Following the successful German campaigns to capture Yugoslavia, Greece and Crete, and the Axis siege of Tobruk in Libya, Churchill and the Chiefs of Staff agreed to send strong tank reinforcements from Britain to Egypt

HM Ships *Renown*, *Ark Royal* and *Manchester* in line ahead at sea in late November 1940.   *(Imperial War Museum A2333)*

in a mission code-named 'Operation Tiger'. Initially it was thought that the tank-carrying convoy would sail via Cape Town, but then it was decided that in order to save precious time it should be routed through the Mediterranean. The convoy consisted of 13 fast merchantmen, seven of which were carrying fuel oil and supplies, while the other six were laden with 295 tanks and 50 aircraft which were urgently needed in Egypt. After leaving Gibraltar Force H steamed out into the Atlantic where, at 5.35pm, eight hours after sailing, they rendezvoused with the convoy WS8A and its escort, which included the battleship HMS *Queen Elizabeth*. The whole force then altered course for the Strait of Gibraltar, through which they passed in the early hours of Tuesday 6 May. Any hopes that their passage through the Strait had gone unnoticed were soon dispelled for later that day, at 7pm, an enemy shadowing plane was reported some 25 miles ahead of the convoy. However, no attacks developed that evening and the following day passed quietly as the convoy steamed eastward. By the morning of Thursday 8 May the convoy was in a position Lat 37° - 41'N/Long 06° - 46'E, off the coast of Algeria and almost due south of Sardinia. With a heavily overcast sky the weather appeared favourable for the Allied ships, but at 11am an Italian reconnaissance seaplane broke through the cloud cover and was fired on by the *Naiad*. Patrolling fighters from the *Ark Royal* pursued the plane, but it managed to escape back into the clouds and to report the convoy's position. By noon that day the ships were south of Sardinia, and at 1.45pm eight Italian torpedo-bombers

attacked the *Ark Royal* and *Renown*, having approached low over the water, thereby avoiding radar detection. Fortunately both ships managed to comb the tracks of the torpedoes, and the carrier's Fulmars were able to engage the enemy aircraft and three were shot down, but not without the loss of a Fulmar and its crew. Soon afterwards, at 4.10pm, a formation of enemy SM 79s was broken up and one was shot down, but once again a Fulmar was lost, although this time the crew were rescued. Fortunately, no damage was done to the convoy, but at just after 6pm a strong force of Ju 87 (Stuka) dive-bombers and ME 110 bombers was detected on the radar rapidly approaching Force H, but this raid was broken up by the carrier's Fulmar fighters. The final incident came at 8.15pm when three torpedo-bombers made a determined attack on the *Ark Royal,* which just succeeded in combing the resulting torpedo tracks. That night the Mediterranean Fleet took over the convoy escort and Force H altered course to return to Gibraltar. The convoy itself almost reached safety unscathed, but on 9 May the 9,000-ton SS *Empire Song* was sunk off Malta after hitting a mine, with the loss of its cargo of tanks. Force H did not encounter any problems and the *Ark Royal* berthed at Gibraltar during the early evening of Monday 12 May. As a result of 'Operation Tiger' Admiral Somerville commended the magnificent effort of the *Ark Royal's* air and ground crews, and Captain Maund's skilful handling of his ship in dodging some very well aimed torpedoes.

Chapter Four

The *Bismarck* And The Final Weeks

After four days in Gibraltar the *Ark Royal* went to sea for 24 hours of flying exercises, returning to harbour during the evening of Saturday 17 May, and at 9.30pm the following evening the *Furious* arrived in the colony and berthed astern of her. She was carrying a further 21 RAF Hurricanes and ten Fulmars to re-equip the *Ark's* depleted squadrons, and no sooner had she secured alongside than a ramp was fitted between the two flight decks for the transfer of the aircraft, which took four and a half hours between 10pm and 2.30am the next morning. Finally, at 2.50am on Monday 19 May, Force H put to sea and steamed out into the Atlantic where they remained all day, well out of sight of land. That evening, at just before midnight, the force passed Cape Spartel and in the early hours of Tuesday 20 May they passed through the Strait of Gibraltar and steamed east. Next day, at between 6am and 6.30am, the 21 Hurricanes were flown off the *Ark Royal* and with 27 from the *Furious* they set course for Malta. The *Ark Royal* arrived back in Gibraltar on the morning of Friday 23 May for a stay of just over 24 hours.

Five days earlier the German battleship *Bismarck,* together with the cruiser *Prinz Eugen*, had left Gdynia to carry out 'Operation Rheineübung', a carefully planned foray into the Atlantic where they would create havoc on convoys. On 23 May they were far north, heading for a gap between Iceland and Greenland. However, on the morning of 24 May, off the south-west coast of Iceland, the unthinkable had happened when the *Bismarck* sank the pride of the Royal Navy, the elderly battlecruiser HMS *Hood*, with the loss of all but three members of her ship's company. Not only had the *Hood* been lost, but the much newer battleship HMS *Prince of Wales* had also been seriously damaged. Fortunately the *Prince of Wales* had inflicted some damage on the *Bismarck,* as did the Swordfish of 825 Squadron flying from HMS *Victorious.* The Royal Navy now needed to avenge the tragedy of the *Hood,* and battleships of the Home

A full flight deck with Swordfish ranged for flying off.

(Fleet Air Arm Museum)

HMS *Ark Royal* engaged on convoy escort duty in the Mediterranean during 1941.   *(Fleet Air Arm Museum)*

Fleet, including *King George V* (Admiral Sir John Tovey, C-in-C Home Fleet) and *Rodney,* four cruisers and a destroyer force joined the search for the German battleship.

In the early hours of Saturday 24 May, whilst the cruisers *Norfolk* and *Suffolk* shadowed the *Bismarck* as she headed for the relative safety of Brest, the *Ark Royal, Renown, Sheffield* and a destroyer screen left Gibraltar to steam out into mid-Atlantic to join the search. However, at about 3am on Sunday 25 May the shadowing cruisers lost contact with the German warships and for five hours Admiral Tovey could only guess at their movements and, to make matters worse, some of his ships were now low on fuel. Then at 8am, Admiral Lutjens, who was flying his flag in the *Bismarck,* sent a long signal to Germany as a result of which direction-finding stations in the UK were able to pinpoint his position and inform Admiral Tovey that the *Bismarck* was making for Brest. It was apparent that only Force H was in a position to intercept the enemy battleship, which had detached from the *Prinz Eugen,* and Admiral Somerville battled through gale force winds to cut off the *Bismarck's* route to safety. At dawn on Monday 26 May the north-westerly Force 10 gales were still blowing and the green Atlantic waves were crashing over the *Ark Royal's* flight deck from a sea which was covered in dense streaks of foam. Normally in such conditions flying operations would have been out of the question, but these

were exceptional circumstances and that morning ten reconnaissance Swordfish were flown off the heaving flight deck to carry out a search for the German battleship. At 10.30am an RAF Catalina flying boat spotted the *Bismarck,* which opened fire on him, but not before he had sent out a report of her position. Soon afterwards the *Ark's* Swordfish located the enemy warship and they shadowed her until they were relieved by two more aircraft. With the battleship fast approaching the range for friendly air cover it was clear that everything hinged on the *Ark Royal's* aircraft being able to slow the *Bismarck* down.

By noon on 26 May the *Ark Royal,* in a position Lat 49°- 20'N/Long 19° - 04'W, had crossed the *Bismarck's* line of advance and she was 50 miles north-east of the battleship. It was at 12.45pm that she was able to fly off a strike force of 15 Swordfish and one of her few remaining Skuas, and no sooner had they become airborne than the *Ark Royal* and Force H passed within firing range of the German submarine *U556.* As it happened, the submarine had no torpedoes left and it could only watch as the aircraft carrier passed by. In the meantime Admiral Somerville had ordered the cruiser HMS *Sheffield* to make contact with and to shadow the *Bismarck,* but the signal had not reached Captain Maund in the carrier. As soon as he became aware of it he sent an immediate signal, 'Look out for *Sheffield'* to the strike force, but unfortunately it was too late, for at

3.40pm Captain Larcom in the cruiser saw the Swordfish about to attack him. He immediately ordered his anti-aircraft gunners to hold fire, which they did with remarkable discipline, and he desperately manoeuvred his ship to dodge the torpedoes. Three of the crews, recognizing the *Sheffield,* pulled out of the attack formation, but the remainder launched their torpedoes which, being armed with magnetic pistols, were designed to explode beneath a ship. However, half of those launched exploded on impact with the sea and the remainder were skilfully dodged by the cruiser. It is said that one aircraft, as it left the scene, signalled to the *Sheffield,* 'Sorry about the kipper.' Soon afterwards Admiral Tovey learned that the attack had been unsuccessful, but when the Swordfish landed back on board the *Ark Royal* at just after 5pm they were immediately refuelled and rearmed, although this time with contact pistols, and at 7.10pm they were flown off for a second strike on the *Bismarck.* This time the antiquated torpedo-bombers found their true target, and in an attack which lasted for 40 minutes they scored two hits on the *Bismarck,* one amidships and one which caused a crippling explosion aft and jammed the battleship's rudder at 12 degrees to port. Although her propellers were still operating, the ship had always been difficult to steer by engines alone, and despite the heroic efforts of her engineers, she was not under control and, in fact, steered very slowly in two complete circles before moving off in a north-westerly direction, away from the coast of France and towards Admiral Tovey's force.

Meanwhile, after carrying out their attack in the face of heavy and accurate anti-aircraft fire, which damaged a number of aircraft, the Swordfish returned to the *Ark Royal's* plunging flight deck where three of them crashed on landing, but fortunately with no casualties. By 11.15pm all the Swordfish were back on board and preparations got under way at once to refuel and rearm all the serviceable aircraft, for at that stage it was not realized that the *Bismarck* had been fatally crippled. However, when two shadowing Swordfish returned at 11.35pm and reported that the German battleship had made two complete circles, the third attack was cancelled. Suddenly the position had been reversed and it was Admiral Tovey who was now in control of the situation. That night the 4th Destroyer Flotilla, under Captain Philip Vian DSO, was ordered to shadow the crippled battleship and in the early hours of Tuesday 27 May HMS *Zulu* fired four torpedoes, but had to withdraw rapidly in the face of accurate gunfire from the battleship. As the night wore on, Vian's destroyers continually harried the *Bismarck* and of 16 torpedoes which they fired, two appeared to hit the battleship, but devastating gunfire kept the destroyers at bay. During the long hours of darkness the ship's company of *Ark Royal* remained at Action Stations, and by first light a range of 12 Swordfish was fully armed and ready to fly off. The final action, however, was to be carried out by the battleships *King George V* and *Rodney,* and at 8.47am on 27 May, steaming in open order from the north-west, they opened fire with their main armament. Initially the return of fire from the *Bismarck* was accurate and she straddled the *Rodney* with her third and fourth salvoes. However, the weight of fire from the two British battleships was overwhelming and soon the *Bismarck* was reduced to a blazing hulk. Overhead the *Ark Royal's* strike force circled the German battleship, but they were unable to attack because of the weight of fire falling on and around the shambles which was once the pride of the German Navy. At 10.36am the *Bismarck,* with her battle ensigns still flying, rolled over and sank, and the cruiser *Dorsetshire* moved in to rescue survivors. On board the *Ark Royal* a member of the Royal Marines detachment described the mood on board, '...how stunned we all were on hearing of the tragic loss of HMS *Hood* and when news came in of the sinking of the *Bismarck,* everyone on board was so uplifted that a cheer went up that should have been heard right across the Bay of Biscay.' The loss of the *Hood* had been avenged.

Meanwhile, at 9.50am, the first German aircraft had arrived over the scene in the form of two Focke-Wulf bombers. Because the *Ark Royal* was carrying out flying operations she was unable to use her guns, but this was more than made up for by the *Renown* and *Sheffield.* At 10.55am more enemy aircraft were engaged as they flew in from the north, but again their bombs fell harmlessly. It then became imperative for the ships of the Home Fleet and Force H to leave the scene immediately for U-boats were converging on the area, and it was this threat that caused the rescuing of the *Bismarck's* survivors to be broken off. It was at 7.47pm on Thursday 29 May that the *Ark Royal* and the ships of Force H arrived back in Gibraltar to the cheers of people on board ships moored in the harbour, the local population and from troops of the garrison. The operation to sink the *Bismarck* had been successful, but on Sunday 1 June, having eluded all the RAF's search patrols, the *Prinz Eugen* arrived safely at Brest.

During the evening of Wednesday 4 June, HMS *Furious* arrived in Gibraltar from the UK laden with Hurricanes and Fulmars, and she berthed astern of the *Ark Royal* where the large wooden ramp was used once again to bridge their respective flight decks. At 9.30pm work began to manhandle the aircraft from the *Furious* to the *Ark* and an hour and a quarter later 24 Hurricanes and nine Fulmars had been transferred. Next morning HMS *Argus* arrived in the colony with yet more Hurricanes and at noon that day the three aircraft carriers, escorted by the *Renown* and *Sheffield,* sailed east into the central Mediterranean. Less than 24 hours later, at 9.55am on Friday 6 June, in a position Lat 37° - 29'N/Long 02° - 27'E, the carriers flew off the Hurricanes, which rendezvoused with RAF Blenheim light bombers that would guide them on the flight to Malta. Next day, at 10.30am, the force arrived back in Gibraltar

A Swordfish takes off from HMS *Ark Royal*.
(*M. D. Walden*)

Below:
Officers on board the cruiser *Hermione* enjoying a siesta on the quarterdeck in the Mediterranean during September 1941. In the background are the *Ark Royal* and the *Rodney*.
(*Imperial War Museum A6138*)

where the *Ark Royal* embarked 877 tons of FFO before she, the *Furious,* and the escorts of Force H sailed once again, this time into the Atlantic where, at 6.50am on Monday 9 June, they rendezvoused with HMS *Victorious* and an escort of destroyers. As the whole force set course for Gibraltar, the ever-faithful cruiser HMS *Sheffield* parted company with Force H and steamed home for a long-overdue refit. Following her departure the three carriers went to Flying Stations to begin a somewhat complicated transfer of aircraft between them in readiness for the passage into the Mediterranean. On the morning of Tuesday 10 June the *Ark Royal* returned to Gibraltar and next morning she was joined by the *Victorious* which moored ahead of her at the South Mole. That morning, with the large wooden ramp in place between the two flight decks, the RAF and Fleet Air Arm personnel on board manhandled 24 Hurricanes from the *Victorious* to the *Ark Royal,* and at just before noon on Friday 13 June the two carriers, escorted by the *Renown,* sailed for their flying-off point south of the island of Formentera. Once in position, during the morning of Saturday 14 June, 47 Hurricanes were flown off the two carriers bound for Malta, but unfortunately two of them crashed en route. No sooner had the force arrived back in Gibraltar on the morning of Sunday 15 June than reports were received that the *Scharnhorst* and *Gneisenau* had left Brest, and at 6pm that evening Force H, reinforced by the *Victorious,* steamed into the Atlantic to search for them. While the force patrolled off Cape Finisterre, daily reconnaissance flights were flown, which revealed that the German warships were obviously still firmly alongside in Brest, and on the morning of Thursday 19 June the *Victorious* parted company and set course for Greenock and three days later the *Ark Royal* returned to Gibraltar.

This gave the *Ark's* ship's company a short break, but during the late afternoon of Wednesday 25 June the *Furious* arrived again loaded with Hurricanes and the well-used ramp was put into position once more to bridge their respective flight decks while 22 partially assembled Hurricane fighters were transferred. The work was completed in the early hours of the following morning when the *Ark Royal,* together with the *Renown* and the cruiser *Hermione,* which had taken the *Sheffield's* place, left for the passage east. Most of the first day at sea was spent completing the construction of the 22 aircraft, and they were flown off early on the morning of Friday 27 June. Once they were safely airborne and getting in position for their rendezvous with the RAF Blenheims which would guide them to their destination, the *Ark Royal* turned round and set course for Gibraltar, arriving there at just before noon on Saturday 28 June. No sooner was she alongside than the RAF maintenance parties began embarking a further 26 Hurricanes from the *Furious.* That same night, just half an hour before midnight, tugs began

pulling the *Ark Royal* from her berth and, struggling against the strong winds of a levanter, it took almost three-quarters of an hour to clear the harbour, then with the *Renown, Hermione, Furious* and a destroyer screen, she steamed east once again to the flying-off position south of the Balearic Islands. At 6am the next morning, Monday 30 June, the Hurricanes began flying off, and by 6.40am they had all taken off safely for Malta. However, on board the *Furious* things did not go so well and one Hurricane, as it was taking off, hit the bridge and burst into flames. As well as the fire damage there were 14 fatalities, and flying operations were cancelled, with six Hurricanes being brought back to Gibraltar. Luckily, 35 had been successfully launched and they all made it safely to Malta. Next day, the first day of July, the force returned to Gibraltar, having assisted in the safe delivery of 145 Hurricane fighters during the month of June.

For the *Ark Royal* and Force H there then followed a ten-day break while preparations were made for 'Operation Substance', a major effort to resupply Malta with 50,000 tons of stores which would be carried in six merchant ships, while 5,500 troops were to be borne in one transport, with the Kings Own Royal Regiment of Lancaster being conveyed in the cruiser HMS *Manchester.* However, the *Ark Royal's* schedule first included 24 hours of flying exercises before the operation began, and on the morning of Friday 11 July she and the *Hermione* left Gibraltar for the nearby exercise areas. That same evening one of the carrier's Swordfish crashed into the sea, but the crew were rescued safely and next evening she was back alongside in Gibraltar. Nine days later, in the early hours of Monday 21 July, the *Ark Royal, Renown, Hermione* and the destroyers of Force H put to sea to rendezvous with the battleship *Nelson* and Force X, which consisted of the cruisers *Edinburgh, Manchester* and *Arethusa,* together with the fast minelayer *Manxman.* In addition eight submarines were stationed off Italy and Sicily, and the Mediterranean Fleet would also stage a diversion in the eastern basin. Fortunately, thick fog on the night of 21 July created welcome cover for the convoy, but the troop transport MV *Leinster* ran aground with the result that 1,000 troops were left behind. Next day, with a calm sea and a clear sky, it was apparent that the convoy's presence would soon become known to the enemy, and Force H steamed to the north of the merchant ships as they progressed east into very dangerous waters. That day the *Ark Royal's* fighters chased off an enemy reconnaissance plane before it spotted the merchant ships, but on the morning of Wednesday 23 July, when the convoy was in a position Lat 37° - 42'N/Long 07° - 41'E, north of Philippeville (Skikda) in Algiers and south-west of Sardinia, the first air attack developed. Since first light the *Ark Royal's* fighters had been flying air patrols overhead and other aircraft were ranged on the flight deck ready for take-off. At 9am radar plotters reported enemy aircraft

Protected by the guns of an escorting battleship, the *Ark* steams through an Atlantic swell. *(Fleet Air Arm Museum)*

approaching and the *Ark Royal's* Fulmars intercepted nine Italian SM 79 high-level bombers about 20 miles from the convoy. The fighters managed to shoot down two of them and the remainder were broken up with the result that their bombs fell harmlessly wide of the convoy. Three of the Fulmars were shot down, but luckily their aircrews were rescued from the sea. However, at 9.45am, whilst the high-level bombers were being intercepted, seven torpedo-bombers dived on the convoy and, despite a terrific anti-aircraft barrage from the fleet, they launched a determined attack. Three of the enemy aircraft were shot down but two of the torpedoes found targets in the cruiser *Manchester* and the destroyer *Fearless*. The destroyer was so badly damaged that she had to be abandoned and sunk, and the *Manchester* was hit in a fuel tank. Initially the cruiser took on an ominous list and although this was soon righted, three of her four engines were out of action and she was ordered back to Gibraltar.

Meanwhile, as the rest of the convoy steamed eastward, a second raid by high-level bombers was broken up and at just after 5pm, with the merchantmen having reached the entrance to the Skerki Channel, the *Ark Royal* and Force H turned to head back for Gibraltar and Force X took up the escort, with the fighters from the *Ark Royal* providing air

cover until after darkness had fallen. Further air attacks that evening damaged the destroyer *Firedrake,* and next day E-boats torpedoed the SS *Sydney Star.* The embarked troops were transferred to a destroyer and with a skeleton crew and listing badly, she made the relative safety of Malta, as did the remainder of the convoy. For the *Ark Royal* the return passage to Gibraltar passed uneventfully, although at 5.30am on Friday 25 July the carrier altered course to avoid an Italian sea rescue craft which was showing a flashing white light, and the mercy vessel was left unharmed by the British fleet. Despite the grounding of the *Leinster* and the damage to the *Manchester,* which resulted in 1,700 troops not reaching Malta, 'Operation Substance' was a success and at 8.20am on Sunday 27 July the *Ark Royal* berthed safely at Gibraltar. Three days later, along with the rest of Force H and the battleship *Nelson,* the carrier was at sea again for it had been decided to send troops from the *Leinster* and the *Manchester* to Malta in the cruisers *Hermione* and *Arethusa,* the fast minelayer *Manxman* and two destroyers. Whilst they were making their passage the *Ark Royal* was to make a diversionary attack on the airfield and harbour at Alghero on the north-west coast of Sardinia. By nightfall on Thursday 31 July, Force H was some 30 miles off Cape Caballeria on the northern coast of

Minorca, and two destroyers were detached to bombard Alghero, which they did at about midnight, destroying the town's Customs House. Just over three hours later, at 3.10am, a strike of nine Swordfish all armed with bombs took off from the *Ark Royal* and made a successful attack on Alghero Airfield despite some accurate anti-aircraft fire. The planes returned to the *Ark Royal* at just after 6am, and 20 minutes later, as the third Swordfish was landing on, tragedy struck. The aircraft was still carrying a 40lb bomb which had jammed on its bomb rack, but as the wheels hit the flight deck it was unleashed and it exploded, killing the pilot, Sub-Lt Jewell, the observer, Sub-Lt Royal and the TAG, Ldg Airman Huxley. The explosion and blast also killed three members of the flight deck party, Lts Bowker and Gay, and Stoker Hunt, as well as blowing a hole in the deck and damaging the arrester gear. With the six remaining Swordfish still circling the ship, temporary repairs were quickly effected, and with fuel to spare they were able to land on safely. At 5.30pm a funeral service was held for the six men killed in the tragic incident, and an hour later the ship steamed from a calm, flat sea into torrential rain and severe thunderstorms, which at least provided cover from enemy air attacks.

Meanwhile, Force X was steaming hard towards Malta which they reached on the morning of Saturday 2 August, receiving an enthusiastic welcome as they entered Grand Harbour. Later in the day, after disembarking the troops, they left the port to make an equally fast westward passage back to Gibraltar and at 8.34am on Sunday 3 August, in a position Lat 38° - 06'N/Long 07° - 20'E, just south-east of the Balearic Islands, they met the *Ark Royal, Renown* and *Nelson,* and the whole force returned to Gibraltar on the evening of Monday 4 August. It was to be the *Ark Royal's* final operational sortie with her faithful companion, the battlecruiser HMS *Renown*, for on Friday 8 August she left Gibraltar for the UK and a refit. Admiral Somerville transferred his flag to the battleship *Nelson* and of the original trio of capital ships which had made up Force H, only the *Ark Royal* remained.

Six days after the departure of the *Renown*, the *Ark Royal, Nelson* and *Hermione* put to sea for three days of exercises together in the eastern approaches of the Mediterranean, but by lunchtime on Sunday 17 August they were back in the colony. Four days later, at 9.20pm, the three ships slipped their moorings once again and set course eastward. They were steaming towards Sardinia where they were to make a diversionary attack on cork plantations near the town of Tempio in the north of the island, while the fast minelayer *Manxman* laid a minefield off the Italian port of Leghorn. The diversion worked well, with the Italian High Command anticipating an eastbound convoy and the Italian Navy dispatched two battleships and four cruisers down the west coast of Sardinia from where they could ambush the 'convoy' as it passed to the south.

Following the unopposed attack on the cork plantations, Admiral Somerville wanted to launch a torpedo attack on the Italian fleet, but reconnaissance flights failed to locate any vessels, and by 4pm on Tuesday 26 August the *Ark Royal* and Force H were back alongside in Gibraltar for a well-earned rest before the next forays into the Mediterranean.

It was Monday 8 September when the *Ark Royal* and the *Hermione* left Gibraltar again to ferry Hurricanes to the flying-off position, but owing to the lack of Blenheims to act as guides, only 12 aircraft were flown off and the force returned to Gibraltar on the morning of Wednesday 10 September. It turned out to be a very busy day on board the *Ark Royal* as 26 more Hurricanes were transferred from the *Furious,* as well as the Swordfish of 312 Squadron which were replacing those of 310 Squadron, with over 50 aircraft in total being manhandled between the two carriers. That evening, at 9pm, with the work having been completed, the *Nelson, Ark Royal, Furious, Hermione* and an escort of destroyers left Gibraltar for the flying-off position at Lat 38° - 11'N/Long 04° - 19'E in the Mediterranean, where 45 Hurricanes were dispatched to Malta, guided by seven RAF Blenheims. During the return passage to Gibraltar on Sunday 14 September, one of the *Ark Royal's* Fulmars crashed into the sea, but the crew were safely rescued by the *Hermione* and that evening, at just after 8pm, the whole of Force H docked in Gibraltar once again. This time there was a break of just one full day before the *Ark Royal, Nelson* and *Hermione* were at sea again for two days of exercises, during which 312 Squadron practised dummy torpedo attacks on the force. During the manoeuvres one Swordfish crashed into the sea, but fortunately the crew were safely rescued and on the afternoon of Wednesday 17 September the *Ark Royal* returned to her berth in Gibraltar. Two days later the Italian submarine *Scire,* which had been modified to carry three human torpedoes in canisters forward and aft of the conning tower, manoeuvred unobserved into Gibraltar Bay, where it lay on the bottom until 1am on Saturday 20 September, when it surfaced and the three chariots set off for the harbour. These were operations at which the Italian Navy excelled, although the first chariot found the harbour defences were so good that its crew laid their explosive charges on the hull of the storage hulk *Fiona Shell* which was anchored in the commercial anchorage of Gibraltar Bay. The second chariot encountered the same problem and so placed their charges beneath the 11,000-ton motor ship *Durham* which was anchored close to the *Fiona Shell.* The third team had been detailed to attack the *Ark Royal* which was lying alongside 43 berth on the South Mole, well inside the harbour defences. Lt Visitini and PO Magno, the crew of chariot three, eventually managed to penetrate the southern entrance to the harbour, despite the patrols who regularly dropped exploding charges into the

The destroyer *Legion* evacuating the *Ark Royal's* ship's company as the carrier lists to starboard after she was hit by a torpedo within 18 miles of the coast of southern Spain during the afternoon of 13 November 1941. The wartime censor has obliterated the pennant number of the destroyer.

(Imperial War Museum A6332)

The ship's company transfer to HMS *Legion*.   *(Fleet Air Arm Museum)*

water, and once inside they surfaced in order to get their bearings. By this time dawn was fast approaching and the two men decided they did not have enough time to make a successful attack on the *Ark Royal*, and so instead they attached their charges to the starboard side of the 8,145-ton oil tanker RFA *Derbydale* which was moored alongside the detached mole. Having completed their task the two men managed to make their way out of the harbour, where they scuttled their chariot and swam ashore to the Spanish side of the Bay. Shortly after they had scrambled ashore at 7.45am the first massive explosion underneath the *Derbydale* told the harbour authorities that something was clearly wrong, and three-quarters of an hour later two more explosions tore into the hulls of the *Durham* and the hulk *Fiona Shell*, which sank rapidly while tugs struggled to

beach the first stricken vessel. On board the *Ark Royal* there was frantic activity as all the watertight doors were shut and the engineers laboured to raise steam for full power. That morning the dockyard was a hive of activity with harbour craft and divers checking the moorings and the ships' underwater hulls, but by midday the authorities were confident that no more charges had been planted and the *Ark Royal* returned to four hours' notice for steam. Despite the fact that the *Ark Royal* had eluded them, the Italian Navy considered it to have been a successful day and a prelude to the devastating attack they planned at Alexandria Harbour in which the battleships *Queen Elizabeth* and *Valiant* would be severely damaged and disabled.

Four days after the Italian attack on the ships at Gibraltar the *Ark Royal*, together with the rest of Force H, left the colony to escort a convoy of nine merchant ships carrying stores and ammunition to Malta. For this mission, code-named 'Operation Halberd', Force H was reinforced by the battleships *Rodney* and *Prince of Wales*, as well as four cruisers, with whom they rendezvoused at 7.35am on Saturday 27 September in a position Lat 37°- 31'N/Long 08° - 38'E. At 12.26pm that afternoon a force of 12 Italian torpedo-bombers were in the vicinity of the convoy, but they were intercepted and broken up by the *Ark Royal's* Fulmars, and although six of them got through with their torpedoes, these were skilfully avoided. By 1.10pm the raid was over, but 25 minutes later came renewed attacks by torpedo-bombers, and 14 Fulmars were scrambled to intercept them. Despite the efforts of the fighters, the brave and determined Italian pilots pressed home a low-level attack on the battleship *Nelson* which was hit forward by a torpedo. These enemy bombers were shot down, but so too was one of the *Ark Royal's* Fulmars, sadly by anti-aircraft fire from the *Rodney*. Hardly had the noise of gunfire from this engagement died away than a third attack developed, and one very determined enemy bomber was shot down as it approached the carrier, just seconds from dropping its torpedo. During this third onslaught a report was received that two enemy battleships, four cruisers and eight destroyers were just 15 miles to the south-west and the *Prince of Wales, Nelson* and *Rodney*, together with two cruisers, were detached to locate them. Meanwhile, on board the *Ark Royal* a strike force of Swordfish were prepared to fly off as soon as the enemy's position was confirmed. However, due to inaccurate reconnaissance reports from the RAF, the two fleets did not encounter each other and the carrier's strike force returned that evening after a fruitless search for the Italian vessels. At 8.40pm the three battleships and two cruisers rejoined the

The view from the flight deck as the *Ark Royal* lists to starboard. Swordfish aircraft are still parked on deck.

(Fleet Air Arm Museum)

convoy, and although the *Hermione* bombarded the Sicilian coast that night, there were no more attacks on the convoy which reached Malta safely, after which Force H returned to Gibraltar on 1 October, where the *Ark Royal* could undergo some much needed maintenance. By now it was clear that the carrier was in need of a refit and rumours abounded that she would return home for Christmas. However, that was still some ten weeks away and on 16 October, together with the *Rodney* (which had replaced the damaged *Nelson*), the *Hermione* and a destroyer screen, the *Ark Royal* sailed from Gibraltar to fly off 828 Albacore Squadron to Malta and to create a diversion aimed at drawing enemy attention from the cruisers *Aurora* and *Penelope* and two destroyers, code-named Force K, which were reinforcing the Mediterranean Fleet. Next day, as the *Ark Royal* and her escorts steamed east, fighters shot down an enemy reconnaissance plane and in the early hours of Saturday 18 October the 11 Albacores and two Swordfish were flown off, with all but one Swordfish arriving safely in Malta. Next day Force H turned back for Gibraltar, leaving the two cruisers and destroyers to

make the fast passage to Grand Harbour, where they arrived on Tuesday 21 October, the day after Force H reached Gibraltar. The officers and men on board the *Ark Royal* could now enjoy a welcome break before the next foray into the Mediterranean.

It was at 7.30pm on Monday 10 November that the *Ark Royal, Argus, Malaya* (which had now taken the place of the *Nelson*), *Hermione* and a destroyer screen, which included the *Legion* and *Laforey,* left Gibraltar on what had become a rather routine passage into the Mediterranean to fly off Hurricane fighters to Malta. Because of thick fog the flying off was delayed until Wednesday 12 November, and upon completion of the task Force H turned round and set course for Gibraltar. During the afternoon shadowing aircraft were sighted and submarine activity was reported west of Ceuta, the Spanish enclave on the coast of North Africa, and later in the day Admiral Somerville received reports of a U-boat on the surface off the Spanish coast, north-west of Alboran Island. Both submarines would be very close to Force H's route, and that night the force had to reduce speed in stormy weather conditions. At just after 4am the destroyer *Legion* reported a loud underwater explosion in her wake, which was thought to be the premature explosion of a torpedo. During the morning of Thursday 13 November weather conditions improved and in the early afternoon the *Malaya* carried out gunnery exercises. The *Ark Royal* had been flying anti-submarine patrols since 6.45am, and at 3.29pm, whilst steaming at 18 knots, she altered course into the wind to 286 degrees so that she could operate aircraft independently inside the destroyer screen. During the following six minutes six Swordfish and two Fulmars were flown off, and five Swordfish were landed on before the carrier returned to her position in the line at 24 knots. By now the mountains of Spain and the coastline of the Costa del Sol in the Malaga region were clearly visible less than 18 miles away. At 3.41pm, when the carrier was in a position Lat 36° - 03'N/Long 04° - 45'W, approximately 30 miles east of Gibraltar, in Captain Maund's words, 'A severe explosion took place on the starboard side abreast the Admiral's bridge.' Those who witnessed the explosion reported a huge mass of water rushing up on the *Ark Royal's* starboard side, but no one on the carrier's bridge had seen any sign of a torpedo track and initially it was thought that there had been an internal explosion in the bomb room. However, Captain Maund quickly realized that had this been the case then there would probably have been little left of the centre section of the ship. Furthermore it was unlikely that an internal explosion could have caused a column of water to rise up and wreck the starboard seaboat. So fierce was the explosion that it blew open the bomb lift doors under the bridge from where smoke billowed out, and the whole ship whipped so violently that five aircraft parked at the forward end of the flight deck were thrown up into the air with such force that they bounced back on deck three times. In fact, the *Ark Royal* had been hit by a single torpedo fired by KLt Friedrich Guggenberger in the submarine *U81*, which had made a skilful submerged attack on the carrier.

The *Ark Royal* immediately took on a 10° list to starboard and within three minutes this had increased to 12 degrees. As she continued to steam ahead at over 20 knots, she swung to port and passed between the *Malaya* and the *Argus*, whilst on the bridge attempts were made to reverse the engines and to midship the helm, but all the telegraphs were jammed and the telephone system was out of action. Immediately after the explosion 'Action Stations' was sounded over the tannoy, which was still working, and by bugle and word of mouth. As the failure of communications had isolated the bridge it was clear that way could only be taken off the ship by verbal orders and that a new control centre would be required as the carrier steamed on at 18 knots. Captain Maund left the bridge and went to the engine control room to obtain first-hand information about the situation below and here he gave the order 'half

speed astern all engines' and had the wheel put amidships. Having given the orders to bring the ship to rest he ordered the flooding of the port rapid flood compartments and the transfer of fuel oil from starboard to port. By now the ship was listing 15 degrees to port, the switchboard was out of action, there was no power to the two 250-ton pumps forward, the starboard boiler room was flooded and the watertight hatches in the fan intakes were open. However, the hatches in the centre boiler room were shut and the watertight doors between the fan space and the armoured passageway were closed. The evaporator room was partially flooded and, owing to the lack of forced lubrication pressure, the starboard engines were out of action, but the flooding in the starboard engine room was being dealt with by the electrical fire and bilge pump.

On his return to the flight deck Captain Maund stationed ratings along the route to the engine control room, by way of the forward cabin flat, the port side of the lower hangar deck and so up to the flight deck, and this provided the main line of communication between the commanding officer and the engineers in the machinery spaces. In addition Captain Maund gave orders to rig a telephone line to replace the human chain but, initially, only one handset could be found. Fortunately, information soon came in that all available pumps were being installed in the servery flat, the Marines' mess deck and the Boys' bathroom flat, where the flooding appeared to be worst. The *Hermione*, which was standing by, was requested to send over as many portable pumps, with hoses and cable, as she could spare and they duly arrived, together with a working party. By 4pm, with the ship having heeled over to an angle of 17 degrees, much of it in darkness, and with the telephones out of action, it was very difficult for the shipwrights to assess the full extent of the damage which had been caused by the torpedo. Additionally, with the list increasing, Captain Maund realized that his ship might well continue on this track and capsize very quickly, and he therefore considered it essential to evacuate as many of the *Ark Royal's* 1,600-strong ship's company as possible. Consequently he gave the order over the tannoy, 'Hands to Abandon Ship Stations', with the first part of the port watch of seamen, repair parties and the steaming watch to muster on the flight deck. He also ordered everyone over the port side and at the same time sent a signal to the destroyer *Legion* to come along the port side aft. This was not an easy manoeuvre for the destroyer's captain since the carrier's wireless masts were down and could not be raised, and the port propeller was visible not far below the water, which meant that the *Legion* had to keep her stern clear of the *Ark Royal* and her mast well away from the carrier's wireless masts. As soon as the *Legion* had nosed her way alongside, around 1,487 officers and men were transferred, some jumping onto hammocks which had been laid on the destroyer's forecastle, while others used lines which had

The view from HMS *Legion* as officers and men are transferred to the destroyer. *(Fleet Air Arm Museum)*

been rigged from the ship. One of the ship's cats escaped in the arms of a member of the Royal Marines detachment, and the Paymaster Commander saved two suitcases full of money, having emptied the ship's safe. During this very unusual disembarkation there was inevitably much shouting and calling as men on board the *Legion* helped and encouraged the *Ark Royal's* ship's company to either jump or slide down one of the many lines, but a whistle got immediate silence and orders were passed to those who had transferred to move aft and go below in the destroyer. Finally, at 4.48pm, and carrying almost 1,800 men, the *Legion* cast off.

At 4.30pm, while the disembarkation was under way, the engine room ratings who were on the flight deck were ordered below to raise steam and the seamen were divided into three parties. One team under the Gunnery Officer went to the forecastle to get the ship under tow when tugs arrived and the other groups acted as working parties on the lower hangar deck. However, although all the bulkheads were holding, in the engine room department the situation was deteriorating. The starboard boiler room was now full of water and this overflowed through the uptake casing into the centre boiler room which in turn became flooded. In addition the machinery control room was flooding rapidly through shattered pipes and through welded seams which had split, allowing water in from the centre boiler room. Although sea water had entered the

starboard engine room, as long as the ship had electrical power then the fire and bilge pump could easily cope with it. At about 5pm it was found that steam could not be maintained in the port boiler room owing to the listing of the ship, which meant that suction could not be obtained on the boiler water feed pump, and as the *Ark Royal* had no diesel generators, the lack of steam meant that all electrical power would be lost. Up until that point the pumping and counter-flooding of the rapid flood compartments had allowed the list to be reduced to 14 degrees. The priority now was to restore electrical power and to obtain 40 tons of distilled water for the boiler, and although daylight was fading fast, at 5.30pm the destroyer *Laforey* came alongside. Labouring in almost total darkness the working parties began transferring portable pumps to the carrier, and yards of heavy electrical cables. However, it soon became clear that more men were required on board and a signal was sent to the *Legion* requesting the return of 80 technical ratings, who duly arrived back at 9.40pm. By this time there was enough fresh water on board to raise steam in one of the port boilers and soon two boilers were steaming.

Shortly after nightfall the tug *St Day* arrived on the scene and, according to Captain Maund, '...made a pitiable exhibition. It certainly took her four times the time it should have done to get the ship in tow, and when she had achieved this, she found herself facing aft alongside the starboard side and eventually had to slip her tow; she was not seen again for some two hours.' Fortunately, the tug *Thames* arrived soon afterwards and by 8.35pm the *Ark Royal* was in tow and going ahead at two knots. Despite atrocious conditions in the engine and boiler rooms, where the engineers had to contend with the terrific heat, very little ventilation, greasy decks underfoot and of course the heavy list, they had raised steam by 9.15pm and by 9.50pm two turbo-generators were running. Once this stage had been reached it was decided that the *Laforey* should cast off as she was running the risk of being damaged by the *Ark Royal's* port propeller. In addition, there were high hopes that the carrier would be able to get under way on that propeller. It was at 10.15pm when the *Laforey* slipped, but the changeover to the *Ark Royal's* own power supply was slow, mainly because of the darkness and the heavy list. However, once electrical power became available, pumps were immediately started up, light was restored to the engine and boiler rooms, and the engine room fans became operational again.

At 10.30pm, with the list having increased by only one or two degrees in eight hours, expectations were high that the *Ark Royal* would be brought safely into Gibraltar where she could be docked. The pumps were successfully reducing the level of water in the servery flat, the Royal Marines' mess deck, and the Boys' bathroom, and it was estimated that once there was steam on the port engines a speed of six knots could be expected. However, at about 2.15 am on Friday 14 November, Commander (E) reported that despite the successful pumping, the list on the ship was slowly increasing and he was unable to carry out any further counter-flooding. Meanwhile, on the flight deck, the Navigating Officer had been assisting the tug *Thames* to keep a good course when suddenly, out of the night, the *St Day* reappeared and with some difficulty was secured alongside the port side to help the tow. The *Ark Royal's* speed was then increased, but at this point steam and smoke were seen pouring from the fan flat and it was learned that there had been a fire in the port boiler room. By this time Warrant Engineer S. A. Woodriffe, Chief Stoker H. Walley, Stoker PO Winscott, Ldg Stoker C. Feaver and Stoker T. W. Scott had been toiling for over eight hours in atrocious conditions, first to raise steam and then to maintain it. Likewise, in the port engine room ERA Cleale and Ldg Stoker Church were working in appalling conditions, with no ventilation, to keep the turbo-generator running, but it was all to no avail for fires started breaking out in the boiler casings and the smoke and fumes were blinding and choking the dedicated engineers. It was discovered that the funnel uptake had flooded and so the furnace gases could not escape through the funnel. With the crews barely able to see or breathe, and with the steam pressure rapidly falling, the Senior Engineer ordered the boiler room to be evacuated, before he himself collapsed. Fortunately PO Winscott managed to

rescue him but, once again, all the lights went out and the vital pumps came to a standstill.

In order to continue the pumping, the *Laforey* was again signalled to come alongside, but as the list had now increased to 20 degrees and it was too dangerous to go alongside aft, because of the propeller, she was secured outboard of the *St Day* and within a few minutes power was once again restored to the pumps. This was at 3.40am, but from that time on the list steadily increased because the pumps were making little difference to the situation. Conditions below deck were atrocious with water and oil swilling around on the decks, and the list making it impossible to stand up without holding on to some fixed object. The heat and the lack of ventilation added to the trying conditions, but despite all this the remaining members of the ship's company did their best to keep the pumps in action. Although the speed of the tow was increased, the carrier was still some 30 miles from port and a large-output pump was brought out by the sloop *Penstemon*. However, the list of the carrier was so steep that it could not be transferred, and it was clear that the end was approaching rapidly for the *Ark Royal*.

At 4am, with the list having increased to 23 degrees, the Navigating Officer and those manning the communications centre on the flight deck could no longer stand up, and with nothing to hang on to they were ordered down to the lower hangar deck. At about the same time Commander (E) reported that there was little more that his men could do as, despite the pumping, the list was increasing rapidly and it soon reached 27 degrees. Captain Maund then instructed the seamen to take all available ropes forward and to secure them inboard so that the 250 men remaining on board could leave the ship quickly. Within minutes of this task having been completed the list had increased to 28 degrees and as movement could not be made on any deck without holding on, Captain Maund ordered all men on deck to slip down to the tug *St Day* and he also ordered everyone up from below. At 4.30am, with the ship listing at 35 degrees, Captain Maund was the last man to slide down into the *St Day*, where he was greeted with cheering as the tug and the *Laforey* cast off.

The *Ark Royal* remained afloat for another hour and 40 minutes and for a time she hung, as though suspended, at an angle of 45 degrees. Then the island superstructure disappeared beneath the waves with the flight deck at right angles to the sea. Lt Heather RNVR, who was standing by in a motor launch about 50 yards from the *Ark Royal*, recalled: 'The ship continued to heel almost until she had rolled beyond 180 degrees, when I noticed against the sky the starboard bilge keel, and with an Aldis lamp I saw a large rent abaft the position of the funnel extending 130 to 150 feet longer than my ship (which was 112 feet). This hole was between the centre line of the ship and the starboard bilge keel, extending to the ship's side at the after

Two views of the carrier as she lies crippled and helpless in the water. She finally sank early the following morning.

(Fleet Air Arm Museum)

end. The hole was at both ends a V shape, and the after end was broader than the forward end.'

Finally, at 6.13am on Thursday 14 November 1941, fourteen and a half hours after she had been torpedoed, and with only one fatality out of a complement of 1,749, the *Ark Royal* sank beneath the waves. During her eventful career of just three years the name of the *Ark Royal* had become a legend the world over, a name which would be inherited by one of the Royal Navy's most powerful aircraft carriers.

Soon after the sinking the ship's canteen committee decided to purchase a silver bell from the balance of the ship's fund which had been rescued from the safe by Commander Steele, for presentation to future ships which bore the name *Ark Royal*, and it was cast by Gillet & Johnson of Croydon in 1943 at a ceremony which was attended by the First Lord of the Admiralty and by officers and men from the ill-fated ship. The bell is in solid sterling silver weighing about two hundredweights and measuring 19 inches in diameter at the mouth. The clapper consists of a cast iron shank with a silver nickel ball and the cost was £598.

Commanding Officers:

Captain A. J. Power CVO RN	17 January 1938
Captain C. S. Holland RN	10 April 1940
Captain L. E. H. Maund RN	19 April 1941

Principal Particulars:

Length Overall:	800ft
Beam:	112ft
Draught:	27ft 9in
Main Propulsion Machinery:	Three shaft. Parsons geared turbines. Six Admiralty three-drum boilers. 102,000 SHP: 31 knots.
Armament:	Eight twin 4.5-inch HA guns. Four mountings multiple pom-poms.

Part Two

HMS *Ark Royal*
1955-1979

Chapter Five

The Early Years 1942-1958

On 19 March 1942, just four months after the loss of the *Ark Royal,* a top secret letter was dispatched from the Admiralty offices in Bath addressed to the directors of the shipbuilding firm Cammell Laird & Company of Birkenhead. The letter was headed: 'Aircraft Carrier', and it began: 'Gentlemen, I have to request that you will proceed with the construction and completion in all respects of the hull and machinery of one aircraft carrier for HM Navy.'

In Britain the early months of 1942 were dark days, with unmitigated disasters in the Far East bringing the grim realization that the country was too weak to fight a major war in the West and in the Far East at the same time. What was clear was the fact that the aircraft carrier

had superseded the battleship as the new capital ship, and that in the pre-war years the Fleet Air Arm had been a very neglected force within the Royal Navy. The Admiralty's 1942 building programme had provided for four large fleet aircraft carriers which were to be named *Audacious, Africa, Eagle* and *Irresistible,* and it was the latter which was to be built at Birkenhead by Cammell Laird & Company. The new vessels, at 31,600 tons, were to be much improved versions of the last two modified Illustrious-class carriers, *Indefatigable* and *Implacable,* with an overall length of 790 feet, a beam of 109 feet, and two full-length aircraft hangars measuring 412 feet by 62 feet, with a height of 14ft - 6in. These would accommodate the larger, faster US aircraft which were coming into service with the Fleet Air

Her Majesty Queen Elizabeth arrives at the Birkenhead shipyard of Cammell Laird & Co on Wednesday 3 May 1950, to launch the fourth *Ark Royal.* Here she inspects the Guard of Honour before the ceremony.   *(Fleet Air Arm Museum)*

Her Majesty The Queen about to launch the new carrier, and . . .

. . . the *Ark Royal* moves down the same slipway where, 13 years previously, the third ship of the name had taken to the water. *(Fleet Air Arm Museum)*

Arm, and with two aircraft lifts measuring 45 feet by 33 feet it was envisaged that the new ships would be able to carry at least 72 aircraft. Their main defensive armament was to consist of 16, 4.5-inch guns and their four sets of Parsons single-reduction geared turbines, steam for which would be provided by eight Admiralty three-drum boilers, would give them a speed of 31 knots.

It was over 12 months after the order was placed, on Monday 3 May 1943, in a secret ceremony at Cammell Laird's Birkenhead shipyard, that The Princess Marina, Duchess of Kent, laid the first keel plates for HMS *Irresistible,* and five months later the keel of the *Audacious* was laid at Harland & Wolff's Belfast yard. When the Second World War ended on 2 September 1945, the two hulls were still on the stocks at their respective shipyards, with work on both of them reasonably well advanced. A third vessel, which was to have been named *Eagle,* was on the stocks at Walker on Tyne, but the fourth carrier, the *Africa,* had not progressed beyond the drawing board. With the end of hostilities it was decided that there was no need for four large fleet carriers of the Audacious class and in

October 1945 the order for *Africa* was cancelled. Three months later, in January 1946, the *Irresistible* was renamed *Ark Royal,* as a successor to the legendary aircraft carrier which had been lost in November 1941. Soon afterwards work was stopped on the *Eagle* which was under construction on the River Tyne, and with the cancellation of that contract the shipyard workers were transferred to work on merchant ships being built at the yard. Meanwhile, at Belfast, the *Audacious* was renamed *Eagle* in honour of her predecessor which had been torpedoed and sunk in the Mediterranean on 11 August 1942, with the loss of 160 lives. Now, with the war having been over for four months, it was publicly announced that the two aircraft carriers were under construction, and on 14 January 1946 the chairman of Cammell Laird, Sir Robert Johnson, announced that the *Ark Royal* would be launched at the end of 1946 and be completed by the summer of 1948. It seemed that both the *Ark Royal* and the *Eagle* would be in commission by 1949, particularly as the latter ship was launched on 19 March 1946, but it was not to be, for soon afterwards work on the *Ark Royal* was halted and

On 10 July 1952, the *Ark Royal* was towed across the Mersey from Birkenhead to the Gladstone Dock on the Liverpool side of the river. *(Fleet Air Arm Museum)*

the massive hull lay incomplete and idle on the largest and most prestigious slipway in Cammell Laird's shipyard for almost four years, much to the frustration of the Cammell Laird directors who were unable to utilize the slipway for the building of large merchant ships. Then in 1949 work was resumed and on 2 December that year it was announced that Her Majesty Queen Elizabeth would launch the new aircraft carrier on Wednesday 3 May 1950. As the date for the great event approached, it was announced that links with the old *Ark Royal* would be strengthened by inviting 100 of her officers and 300 of her men to attend the ceremony, with leave being granted to those who were still serving in the Navy, to allow them to be present.

When the day arrived it was warm but overcast, and gathered at the shipyard for one of Merseyside's biggest occasions since the launching of the Cunard liner *Mauretania* in July 1938 were some 50,000 people, while off the slipway a large fleet of boats and small ships had gathered, all steaming up and down waiting for the new carrier to take to the water. Anchored in midstream, dressed overall and looking very smart, was the aircraft carrier *Illustrious* which, with the destroyer *Wizard*, had come to the Mersey especially for the ceremony. She had embarked the First Lord of the Admiralty, Viscount Hall, the C-in-C Plymouth, Admiral Sir Rhoderick McGrigor, and Rear-Admiral Guy Royle, the first Admiral

The fourth *Ark Royal* on her contractor's sea trials in the autumn of 1954.

(Fleet Air Arm Museum)

(Air) in the old *Ark Royal,* at Devonport on 1 May before sailing north for the River Mersey. She arrived alongside Princes Landing Stage, Liverpool, during the afternoon of the next day and at 9am on Wednesday 3 May, the day of the launch, she slipped her moorings and steamed out into midstream where she took up her position off Cammell Laird's shipyard. A Royal Marine who was also present recalls the event: 'At noon, the salute of 21 guns heralded the arrival of the Queen, accompanied by the chairman of Cammell Laird's. After the dedication by the Bishop of Chester, the Queen named the new ship and broke the customary bottle of wine over the bows. A moment of intense stillness and the majestic shape started moving

down the slipway. This was the signal for a fresh outburst of cheering and the hooting of the vessels lying in the river. With a dip symbolic of her "first curtsey" to the royal sponsor who launched her, the new *Ark Royal* entered the water and so started her career.' One small boy, John Crellin, whose family took him to watch the launch, and who later served in the ship, recalls watching the event from one of the Wallasey ferries which had been pressed into service as a sightseeing boat: 'Eventually she began to slide and she emerged clear of the screen of cranes, followed by a cloud of dust from the drag chains. The river came alive with the sound of whistles and sirens as she became waterborne, with little perceptible backwash, and then stopped clear of the slipway. She looked clean and impressive, riding high in the water, her outline as yet unbroken by the addition of the island and the myriad encumbrances and extensions of later years.' Once into the river the *Ark Royal* joined the *Illustrious* as 40 Fleet Air Arm aircraft flew past in salute, while tugs towed the new carrier round to the company's fitting-out basin, where she would dominate the scene for the next four years.

At the luncheon which followed the ceremony Sir Robert Johnson told the assembled guests that his company hoped to finish the *Ark Royal* in a little over two years, but Sir Robert, who was very conscious of the fact that the carrier had occupied his best slipway for seven years and that it was now taking up most of his fitting-out basin, had not reckoned with the rapid advances which were being made in naval aviation. The Queen in her speech to the assembled guests recalled the histories of the three preceding *Ark Royals,* from the first which had served as the flagship of Lord Howard of Effingham, to the third which, as everyone knew, had been lost during the Second World War. Her Majesty referred to the many members of that carrier's ship's company, and said that she was sure they would recognize in the new *Ark Royal* a truly worthy successor, and that those who were to serve in her were inheriting both a great name and a great example. Viscount Hall, the First Lord of the Admiralty, spoke of the vital function which aviation had in the Royal Navy, and he informed the guests that the *Ark Royal,* together with her sister HMS *Eagle,* would be the most formidable warships ever to have served in the Royal Navy and that they would be the envy of all nations. As the luncheon ended and all the guests began to disperse, work was already under way on the *Ark Royal,* now secured alongside the fitting-out basin.

Unfortunately, Sir Robert Johnson's estimate of just over two years for completion was to be sadly awry, for more time was needed for the implementation of some very important developments which were almost ready to go into operational service, the most significant of these being the angled flight deck. However, in July 1952, with most of the fitting-out work having been completed, the *Ark Royal* was towed from the basin where she had been since the day of her launch, out into the River Mersey then downriver and across to the Liverpool side where, from 10 July to 7 August, she was dry docked in the Gladstone Graving Dock. On Monday 18 May 1953, nine months after her return to the fitting-out basin at Cammell Laird's shipyard, the Admiralty Board first discussed the proposal that 'an interim form of angled deck' be fitted in the new carrier. It was explained that there would be no other opportunity, without great expense, to provide the ship with an angled deck and that, possibly, funds would never be available to put in a fully-angled deck at a later stage in her career. The meeting was told that there had been great difficulties in designing a barrier which was capable of stopping delta-winged fighters and without an angled deck of some kind

the *Ark Royal,* '...might not be able to operate the naval fighters of the future.' Having decided to go ahead with installing an interim angled deck, the meeting decided that the changes proposed should only mean two months' delay in the completion of the ship, but they were obviously worried that the builders might use these changes as an excuse for much longer delays and a minute was added instructing the Controller of the Navy to discuss this question with the builders immediately. They also added a rider to the effect that if it were considered likely that the addition of the angled deck would result in a long delay, then the Board would reconsider the whole question of adding the angled deck.

In the event Cammell Laird estimated that there would be a delay of only two months, and so the Admiralty decided to go ahead with an angle of five degrees, as opposed to the eight to nine degrees which was planned for the *Hermes.* The main reason for this decision was the recognition that the fitting of a fully-angled deck would be a major operation involving much redesigning and additional cost. The actual alterations involved the fitting of a small sponson at the forward end of the deck edge lift, which was to be the first such lift to be fitted in a British aircraft carrier, as well as the rearrangement of the arresting gear sheaves. However, due to the additional sponson, one six-barrelled and one single-barrelled Bofors were lost which left the ship armed with eight 4.5-inch twin mountings, five six-barrelled Bofors and three single Bofors guns. It was also envisaged that the resulting deck park forward of the island superstructure would be large enough to take about 16 N113 aircraft (subsequently the Supermarine Scimitar). In addition to the angled flight deck the *Ark Royal* would be fitted with the new BS4 steam catapults, as it was apparent that aircraft weights and performances were rising fast, and the steam catapult was flexible enough to cope with the heaviest and fastest aircraft which could be visualized at that time. The resulting cost to the Admiralty for these modifications was an additional £25,140 on the tender price.

No sooner had work started on the fitting of the angled deck, than the builders began informing the Admiralty that they were experiencing problems with modifications to the main turbines, and that they envisaged completion of all their building work during November 1954, which would be 12 years after the laying of the keel. In March 1954 the *Ark Royal's* first commanding officer, Captain D. R. F. Cambell DSO RN, was appointed to the ship following the cancellation of his appointment to the *Bulwark* which was fitting out at Belfast. The choice of Captain Cambell as the commanding officer of the Royal Navy's most modern and most powerful aircraft carrier was a logical one, for it was he who, in August 1951, had first suggested the idea of the angled flight deck, so that aircraft landing on it could be quickly pulled to one side and be prepared for

The *Ark Royal* enters Portsmouth Harbour for the first time during the afternoon of Friday 25 March 1955. Southsea Common can be seen in the background as she passes Clarence Pier, where the funfair is under construction.

(Imperial War Museum FL5674)

An aerial view of the new carrier showing her deck edge lift which was unique in a British aircraft carrier, but which was never really a success.　　　*(Fleet Air Arm Museum)*

in 1948 when he was appointed to the frigate HMS *Tintagel Castle,* which formed part of the 2nd Training Squadron based at Portland. Promoted Captain in 1949 he took up an appointment at the Admiralty Research Establishment, and it was during his four years there that he developed his idea of the angled flight deck.

By the beginning of May 1954 the *Ark Royal* was almost ready to undergo her Contractors' Sea Trials, but first she had to be dry docked and on Monday 3 May she once again made the four and a half mile passage from Cammell Laird's Birkenhead yard to the Gladstone Graving Dock at Liverpool. Not only was she going to have her underwater hull scraped and repainted, but she was to have new propellers fitted before carrying out her trials. However, as she was leaving Birkenhead, the starboard side of the carrier scraped the quay, crushing a ventilator cowling in the forward part of the ship, and shearing off a number of bilge outlet flanges aft. At the entrance to the Gladstone Graving Dock at the other side of the river, the port side of the ship swung against the quay, splintering a protective timber fender and taking off eight feet of paintwork amidships. A few minutes later, as she rounded the knuckle leading into the dry dock, the starboard side of the ship grazed the quay, scraping off yet more paint and snapping a one-inch hawser. Despite the mishaps and the fact that a flotilla of 12 fussing tugs, which were escorting and guiding the carrier, were belching black smoke which formed an effective screen round her, hundreds of Merseysiders turned out on the river front, in ferry boats, on the overhead railway and at the dock gates to see the new aircraft carrier. Six weeks later, with all the scheduled work completed and the accident damage repaired, the *Ark Royal* left the Mersey under her own steam, flying the Red Ensign, for her Contractors' Sea Trials, but a week later she was back alongside at Cammell Laird's shipyard for the final month of her fitting out.

In the autumn of 1954, on Monday 20 September, the *Ark Royal* began four more days of steaming trials in the Firth of Clyde, following which she returned once again to Cammel Laird's fitting-out basin at Birkenhead. Four months later, on Sunday 9 January 1955, the carrier made her third passage from Birkenhead to the Gladstone Dry Dock, where she underwent heeling trials which involved listing at 15 degrees both to port and starboard, and 14 days later she was back at Birkenhead and this time she was almost ready to embark her ship's company. At 4pm on Thursday 17 February 1955 the advance party joined her at Birkenhead, and over the following four days the main drafts of the ship's company joined the *Ark Royal,* and during the afternoon of Monday 21 February Captain

catapulting once again. The idea was taken up by the Royal Aircraft Establishment where it was concluded that trials should take place, and as a result, in early 1952, an angled deck was painted onto the flight deck of HMS *Triumph* and a variety of aircraft carried out touch and go circuits. The success of the trials was a major factor in the decision to go ahead with the *Ark Royal's* angled deck.

Captain Cambell had joined the Royal Navy in 1925 and trained as a Fleet Air Arm pilot six years later. During the 1930s he served as a pilot in various naval fighter squadrons and aircraft carriers, and in 1939 he commanded 803 Squadron in the third *Ark Royal.* Following this he served in HMS *Argus,* before becoming a naval test pilot and being promoted to Commander. In the last years of the Second World War he served on the British Air Commission in the USA and in 1947 he was appointed Commander (Air) in HMS *Glory.* His first command came

Cambell addressed them for the first time. Next morning there was an early start for a rehearsal for the commissioning ceremony and then, at 2.55pm, the guests began to arrive on board for this important milestone in the ship's career. The ceremony was held in the upper hangar and presided over by Captain Cambell who read out a message which had been sent by the vessel's royal sponsor. It said: 'I am happy to send this message of goodwill to the *Ark Royal* and all her company. She bears a name which has won great renown through all the long years of this country's mastery of the sea. Those who set forth in her have a proud inheritance and a great fame to uphold. I do not doubt that they will bring to her service the loyalty, seamanship and courage, which is her right, and I send my good wishes to all who put to sea in the *Ark Royal*.'

On Thursday 24 February the girls of the Littlewoods department store in Birkenhead laid on a dance for the ship's company at the town's Tower Ballroom, New Brighton, and one Royal Marines Corporal recalls the bitterly cold weather that night as he walked back to the ship through a blinding blizzard, looking like a snowman and having to shin up signposts to wipe away the snow and read the directions. In the event he arrived back before 11am on Friday 25 February 1955, when Special Sea Dutymen were called to their stations for the first time. Thirty-five minutes later flight deck manning parties closed up as the ship prepared to sail for her acceptance trials. The

carrier was still flying the Red Ensign and she was in the charge of Cammell Laird's trials master, Captain C. N. Lentaigne DSO RN (Retd). At 11.41am the ship was clear of the basin, and eight minutes later all the tugs had slipped their towing ropes as the *Ark Royal* steamed slowly down the River Mersey. That afternoon, in the Irish Sea, the main propulsion machinery was worked up to two-thirds of full power as tests of the remote controls for X and Y engine rooms were carried out. That evening, at 7.25pm, the ship anchored for the night off Port Erin, Isle of Man. On the next day sailing was delayed until 11am, because of problems with the turning gear of A engine room, and once under way full-power trials were carried out off Ailsa Craig. Unfortunately, acceptance was delayed by a lubrication failure in Y engine room but finally, at 6.31pm, Captain Cambell signed the Provisional Acceptance Certificate and the White Ensign was hoisted at the masthead. Two hours later, with the ship at Greenock, Cammell Laird's contractors were landed and the RFA *Wave Liberator* came alongside to refuel the carrier. On leaving she carried away some of the awning stanchions on her poop through scraping the overhang on the starboard side. Next day, with fuelling completed, the *Ark Royal* weighed anchor at 8pm and, with a southerly gale blowing, she steamed to Loch Ewe for steering trials. However, the strong winds made it too hazardous to enter the loch and the trials were carried out off Skye, but during the late afternoon of Tuesday

The *Ark Royal* at Spithead with a full range of aircraft. *(Fleet Air Arm Museum)*

1 March Captain Cambell did anchor in Loch Ewe, where good progress was made in cleaning the ship and exercising different evolutions, although the adverse weather limited recreational possibilities somewhat. It was at 5pm on Friday 4 March that the *Ark Royal* weighed anchor and left Loch Ewe bound for the anchorage of St Helen's Roads off the Isle of Wight. During the passage manoeuvring trials and seaboat drills were carried out, although with north-easterly gales blowing, the latter were severely limited. At 7am on Monday 7 March the *Ark Royal* anchored in St Helen's Roads and three hours later Captain Cambell went ashore to Gosport by boat. Two hours later, piloting one of the ship's Dragonfly helicopters, he returned on board, thus making the first aircraft landing onto the *Ark Royal*. The cost of building the new ship was £16,155,700 and although she still had to undergo more trials, the Royal Navy's most modern aircraft carrier was now part of the fleet.

After arriving off the Isle of Wight on 7 March 1955, the *Ark Royal* remained at anchor in St Helen's Roads for four days while the ship's radar calibrations were carried out, but leave was restricted by strong south-westerly gales. On the morning of Friday 11 March she shifted to a Spithead anchorage, but with strong winds still blowing,

the leave situation was only slightly alleviated. At just after 8am on Monday 14 March the *Ark Royal* began radio sea trials and gunnery firings for radio shock trials in the Portsmouth exercise areas, south-east of the Isle of Wight. These trials were carried out over a period of 11 days, and each evening the ship would return to her anchorage at Spithead. At 2pm on Friday 18 March a Firefly aircraft from RNAS Ford, which was co-operating with the carrier on radio sea trials, suffered an engine failure and force-landed in the sea about five miles from Ford, but fortunately the pilot was recovered safely by a helicopter from the naval air station and no action was required by the ship. At 10.22am the next day, while Marine C. Johnson was on duty as lifebuoy sentry, he suddenly saw someone jump into the sea from the starboard forward end of the ship. He immediately threw the man a lifebuoy and rang the alarm and it was his prompt actions, and that of the Officer of the Day, Lt-Cdr J. S. Wilson, in getting away one of the port motor boats, which were the main contributory factors in saving the man's life, for the only seaboat was unserviceable at that time, with starting trouble. In the event the rating, who was later disembarked for psychiatric treatment, was saved and the incident served as a valuable test of the ship's organization. In the words of Captain Cambell, 'In the event, nothing but good resulted and the ship's company were greatly heartened at the quick saving of the man, and highly amused at the somewhat ludicrous background of the case.'

The weekend of 19/20 March was spent at Spithead, but once again gales restricted leave and at one stage all boat traffic between the ship and the shore was suspended. On Tuesday 22 March the carrier resumed her radio sea trials in company with the frigate *Fleetwood*, and that afternoon she encountered a Russian fleet of two small merchant ships, two tugs and five fishing vessels, whereupon photographs were duly taken by both sides. That evening the *Ark Royal* anchored at Spithead prior to entering Portsmouth Harbour the following day, but severe gales prevented the ship's movement up harbour for two days, and also got her some unwelcome newspaper publicity.

On Wednesday 23 March, with gale force winds blowing across the Solent and Spithead and with the ship light in the water, she developed a $1\frac{1}{2}°$ list which in turn caused an oil leakage from one of the service fuel tanks containing heavy furnace fuel oil. The spillage, which consisted of about two tons of oil, was widely dispersed by the gales and strong tides, causing pollution along the shoreline at Southsea and on the Isle of Wight. So, with a furore raging in the local and national press, the *Ark Royal* steamed up harbour and at 1pm on Friday 25 March she secured alongside Portsmouth's South Railway Jetty.

Whilst she was alongside at Portsmouth, a ceremony was held in the ship's upper hangar during the morning of Saturday 26 March, at which the Flag Officer Air (Home), Vice-Admiral Sir John Eccles, and ex-CPO (Cook) T. Vatcher presented the solid silver bell, complete with its own wooden tabernacle, which had been bought from the previous *Ark Royal's* welfare fund, to the ship. Following the presentation a reception was held for 300 former members of the third *Ark Royal's* ship's company. As Captain Cambell reported to the Admiralty: 'The task of bringing to life such a large and complex ship has been greatly aided by the legacy of a strong *"Ark Royal"* tradition. The presentation of the silver bell, the links with the ship's sponsors and adopters (City of Leeds and Lloyds of London) and the goodwill of Cammell Laird's and of Merseyside – all these have greatly contributed to the establishment of a sound ship-spirit at the outset.'

The *Ark Royal* left Portsmouth during the afternoon of Monday 28 March, bound for the Plymouth area, and next morning she carried out a number of runs on the measured mile off Polperro. That same morning, at 10.26am, the *Ark Royal* met her older sister, HMS *Eagle*, for the first time. The *Eagle* had left Devonport to carry out flying trials in the Channel, and after exchanging courtesies they went their separate ways. That evening the *Ark Royal* anchored in Whitsand Bay, and at 7.30am on Wednesday 30 March she

weighed anchor and, with full ceremony, steamed up harbour to berth alongside 5 and 6 wharves of Devonport Dockyard. In early April dockyard maintenance work started on the ship, while the ship's company went on seasonal leave. On Friday 8 April the first catapult deadload trials got off to a rather slow start and 13 days later, whilst a 40,000lb deadload was being moved by crane, a holding eye gave way and the deadload fell onto the flight deck, damaging both the deck and supporting pillars. The damage was soon put right and despite two more minor accidents, the catapult trials were completed on Wednesday 25 May. The 1955 Navy Days at Devonport were held during the three-day Whitsun holiday weekend from Saturday 28 to Monday 30 May, and the *Ark Royal* proved to be the star attraction, with 26,226 visitors. Amongst the treats they enjoyed were static displays in the lower hangar, tea and sticky buns in the upper hangar and helicopter displays on the flight deck. Following this hectic weekend, the *Ark Royal* left Devonport at 2pm on the last day of May and set course for Gibraltar where she was to carry out a series of shakedown exercises.

Three days after leaving Plymouth Sound the *Ark Royal* arrived in the colony, and after a full ceremonial entry into the harbour she secured alongside the South Mole for her first 'foreign' visit. The exercises began on the morning of Monday 6 June and after leaving harbour at 8am she remained in the vicinity of Gibraltar before stopping at noon over the position where her predecessor had sunk some 14 years previously. To mark the carrier's first visit to the spot, a service was held on the flight deck during which a wreath was dropped into the sea. After this, for two weeks, it seemed to the ship's company that life was one long round of evolutions as the ship carried out exercises off Gibraltar, anchoring each evening in Gibraltar Bay, with weekends alongside in the colony. On Sunday 19 June the Governor of Gibraltar visited the ship and that afternoon she was opened to visitors, which proved very popular. Next day, with the first phase of the shakedown exercises completed, the *Ark Royal* left Gibraltar at 8am and set course for home waters where she was to start her flying trials. On the morning of Thursday 23 June she arrived back at Spithead, and that weekend she was visited by a number of ex-members of her predecessor's ship's company. Her flying trials began on Monday 27 June when, at just before 8am, Commander (Air) R. Fell RN left the ship by helicopter and 15 minutes later she got under way, bound for the Portsmouth exercise areas. At 9.40am Commander Fell returned to the ship flying an Avenger from RNAS Ford and, after making a circuit of the carrier, he made the first fixed-wing deck landing onto HMS *Ark Royal*. He followed this up with a number of free take-offs and landings, then touch and go circuits, before landing on at 11.50am to complete the morning's flying programme. That afternoon, at 2.30pm, Commander Fell started the

The *Ark Royal* arrives in Bighi Bay, Grand Harbour, Malta, during the morning of 18 November 1955 to carry out maintenance. *(Fleet Air Arm Museum)*

With aircraft ranged and the flight deck manned, HMS *Ark Royal* makes a ceremonial entry into harbour during 1955. *(Fleet Air Arm Museum)*

second half of the day's flying schedule by making the first catapult-assisted take-off from the carrier. He was followed by a Sea Hawk of 800 Squadron, a Wyvern, two Gannets and a Skyraider from RNAS Ford, which made a number of deck landings and launchings. Late that afternoon the carrier anchored in Sandown Bay and next morning the flying trials started early with the ship leaving her anchorage and operating Wyverns, Gannets and Sea Hawks, watched by the C-in-C Plymouth, who arrived by helicopter. The next two days followed the same pattern, although they were marred by catapult failures, and on the morning of Saturday 2 July the *Ark Royal* secured to C buoy in Plymouth Sound where everyone could relax for the weekend. Following the break, the carrier weighed anchor at 8.45am on Monday 11 July and steamed to Weymouth Bay for more flying trials, this time with Sea Venoms. By the end of the month, with the first phase of her trials completed, the *Ark Royal* was back in Devonport Dockyard and during Navy Days over the Bank Holiday weekend she was opened to visitors again. On the final day, Monday 1 August, over 10,000 people toured the ship, which made

her the number one attraction.

On Thursday 1 September, while essential maintenance was being carried out, the First Lord of the Admiralty, Mr J. P. Thomas, together with Admiral Sir Alexander Madden, the C-in-C Plymouth, visited the ship. Later in the month, once work had been completed and any defects made good, the main ground parties of 800 and 898 (Sea Hawk) Squadrons joined the *Ark Royal* and two days later, at 1.30pm on Monday 26 September, she slipped her moorings and steamed out into the Channel for the second phase of her flying trials. By the end of the week the Sea Hawks of both 800 and 898 Squadrons had been embarked, and they had carried out a full flying programme. Following a night at anchor in Sandown Bay, on the morning of Friday 30 September the *Ark Royal* weighed anchor and steamed up harbour to secure alongside Portsmouth's South Railway Jetty at noon. During this stay alongside at Portsmouth four Sea Hawks were successfully catapulted from the stationary aircraft carrier during the morning of Tuesday 4 October, causing the harbour to resound to the roar of their jet engines

Replenishment at sea. The *Ark* refuels from an RFA.   (*R. Lakey*)

overhead; the exercise was not repeated! That afternoon the *Ark Royal* left harbour to carry out further flying exercises off the Isle of Wight.

On Monday 10 October a Press Day was held on board when the ship's remote controls for the main propulsion machinery were demonstrated and a flying display was given by Sea Hawks, Gannets and Skyraiders. Next morning the *Ark Royal* left home waters and set course for Gibraltar and the Mediterranean again, arriving in the exercise areas off the colony on the morning of Friday 14 October. Flying started at 8am, but unfortunately it got off to a tragic start when a Sea Hawk piloted by Lt Morse ditched on take-off from the starboard catapult. Despite the fact that the seaboat was on the scene within ten minutes, there was no trace of the pilot or any wreckage. It was the carrier's first fatal flying accident. After another day's flying off Gibraltar and a weekend alongside, the *Ark Royal* left for Malta on the morning of Monday 24

October. After a fast eastbound passage she arrived off the north coast of the island in the early hours of Wednesday 26 October to be met by a violent storm with wind speeds of 48 knots and torrential rain. Nevertheless, it was possible to fit in three days of flying, during which the ship anchored each night in the Kemmura Channel, and at 2pm on Saturday 29 October she entered Grand Harbour and secured to buoys in Bighi Bay. She remained in Malta for over a week, when she was visited by the First Lord of the Admiralty, and she was also opened to the public, but during the morning of Tuesday 8 November work started in earnest once again when she left harbour for ten days of flying exercises, after which she returned to Grand Harbour to undergo a self-maintenance period.

With all work completed and the ship cleaned up, the carrier left Grand Harbour on the morning of Tuesday 29 November to undertake a goodwill visit to Toulon where she arrived on Friday 2 December and spent four days.

The *Ark Royal* about to pass under the Forth Railway Bridge on 15 May 1957.   *(R. Lakey)*

After leaving the French port on the morning of 6 December she carried out flying exercises before anchoring in the Gulf of Augusta four days later. However, just six hours after dropping anchor she was at sea once again, steaming hard for Malta with an emergency hospital case. The passage from Augusta took just four hours and at 2.40am on the morning of Sunday 11 December the ship was manoeuvred to a stop outside Grand Harbour where the stretcher case was ferried ashore in the ship's seaboat before being transferred to Bighi Hospital. Following this, in company with HMS *Saintes,* the *Ark Royal* continued her flying exercises off the island of Malta, before returning to the port on Friday 16 December for the Christmas and New Year holiday. During the Christmas break the Malta Choral Society paid a visit to the ship and joined in a carol service in the upper hangar, and the C-in-C Mediterranean, Admiral Sir Guy Grantham, also paid a

short visit. On the morning of Friday 13 January 1956 the *Ark Royal* left harbour again to carry out flying exercises off Malta. That afternoon a deadload trial was carried out, with a redundant Sea Hornet being catapulted into the sea, and that was followed by seven days of exercises with the destroyers *Ulysses* and *Saintes,* and the two light fleet carriers *Albion* and *Centaur* which were en route to the Far East for goodwill visits. On Friday 20 January the *Ark Royal* returned to Grand Harbour where she secured to buoys in Bighi Bay. Next morning, as tugs held the carrier steady, 12 Sea Hawks were launched from the starboard catapult to the naval air station at Hal Far, and it was on the last day of January that the *Ark Royal* left Malta for exercises with the Mediterranean Fleet.

'Exercise Febex' was carried out in the Eastern Mediterranean, and taking part with the *Ark Royal* were the *Albion* and *Centaur,* which were bound for Port Said, the

'Operation Steadfast', the Royal Review of the Home Fleet off Invergordon at the end of May 1957. The *Ark* has just steamed past HMY *Britannia,* with the carriers *Ocean* and *Albion* following her. *(R. Lakey)*

On Wednesday 29 May 1957 Her Majesty The Queen visited the *Ark Royal.* Here she inspects the Royal Marines Guard of Honour.
(R. Lakey)

cruiser HMS *Birmingham* and a destroyer screen. During the exercise both FOAC and FO2 Mediterranean Fleet flew their flags in *Ark Royal* and sadly, a Gannet from the *Albion* and its crew were lost. On Friday 10 February the carrier returned to Grand Harbour for an 11-day maintenance period before sailing on Tuesday 21 February to carry out heeling trials before setting course for Naples where, together with the destroyer *Chieftain,* she was to make a very enjoyable five-day courtesy visit, during which there were organized trips to Rome, Capri, Pompeii and Sorrento, which made a pleasant change from Grand Harbour. By now, according to one member of the Royal Marines detachment, canaries and budgerigars had begun to make their appearance in the ship and mess decks were beginning to take on the appearance of aviaries, where even the din of the fans and generators could not drown out the noise of their chirrups and whistles. After leaving Naples on Wednesday 29 February the *Ark Royal* returned to Malta where, whilst at anchor off Grand Harbour, she embarked Vice-Admiral M. Richmond, FO2 Mediterranean Fleet, and sailed with the *Birmingham* and *Aisne* for 'Exercise Cascade'. Three days later came one of the worst days in the *Ark Royal's* career when, at ten past midnight on the morning of Thursday 8 March, whilst 80 miles south-west of Sardinia, Sea Venom 42 disappeared from the radar screens. By 1.15am, with the maximum estimated endurance of the aircraft having long expired, the aircrew, Lt J. D. Ealand RN and FO R. J. Mullard RAF, were posted as 'Missing Presumed Dead'. While the escort screen searched for the missing aircrew, the *Ark Royal* continued to operate with the *Aisne,* but at 1.30am Gannet 383 crashed over the carrier's starboard bow when making a free take-off. Captain Cambell immediately ordered full astern and within minutes the seaboat was away, fully crewed and with Ldg Seaman Ramplin, one of the ship's divers, on board. The *Aisne* joined the search and the crew of the seaboat quickly located the semi-submerged wreck of the Gannet, whereupon Ldg Seaman Ramplin immediately attempted to rescue the pilot, Lt L. M. Tooley RN, and Sub-Lt D. Claxton RN. Suddenly, to the horror of the onlookers, the Gannet sank beneath the waves taking Ldg Seaman Ramplin with it. So rapidly did the Gannet sink, with the diver and his gear apparently entangled with the aircraft, that the seaboat's crew were powerless to help. The *Ark Royal* remained in the vicinity for the remainder of the day, but no survivors were found. Later in the day flying operations resumed following the loss of five members of the *Ark Royal's* ship's company in two tragic accidents within the space of two hours. Four days later the carrier berthed alongside Gibraltar's South Mole.

During the eight-day stay alongside in Gibraltar, Vice-Admiral Richmond took the salute at Divisions before leaving the ship, and three days later, on the morning of Tuesday 20 March, the *Ark Royal* sailed for the Atlantic and

'Exercise Dawn Breeze', a NATO exercise in which she participated whilst on passage to Spithead. On the evening of Monday 26 March she arrived off the Isle of Wight and after anchoring for the night, she secured alongside Portsmouth's South Railway Jetty at just after noon the next day. Two days later, at 11.55am on 29 March, the *Ark Royal's* royal sponsor, now Her Majesty Queen Elizabeth The Queen Mother, visited the ship for the first time where she was welcomed on board by Captain Cambell. After inspecting a Guard of Honour formed by the Royal Marines, she took the salute on the flight deck as nearly 2,000 members of the ship's company marched past. Later, after lunching on board, the Queen Mother watched a film of her arrival and visit, which had been taken by the ship's photographers and which was shown on the internal television system. In those days, before the advent of video recorders, such a TV diffusion system was quite a novelty. Four hours after her arrival, at 3.55pm, the Queen Mother boarded a helicopter on the carrier's flight deck and, cheered by the ship's company, she left to return directly to Buckingham Palace. During the following two days, which were Navy Days at Portsmouth, almost 12,500 people visited the carrier at South Railway Jetty. The *Ark Royal* was scheduled to sail during the afternoon of Tuesday 3 April, but strong winds delayed her departure for 24 hours and she finally got away at 6,30pm on Wednesday 4 April, anchoring then for the night in Sandown Bay. Next morning, after an early start, she flew off all the serviceable aircraft – 28 Sea Hawks, eight Sea Venoms, seven Gannets and four Skyraiders – before preparing for the final assignment of the commission – six days of deck landing and launching trials of the de Havilland 110 day and night all-weather fighter which was destined for the Fleet Air Arm.

The DH 110 was the prototype of the de Havilland Sea Vixen and the aircraft had, in fact, already been ordered for the Fleet Air Arm, but on completion of the trials off the Isle of Wight, the company was able to announce: 'The trials demonstrated the practicability of working a large aircraft like the 110 from a carrier. They appeared to justify the policy of continuing with the large fleet carrier in the new conditions created by the atomic bomb, for they proved that the type of air defence which is necessary for continental strategy can be afforded also for the protection of surface traffic across the wide oceans of the world.'

With the trials successfully completed, the *Ark Royal* secured alongside 6 and 7 wharves at Devonport Dockyard on Friday 20 April 1956, and preparations got under way for a more light-hearted event which was to be held on board. This was a ladies' fashion show during the evening of Thursday 26 April, held in the upper hangar where, instead of the usual parked jet aircraft, glamorous models paraded the latest fashions before a very enthusiastic audience, with the proceeds going to charity. Finally, the

As she crossed the Atlantic in June 1957, the *Ark Royal* met a replica of the 17th-century sailing ship *Mayflower*. (R. Lakey)

Ark Royal was opened to the public during Devonport Navy Days in May, but by then most of the ship's company had dispersed and soon afterwards the ship was taken over by the dockyard.

On Monday 24 September 1956, as the *Ark Royal* lay alongside her berth at Devonport Dockyard, her second commanding officer, Captain F. H. E. Hopkins DSO DSC RN, was appointed to the ship. Captain Hopkins had joined the Royal Navy as a cadet in 1927, and had served as a midshipman in the brand new cruiser HMS *London*. Between 1931 and 1933, as a sub lieutenant and a lieutenant, he served in the destroyers *Vortigern* and *Winchester* and in 1934 he qualified as an observer at Lee-on-the-Solent. From 1934 to 1938 he served in various squadrons aboard the aircraft carriers *Courageous* and *Furious* and after a spell as an instructor at RNAS Ford, he served in 826 Squadron aboard the *Formidable*. During this time he took part in the bombing of ports in Italian Somaliland and Eritrea, the Battle of Matapan, the evacuation of Crete and the bombardment of Tripoli, as well as Army support in the Western Desert. In December 1941 he took command of 830 (Swordfish) Squadron where, until June 1942, the squadron was instrumental in cutting General Rommel's supply line between Italy and Tripoli. In July 1942 he was appointed to the British Naval Air Commission in the USA, where he remained until 1944 before joining the US Navy's fast carrier task force in the Pacific. During the final months of the Second World War he was present at the recapture of the Philippines and other major campaigns. During the war he had trained as a pilot and later became an instructor at the Naval Staff College. In 1950 he joined HMS *Theseus* as Commander (Air) and he was involved in operations off Korea. Prior to his appointment to the *Ark Royal* he served as Captain (D) of the Second Training Squadron at Portland.

During the *Ark Royal's* extended refit a number of modifications were made, the most important being the installation of an Operations Room from where any war operations could be conducted. Another significant alteration was the removal of two gun turrets from the port side forward, which not only enabled the flight deck to be extended, but also provided space in the area vacated by the gunnery machinery for mess deck accommodation for 120 men. The ship's internal television system was also improved and all messes were supplied with television sets.

On Thursday 1 November 1956, the day that Anglo-French naval and air forces embarked on the ill-fated Suez campaign, the *Ark Royal's* recommissioning ceremony was held at Devonport. As well as the official guests, which included the C-in-C Home Fleet, Admiral Sir John Eccles, and the C-in -C Plymouth, Admiral Mark Pizey, some 500 relatives of the ship's company visited the ship to witness the impressive ceremony in the upper hangar. After the official speeches and a short religious service the guests were entertained to lunch in the various dining halls. Writing in a letter to Captain Hopkins, the C-in-C Home Fleet summed up the day thus: 'I am quite sure that the whole ceremony left a very big mark on all those who were present, and as a result, the commission of the *Ark Royal* could not have been started off better.' Just eight days after the recommissioning ceremony, another memorable event for the ship's company was held on board when, on Friday 9 November, the well-known television star, Tonia Berne, visited the ship with her supporting cast and the 'Tonia Berne Show' was put on with great success in the upper hangar to the great delight of a massive audience of the ship's company and their guests. Two of the glamorous chorus girls had no difficulty in persuading a couple of sailors to get up on stage with them, but they did not find it so easy restraining them after that! Tonia Berne herself had the whole audience 'rockin' when she performed some rock 'n' roll, but fortunately the mooring ropes held fast, and meanwhile work continued in other regions of the ship to get ready for sea.

On Wednesday 21 November there was a nasty accident which, if it had not been for the prompt action of PO Electrician Jones, would have been far worse and could have proved fatal. An electrical mechanic was ascending a ladder carrying a jar of sulphuric acid when he slipped and fell, resulting in the contents of the broken jar being spilled all over himself. Hearing screams nearby, PO Jones managed to carry the victim into an adjacent compartment where he thrust the man's face under running fresh water. He then quickly filled a makeshift eyebath with soda solution and thoroughly washed the injured man's eyes. Following this he started to treat the man's legs which were very badly burned, and he was doing this when sickbay attendants arrived to administer further first aid measures. Captain Hopkins later officially commended PO Jones for displaying such initiative which undoubtedly saved the man from much deeper and more serious burns. Next day, having embarked a trials party, the *Ark Royal* left her berth at 7.45am and steamed out to Plymouth Sound where she moored for three days, before leaving for the Channel between the Isle of Wight and Portland to carry out her post-refit trials.

On 2 December the first of a series of flying trials began, initially with Gannets from RNAS Ford, and at 4pm on Monday 3 December there was a serious accident on the flight deck when NA D. Maguire was hit and severely injured by the propeller of a Gannet whilst the aircraft was being loaded onto the catapult. Flying operations were immediately suspended and the ship steamed into Spithead from where the injured rating was transferred to RNH Haslar. When the flying trials resumed after this incident Wyverns of 831 Squadron made a series of deck landings and launchings, and then, on the morning of Saturday 8 December, the carrier returned to Devonport Dockyard where seasonal leave commenced, prior to the Christmas

Both the ship and her ship's company look immaculate as she is dressed overall for the US Navy's International Fleet Review at Norfolk, Virginia. Astern of her is the USS *Saratoga*.

(*R. Lakey*)

and New Year festivities. On the afternoon of Friday 28 December the *Ark Royal* left her berth and steamed out to the Sound where she moored on C buoy, then on New Year's Eve, with most non-duty personnel anxious to go ashore, a thick blanket of fog descended over the Plymouth area and all boat traffic between the ship and shore was suspended, much to everyone's annoyance. Three days later, on the morning of Thursday 3 January 1957, together with the destroyer *Orwell*, the *Ark Royal* put to sea to start another series of flying trials in the Channel. These took place over four days, during which the first of a new generation of naval aircraft, the Supermarine N113, the nuclear capable strike weapon, made its second series of landings on and launchings from the carrier. Later in the commission the N113 would return as the Supermarine Scimitar. After two days moored in Plymouth Sound, during which time the squadron ground parties joined the ship, the *Ark Royal* sailed again, this time to embark the Gannet anti-submarine aircraft of 815 Squadron, the Sea Hawks of 824 and 898 Squadrons, the Wyverns of 831 Squadron, the Sea Venoms of 891 Squadron and the Skyraiders of 849B Flight. After embarking the aircraft and performing deck landing trials off the coast of north Cornwall, the *Ark Royal* set course for Gibraltar and the Mediterranean Fleet. She arrived in Gibraltar on Monday 14 January, remaining alongside for two days before departing in company with HMS *Dainty*, their destination being Marsaxlokk Bay, Malta, which they reached on Saturday 19 January. Three days later, as she carried out flying exercises off the Mediterranean island, the Sea Hawks of 802 Squadron were embarked, and on Friday 25 January, with the FOAC, Vice-Admiral M. L. Power, on board, the *Ark Royal* made a ceremonial entry into Grand Harbour where she secured to a buoy in Bighi Bay. During her stay at Malta the ship's sporting activities got off to a good start when the boxing team took on the combined Mediterranean Fleet team, and won easily.

However, down below in the engine rooms, the ship's propulsion machinery was causing problems for the engineers and it became apparent that the ship would have to return to Devonport early for repairs on the main engines. First of all though, she would spend three more weeks in the Mediterranean and on Tuesday 5 February she left Malta and steamed west for Gibraltar, where she was to carry out flying exercises in the area. At 11.26 am on Wednesday 13 February HRH the Duke of Edinburgh embarked by helicopter and during the course of the day the ship steamed west of Ceuta in North Africa, where the royal visitor was given a flying display before he toured the ship. That afternoon Prince Philip cut the cake which had been baked to celebrate the 1,000th deck landing of the commission by a Sea Venom of 893 Squadron, after which he left the ship by Gannet at 4.20pm for North Front. After carrying out flying exercises with the aircraft carrier

Albion and the fast minelayer *Apollo*, the *Ark Royal* set course for Devonport on the morning of Friday 22 February. Early on Monday 25 February the squadrons were flown off to Culdrose, Ford and Lossiemouth and that afternoon the *Ark Royal* moored in Plymouth Sound. Next day, at just before 3pm, the carrier steamed up harbour to secure alongside Devonport's 6 and 7 wharves, where the ship went into refit routine and the dockyard was able to carry out the repairs to the main turbines.

The *Ark Royal* remained alongside at Devonport until the late afternoon of Monday 29 April, when she steamed out into Plymouth Sound and moored on C buoy, to be joined over the following four days by the squadron personnel. At 9am on Friday 3 May the carrier moved out into the Channel where the Wyverns and Gannets were safely landed on, and after an overnight stop at Spithead she set course for Rosyth, sailing by way of the Strait of Dover and the North Sea. During the morning of Monday 6 May the aircraft of 802, 804, 898 and 849B Squadrons were landed on and in the afternoon the ship herself anchored off Invergordon. Over the next five days the *Ark Royal* carried out intensive flying operations in the area off Lossiemouth, spending Sunday 12 May at anchor before continuing flying operations on the following day. Forty-eight hours later, on Wednesday 15 May, the *Ark Royal* arrived at Rosyth where she was joined by HMS *Albion*, which had returned from the Mediterranean, and other units of the Home Fleet. Both carriers, together with HMS *Ocean*, were to take part in 'Operation Steadfast', a review of ships of the Home Fleet by Her Majesty The Queen. On Tuesday 21 May the *Ark Royal* and the *Albion* left Rosyth bound for the Cromarty Firth, where they were to be spruced up, before the whole fleet rehearsed for the royal steam-past. The Review itself took place over three days between Monday 27 and Wednesday 29 May and during this time the Queen was scheduled to visit the *Ark Royal*. The full three-hour rehearsal of the steam-past was held on the morning of Friday 24 May with the depot ship *Maidstone* assuming the role of the royal yacht. A Royal Marines officer from the *Ark Royal's* detachment describes the second rehearsal: 'The first rehearsal went off without a hitch, but during the second we failed to appreciate that with the ship doing 21 knots there was a wind speed of 45 knots over the deck. The scene from the bridge must have been worth a guinea a minute. Guard and band assembled serenely on the lift in the upper hangar and the order "up lift" was given. Suddenly all hell was let loose. As the first heads appeared above the flight deck a ripple of wind swept through the guard and band; but there was no stopping the lift and it remorselessly continued upwards. My command of "Quick March" produced no effect whatsoever for, with the wind whistling through the ventilation holes of the white helmets, it went unheard and anyhow the wind was pushing the band steadily backwards. Within seconds

The *Ark Royal* steams past the New York skyline as she enters the harbour on 18 June 1957. *(Fleet Air Arm Museum & R. Lakey)*

chaos reigned, with the bass drummer, all the sheet music and five helmets blowing away aft, and to top it all, the lift driver had also been blown over, leaving the guard and band marooned at the mercy of the elements until he had regained his feet. Luckily he did this with commendable speed and we returned, somewhat dishevelled, to the sepulchral stillness of the upper hangar.' On Sunday 26 May, the morning before the Home Fleet was due to steam out to meet *Britannia,* Cromarty Firth was shrouded in a thick heat haze and rather than risk being unable to proceed through the narrow entrance under similar circumstances, that evening the fleet moved to an anchorage off Nairn, outside the Firth. Monday 27 May dawned gloriously bright with the promise of a hot day to come, and by 9.35am the *Ark Royal* and ships of the Review Fleet had taken up their formations. By 10.30am all the ships were fully manned and a quarter of an hour later the *Britannia,* which was returning from a State Visit to Denmark, was sighted. The Review manoeuvres involved the fleet steaming past *Britannia* in two columns on opposite courses and, as they approached the royal yacht, a 21-gun salute was fired. After the two columns had steamed past once, they turned round and steamed past the *Britannia's* starboard side with ships' companies manning decks and cheering as they passed by. Everything went according to plan and at this point the *Ark Royal* parted company with the fleet to fly off aircraft for the ceremonial fly-past. However, shortly after the squadrons had been launched, there was a total lubricating oil pressure failure in Y engine room and the ship had to stop for almost ten minutes while the engineers sorted the problem out. Later that afternoon the whole fleet, together with the *Britannia,* anchored off Invergordon and in the evening all the ships were illuminated. The following day was comparatively quiet for the *Ark Royal* while the Queen and the Duke of Edinburgh visited the *Albion* and other ships of the fleet. That evening Captain Hopkins attended a reception on board the *Britannia,* and afterwards the *Ark Royal's* band provided the Corps of Drums to sound a fanfare for the Queen's arrival at a Fleet Concert which was held in HMS *Albion.* On Wednesday 29 May it was the *Ark Royal's* 'big day', when the Queen and Duke of Edinburgh arrived on board at 9.45am to be greeted by the Senior Officers. They were then taken to the upper hangar to be received by the Royal Marines Guard of Honour, and after the inspection the royal visitors were driven round the Divisions. At 10.15am the *Ark Royal* weighed anchor and steamed out into the North Sea where, from the island superstructure, the royal party watched flying demonstrations for almost two hours. Afterwards there was a small informal reception in the Admiral's cabin, to which a number of ratings were invited, and finally, at just before 1pm, the ship was stopped and the royal visitors disembarked to return to the *Britannia,* accompanied by the cheers of the ship's company who had

manned the flight deck. In the words of one officer: 'It was altogether a memorable visit in that, although all ceremonies were carried out with pomp and precision, an informal atmosphere was prevalent everywhere.'

No sooner had the royal visitors left the ship than the *Ark Royal,* together with the destroyers *Diamond* and *Duchess,* set course for Norfolk, Virginia, which, for most of the ship's company, was to be the highlight of the commission. The transatlantic passage of almost 4,000 miles was hampered by some bad weather and by mechanical problems affecting both main engines. But on a happier note, when the *Ark Royal* was just 24 hours outside US waters she met up with the replica of the 17th-century sailing vessel *Mayflower* which was in the area, although the meeting was only made possible by an extensive air and sea search which found her to be 30 miles north of the carrier's position, and about 200 miles off Bermuda. There was a great deal of interest in the encounter between one of the Royal Navy's most powerful warships and the replica of the sailing vessel which set sail from Plymouth on 16 September 1620 carrying the Pilgrim Fathers (or Religious Separatists as they were originally known) to the New World. The purpose of the *Ark Royal's* visit to the USA was partly to promote goodwill and understanding between Britain and America, and partly to impress upon the Americans that the Royal Navy was still an efficient, modern and powerful fighting force. The visit also coincided with the Jamestown Festival of 1957 which was held to commemorate the first permanent settlement sent out from London by the Virginia Company under the command of Captain John Smith. Sailing across uncharted waters in the tiny sailing ships *Susan Constant, Godspeed* and *Discovery,* they had first made land on the continent of North America on 6 April 1607, finally anchoring off Jamestown Island on 13 May that year. Going ashore they gave thanks to God and planted the British flag on what was to become the first permanent English settlement in North America. It was this landing 350 years earlier that the United States was celebrating with an April to November festival at Jamestown. One of the highlights of the festival was to be the United States Navy's International Naval Review and Fleet Week from 8 to 17 June and the *Ark Royal, Diamond* and *Duchess* were to be honoured guests on this occasion. The last US Navy Review to celebrate a Jamestown Festival had been in 1907 and the 1957 Review was to be the largest such event in world history, involving 103 warships from over 17 nations.

The *Ark Royal* and her escorts arrived alongside the US Naval Yard at Norfolk, Virginia, during the afternoon of Saturday 8 June and during their stay in the naval base they were open daily to the public, which proved to be a great success. For three days the *Ark Royal* was berthed, with the *Diamond* and *Duchess* immediately astern of her, at Pier 5 in the Navy Yard and, as the biggest visiting warship, the carrier attracted a great deal of attention. Opposite the *Ark Royal* was the mighty 60,000-ton USS *Saratoga* ('*Big Sara*' as she was affectionately known in the US Navy), which was the *Ark*'s host ship, and berthed nearby was the graceful Spanish Navy sail training ship *Juan Sebastian de Elcano*. However, in an area of the USA where great pride in their English ancestry is always noticeable, the Royal Navy's ships were made to feel the most welcome. Despite the intense heat and high humidity, queues were always waiting by the gangways and it was estimated that 40,000 people visited the three ships. Although there was no truth in the rumour that one visitor, after a visit to the *Ark Royal*, remarked, 'The British surely are hospitable. I asked for tea and they gave me rum!', the welcome ashore for the ships' companies, and on board for the visitors, was always warm and sincere. The smart appearance and the discipline shown by the Royal Marines as they Beat Retreat and gave concerts ashore was particularly noteworthy and for the public, waiting in seemingly endless queues on the pier, the precise drill of the Marine sentries was a great source of fascination.

At 7.30am on the morning of Tuesday 11 June the *Ark Royal* and her destroyers moved from Pier 5 to their assigned anchorages in Hampton Roads which, for the carrier, was between Fort Monroe and Willoughby Spit at the head of the Review with the US Navy's battleships *Iowa* and *Wisconsin*, the USS *Saratoga* and the French aircraft carrier *Bois Belleau* (ex-USS *Belleau Wood*). Next day, at 1pm, the Review itself got under way when the reviewing ships, led by the USS *Canberra*, with the US Secretary of Defence, Charles P. Wilson, embarked, and closely followed by the USS *Boston* (sister to the USS *Canberra*), left their pier to simultaneous gun salutes crashing out from all the ships in the Review. The whole review of the seven-mile-long lines of warships, including a fly-past by naval aircraft, took four and a half hours, and on the following morning the *Ark Royal* and the two destroyers returned to their berths, after which the ships' companies were able to enjoy another four days ashore in that hospitable part of the United States.

On leaving Norfolk during the morning of Monday 17 June 1957, the *Ark Royal* parted company with the *Diamond* and *Duchess* and while on passage north to New York she carried out cross-operating exercises with the USS *Saratoga*, which served as a rehearsal for a forthcoming NATO exercise, 'Strikeback', which was to be held in September that year. The exercises were carried out when the two carriers were three to five miles apart, with the US Navy aircraft landing on and taking off from the *Ark Royal*'s flight deck, guided by a team of US Navy officers in the Operations Room. Similarly her own officers controlled the *Ark Royal*'s aircraft as they landed and took off from the *Saratoga*. In all the British carrier operated five types of US naval aircraft; the Banshee and Fury fighters, the long-

nosed, delta-winged Skyray interceptor, the Tracker (the heavier counterpart of the Gannet) and the Skyraider. In its turn the *Saratoga* operated Sea Hawks, Sea Venoms and Gannets. At 3pm on Tuesday 18 June the *Ark Royal* passed the Statue of Liberty and just over an hour later she secured alongside New York's Pier 88, close to the liner *Queen Mary*. As at Norfolk the ship's company were the guests of the US Navy and throughout the two-day stay the goodwill and friendliness of New Yorkers was much in evidence and, as a special concession, the men were paid three weeks' wages in dollars, but on going into the city in uniform many of them found the hospitality such that they were often dissuaded from parting with more than a little of their cash. It was at 1.15pm on Thursday 20 June that the *Ark Royal*, together with her faithful destroyers *Diamond* and *Duchess*, left New York for the eastbound transatlantic crossing, during which Admiral Power carried out his Sea Inspection. Also during the passage a sick French seaman, who had suffered a brain haemorrhage, was picked up from the trawler *Jean Charcot* and when the *Ark Royal* anchored in Falmouth Bay at 7pm on Friday 28 June, the man was taken ashore. The trip to the United States had been an unqualified success and throughout the visit the officers and men from the *Ark Royal* had proved to be good ambassadors for Britain. There were regrets that the next Jamestown Festival was not due until 2007.

After two days at anchor in Falmouth Bay, during which time the ship was opened to visitors, the *Ark Royal* steamed to Portsmouth where she spent nine days alongside before carrying out flying exercises off the Isle of Wight. During July an anti-submarine Gannet AS4 successfully dropped the Mk 30 torpedo, and further deck landing trials were made by the Scimitar, formerly the N113. On Thursday 25 July the two Scimitars SC125 and SC134, which had made a temporary home in the *Ark Royal*, flew back to shore, and on the following day the carrier returned to Devonport and to No 10 dry dock where she remained until mid-August when she was moved to 5 and 6 wharves for her refit to be completed. In early August it was announced that the standard displacement of the *Ark Royal* and *Eagle* had been reassessed, and that instead of the original 36,800 tons, their new tonnage was 43,340 tons, which put them on a par with the USS *Midway*. With a full load of over 50,000 tons they were almost the heaviest ships to serve in the Royal Navy.

The *Ark Royal* put to sea again at 7.45am on Wednesday 28 August, flying the flag of FOAC, Vice-Admiral M. L. Power, and also with 200 relatives of the officers and men embarked. They were on board for a special Families Day, part of which was a cruise round the Eddystone Lighthouse where the ship's squadrons performed a fly-past and 815 Squadron was embarked, before the *Ark Royal* returned to Cawsand Bay for the families to go ashore. Soon afterwards the carrier left Plymouth to steam north for the colder waters of the North Sea, and at the end of the month she

During her visit to New York the *Ark* was berthed close to Cunard's liner, *Queen Mary*.　　　　(R. Lakey)

joined her older sister *Eagle* and the *Bulwark* at anchor off Lossiemouth. Two days later all three carriers sailed to carry out exercises in preparation for the NATO exercise 'Strikeback', but the *Eagle* soon had to put in at Rosyth as an outbreak of influenza swept through her ship's company. However, the *Ark Royal* and the *Bulwark* continued flying exercises off the coast of Scotland and after a long weekend at anchor in the Clyde off Gourock, 'Exercise Strikeback' got under way on Tuesday 17 September, when both carriers joined the US Navy's *Forrestal, Essex* and *Canberra* off the west coast of the Hebrides. The fleet steamed north of the Arctic Circle from where aircraft from all the carriers launched attacks on ground targets from northern Norway to Denmark, and the fleet also exercised procedures for steaming through an area of radioactive fallout, should they encounter nuclear weapons. On conclusion of the exercise the *Ark Royal* returned to Spithead on 28 September and anchored for a weekend break.

Unfortunately, during the exercises, further problems had been experienced with the carrier's main propulsion machinery, which necessitated dry docking, and the only suitable graving dock was at Southampton Docks. So, at 2.45pm on Tuesday 1 October, the *Ark Royal* weighed anchor to steam up Southampton Water to the commercial docks, and by 6.30pm she was safely secured in the King George V dry dock off the city's Millbrook Road. During the ten-day docking period Rear-Admiral Maclean relieved Vice-Admiral Power as FOAC, hoisting his flag in the *Ark Royal*. Two days later, during the morning of Friday 11 October, the carrier left Southampton and immediately set course for the Atlantic and NATO's 'Exercise Pipedown', which consisted of five events; 'Touchdown', 'Snapper', 'Angel', 'Mercury' and a search and strike exercise. By far the most important part of the exercise was 'Touchdown', which was to demonstrate the capability of the USS *Saratoga* and *Ark Royal* to operate each other's aircraft. This

The *Ark Royal* ploughs through heavy seas during 'Exercise Phoenix II' in the North Atlantic during November 1957.
(Imperial War Museum HU75014)

was successfully completed in two days, despite poor visibility, after which came 'Snapper', an anti-submarine exercise which was run in conjunction with 'Angel', an air defence exercise, both of which were designed to increase the efficiency of the anti-submarine and fighter defence of a large NATO fleet at sea. During 'Mercury' the US battleship *Wisconsin* and two destroyers took the part of surface raiders, and they succeeded in evading the search in bad weather and carrying out dummy attacks on the fleet. Finally the British and US units separated and carried out a free-for-all to display to each other their strike potential, before both fleets departed and went their various ways, with the *Ark Royal* and *Albion* setting course for Gibraltar. Unfortunately, low cloud prevented 16 Sea Venoms and 32 Sea Hawks carrying out a fly-past over the 'Rock', but that afternoon the two carriers berthed alongside the colony's South Mole. Three days later, after a spruce-up at Gibraltar, the *Ark Royal* and *Albion* left for a courtesy visit to Lisbon, and after carrying out joint exercises with the USS *Lake Champlain*, they arrived in the River Tagus on the

following day, with the *Ark Royal* anchoring in mid-river at 4pm on Tuesday 22 October. Both carriers left Lisbon during the afternoon of Saturday 26 and next day, in company with the *Eagle*, the *Albion* left for Portsmouth and the end of her commission, while the *Ark Royal's* ship's company manned ship and cheered the light fleet carrier as she parted company.

On the first day of November the *Ark Royal* rendezvoused with HMS *Bulwark* in the Channel where the Whirlwind helicopters of 845 Squadron transferred to the *Ark* and the smaller carrier left for Portsmouth. The *Ark Royal*, meanwhile, returned to Devonport where she secured alongside 6 and 7 wharves at 2pm on Saturday 2 November. On the morning of Wednesday 13 November, after embarking the C-in-C Plymouth, the *Ark Royal* left Devonport to recover her air group, after which the C-in-C left the ship and the *Ark Royal* set course for Rosyth, where she arrived three days later. After a weekend in the Firth of Forth the carrier left to rendezvous with the *Eagle* and the *Bulwark* to take part in 'Exercise Phoenix II', which they had to see through in atrocious weather in Scottish waters. On Tuesday 19 November the ships ran into severe gales, which led to the CAP aircraft of three Wyverns being recalled. The first Wyvern was damaged on landing and it then caught fire just aft of the side lift. Although there were no injuries in this instance, the other two aircraft were diverted to the *Eagle* where they landed safely, but as the *Ark Royal* steamed into heavy seas and Force 10 winds she still had to recover eight Sea Hawks which were airborne. Despite the fact that the flight deck was rising and falling 40 to 50 feet at its extremities, all the Sea Hawks landed safely, with only an undercarriage or two suffering any damage. Following the end of the exercise the *Ark Royal* steamed back to Rosyth, and after a weekend at anchor there she returned to Devonport on Friday 29 November to carry out a maintenance period and to take some well-earned respite and Christmas and New Year leave. By late January 1958 the *Ark Royal* was at sea once again, and after embarking her squadrons and spending a night at anchor in Weymouth Bay, she made a three-day passage south, arriving in Gibraltar on the last day of the month to start a six-month deployment with the Mediterranean Fleet.

In early 1958, in the aftermath of the Anglo-French debacle at Suez and with the rise of Arab nationalism alongside an aggressive foreign policy in Israel, it was clear that the Middle East was very unstable. President Nasser of Egypt had united his country with the Sudan to form the United Arab Republic, and Jordan and Iraq were about to set up an alliance known as the Arab Federation. The political situation was further complicated by France's problems with its North African colony of Algeria and by President Nasser's strident Arab nationalist broadcasts which were being transmitted to surrounding countries. It was in this atmosphere that the British Government had decided to send its two most powerful aircraft carriers to the area, and during the passage to Gibraltar the *Ark Royal* and *Eagle* rendezvoused for the voyage south. They remained in the colony for only three days before steaming east for Malta, and on Friday 7 February five squadrons of Sea Hawks and two squadrons of Sea Venoms, comprising 65 naval aircraft from the two carriers, took part in a fly-past over Valletta as *Ark Royal* and *Eagle* joined the Mediterranean Station and berthed in the city's Grand Harbour. After a long weekend in harbour the *Ark Royal* put to sea to carry out flying exercises off the coast of Libya, before returning to Grand Harbour for another long weekend there. It was on the morning of Tuesday 25 February that both the *Ark Royal* and *Eagle* left Malta for more flying exercises in the area, which got off to a bad start when a pilot from the *Eagle* lost his life. Four days later, at 8.15am on 1 March, a Sea Hawk piloted by Lt E. J. Kay RN crashed over the port side of the *Ark Royal* while landing. Despite a thorough search of the area, no trace of the pilot or his aircraft was found and next day a memorial

service was held over the spot at which the accident had happened, Lat 35° – 28'N/Long 14° – 27'E. Two days later the carriers were joined by the *Ark Royal's* old friend, USS *Saratoga*, which was accompanied by the USS *Essex* for 'Exercise Marjex'. After this six-day exercise the *Ark Royal* headed for Genoa, where she anchored on the morning of Monday 10 March for a seven-day visit. Following this she returned to Malta for an 18-day self-maintenance period and a break from the intensive flying programme which she had been carrying out.

On Tuesday 8 April, with the *Eagle* having returned to Devonport for dry docking, the *Ark Royal* left Malta to undertake further flying exercises with the frigate *Salisbury* and the destroyer *Contest*. After three days of flying, and a weekend break off Palermo, the carrier returned to the exercise areas off Malta, and during night-flying exercises on Monday 14 April, a Sea Venom ditched into the sea immediately after launching at 9.35pm. Although the *Ark Royal* stopped her engines immediately, the *Contest* was the first to reach the scene and the two injured aircrew, Lts Webster and Schofield, were rescued by the destroyer. After the Medical Officer had been transferred to the destroyer, the two injured men were taken to Marsaxlokk where they could be admitted to hospital. Five days later the *Ark Royal* returned to Grand Harbour for a short weekend break before leaving for a visit to Naples, where she arrived on Tuesday 29 April. The extended courtesy visit to the Italian port lasted for 12 days and during that time a BBC film unit embarked in order to produce a series of features showing life in the carrier for a children's documentary, and to film the carrier at work on a Mediterranean exercise. After leaving Naples during the morning of Saturday 10 May the *Ark Royal* returned to the area off Malta where, at 8.48pm on Thursday 15 May, one of her Gannets crashed into the sea whilst attempting to land on board. Fortunately, both crew members were rescued by the planeguard frigate, HMS *Salisbury*. Four days later came 'Exercise Medflex Fort', but it was to be quickly overshadowed by political problems in the Middle East. However, soon after the start of the exercise, in a position Lat 35° – 40'N/Long 30° – 10'E, some 120 miles west of Cyprus, a Sea Venom ditched on launching. The pilot was quickly picked up by the planeguard destroyer, but the observer, Sub-Lt M. H. Goodwin RN, could not be found and it was soon realized that he had not escaped from the aircraft and sadly he was posted as 'Missing Presumed Dead'.

That night the ships taking part in the exercise were put on alert to evacuate British subjects from the Lebanon where anti-government disturbances had been taking place. Although 'Exercise Medflex Fort' concluded on Thursday 22 May, the *Ark Royal* remained off the coast of Cyprus in the area of Akrotiri Bay where, occasionally, despite the EOKA terrorist campaign, recreational leave was given. During a night encounter exercise on Monday 26 May, Lt John Herringshaw

RN, flying a Sea Venom of 893 Squadron, performed the 10,000th deck landing of the second commission and also completed 1,000 flying hours during his flight.

On the morning of Tuesday 10 June the *Eagle* arrived to relieve the *Ark Royal* and the helicopters of 820 Squadron transferred all their stores, personnel and aircraft to the newly arrived carrier. Next morning, at 8am, the *Ark Royal* weighed anchor and set course for Malta, from where, after a ten-hour stop in Marsaxlokk Bay, she left for Gibraltar. During the five-day stay alongside in the colony, Ceremonial Divisions were rehearsed in preparation for a forthcoming visit by the ship's royal sponsor, the Queen Mother, who was due to visit the carrier at Devonport. After leaving Gibraltar on Monday 23 June, the *Ark Royal* entered the Channel in the early hours of Thursday 26 June and by 8.30am that morning she was secured alongside South Railway Jetty in Portsmouth Dockyard. However, the commission was not quite over for, on the last day of June, after embarking the C-in-C Portsmouth and other VIP guests, the carrier put to sea for the exercise area south-west of the Isle of Wight to carry out a series of 'Shop Window' displays. These continued for the rest of the week, with a variety of official guests, including the Minister of Defence and the First Sea Lord, embarking to watch proceedings, with the ship anchoring in Sandown Bay each evening. On the final day, Friday 4 July, the last

deck landings and launchings were made by Gannets flown by Sub-Lt Bevan and Lt-Cdr Mortimer respectively and that evening, after disembarking all the official guests and a large number of squadron personnel off the Isle of Wight, the *Ark Royal* set course for Devonport, arriving alongside 6 and 7 wharves at 9.35am the following morning.

The final event of the commission took place with the ship in dry dock on Friday 11 July 1958, when the Queen Mother visited the ship and arrived on board in a Whirlwind helicopter which had brought her from Exeter. After her previous visit to the carrier in March 1956 the Queen Mother expressed a wish to make a presentation to the ship, and Captain Hopkins had intimated that he would be pleased to receive a ceremonial sash for the drum major of the volunteer band. After inspecting Divisions from the ship's Land Rover, the Queen Mother addressed the officers and ratings before presenting the sash to AB Clive Gable. This was followed by lunch with the C-in-C Plymouth and Captain Hopkins, after which the Queen Mother left the carrier at 2.20pm, her visit having lasted just under three hours.

Next day the *Ark Royal* went into refit routine and on Wednesday 16 July Captain Hopkins handed over command to his Executive Officer, Commander I. S. McIntosh, before leaving the ship. It was the end of a long, busy, and successful second commission.

Her Majesty Queen Elizabeth The Queen Mother inspects Divisions on Friday 11 July 1958, at the end of the ship's second commission. *(R Lakey)*

Chapter Six

The Middle Years 1959-1966

Following the end of her second commission the *Ark Royal* was taken in hand by Devonport Dockyard for an extensive refit, but nine months into the work there was a serious setback. At just after 3pm on Wednesday 8 April 1959 fire broke out in the bilges below X boiler room, which was situated below the lower hangar, and quickly spread to a fitting shop, storerooms and adjacent compartments. At the time there were several hundred dockyard workers on board, but only a handful of ship's company, and although fire parties tackled the blaze, and the Dockyard and City Fire Brigades were quickly on the scene, nine dockyard workers were trapped in a compartment above the boiler room. In the event they managed to escape unscathed by climbing through a

scuttle and swimming ashore where they were treated in a sickbay. The firefighters, assisted by men from HMS *Centaur* which was berthed nearby, faced intense heat in tackling the blaze, along with the additional hazard of dense smoke. Although they used self-contained breathing apparatus, they were unable to work for long periods in the confined spaces and frequent changes of manpower were necessary. Eventually, by 5pm, using three pumps and six jets of water simultaneously, the fire was brought under control and then extinguished soon afterwards. Initially it was thought that the damage caused must be considerable, but a full survey revealed that the worst of the fire had been confined to X boiler room and the adjoining fitting shop. Since a large proportion of the auxiliary machinery was being refitted

During the 1958-1959 refit the deck edge lift was removed. This view shows a pilot's eye view of the flight deck.
(Fleet Air Arm Museum)

ashore and much of the damaged electrical wiring had been due for replacement in any case, the refit was not prolonged as severely as had been first feared, but it served as a sober reminder of the grave hazards caused by fire in a ship. During the refit the deck-edge lift on the port side was removed, as were the two starboard forward 4.5-inch guns and the single bofors guns situated around the island superstructure.

On 1 October 1959 the *Ark Royal's* new commanding officer, Captain P. J. Hill-Norton, joined the ship to take command. Captain Hill-Norton had joined the Royal Navy as a cadet at the Royal Naval College, Dartmouth, and he first went to sea as a midshipman in 1932. In early 1939 he specialized in gunnery and during the Second World War he served in Arctic convoys and on board destroyers in the North-Western Approaches. He was promoted Captain in 1952 and over the following three years he served as Naval Attaché in Argentina, Uruguay and Paraguay. Following these postings he commanded the Daring-class destroyer HMS *Decoy,* before being appointed to command the *Ark Royal.*

It was on Tuesday 1 December 1959 that the main body of the ship's company began to join the carrier, and 14 days later the Royal Marines Band arrived. Despite this, however, the *Ark Royal* was still very much in dockyard hands and conditions on board were somewhat chaotic,

with, for instance, compressed air hoses and electrical cables winding their way through the passageways. However, no sooner had many of the ship's company joined the ship than they were ashore again and taking their Christmas leave. In the third week of December there was a flurry of activity as the ship was cleaned up for the commissioning ceremony, which took place on Monday 28 December 1959. At 2pm that day guests began to arrive, being welcomed on board by the Royal Marines Band playing military music on the quarterdeck, as they assembled in the upper hangar. At just after 3pm the official guests came aboard, among them the C-in-C Plymouth, Admiral Sir Richard Onslow, the Lord Mayor of Plymouth and the Flag Officer Aircraft Carriers, Rear-Admiral Charles Evans. The Royal Marines Band provided the music for the short religious service and the cake was cut by Mrs Margaret Hill-Norton during the ceremony which was televised by the BBC. One of the Royal Marines later remarked about the footage that: 'The cameraman showed considerable ingenuity and skill in being able to film all the important visitors coming on board without including a single glimpse of any member of the guard or band.' By 4.30pm the ceremony was over and the guests were departing, after which work continued apace to clean up the ship and prepare her for sea.

The New Year of 1960 came and went and a week later,

at noon on Friday 8 January, the *Ark Royal* tore herself away from the dockyard wall and steamed out to C buoy in Plymouth Sound from where, after a weekend moored within sight of the open sea, she left to start her post-refit trials. Everything went surprisingly smoothly, with no indications of the serious fire which had caused so much damage less than a year before, which was a tribute to the efforts of the men of Devonport Dockyard. The *Ark Royal* remained at sea for the rest of January, although on most nights she anchored off Weymouth or in Plymouth Sound, and on Tuesday 2 February she began her flying trials in the Channel. These commenced with Sea Hawks and Gannets, and it was not long before Sea Vixens and Scimitars were also performing deck landing and launching trials. By the afternoon of Tuesday 9 February the carrier was back alongside 5 and 6 wharves at Devonport Dockyard where the advance parties of 800 and 807 (Scimitar) Squadrons, 820 and 824 (Whirlwind) Squadrons, 892 (Sea Vixen) Squadron, and 849A (Gannet) Flight joined the ship. During her stay alongside a procession of senior officers visited the *Ark Royal* and at 9.30am on Tuesday 1 March 1960, the newly appointed FOAC, Rear-Admiral R. M. Smeeton, embarked. One hour later Vice-Admiral Evans lowered his flag and left the ship, with Admiral Smeeton hoisting his flag later in the day. At 8am on Thursday 3 March the *Ark Royal* slipped her moorings and left for the Channel, where she embarked all her squadrons and set course for Gibraltar and the Mediterranean Fleet.

After a 48-hour stopover in Gibraltar the carrier steamed east for Malta, and at 6pm on Friday 11 March she entered Grand Harbour where she joined HMS *Albion,* which was on her last commission as a fixed-wing carrier. After another brief stay in port she put to sea on Monday 14 March to carry out the first phase of her work-up in the exercise areas off Malta. This consisted of almost two weeks of intensive flying operations before, on Friday 25 March, the *Ark Royal* anchored off Palermo where everyone was able to relax and enjoy life in the town, the capital of what had been the kingdom of Sicily. Following the weekend break flying operations were resumed off Malta, and during the afternoon of Wednesday 30 March there was a fire in Y boiler room, but this was soon brought under control and it did not disrupt the carrier's flying programme. During the late afternoon of Wednesday 6 April one of the anti-submarine helicopters ditched about a mile away from the ship, but the SAR helicopter and the submarine HMS *Token* were soon on the scene and the crew of three were rescued safely. Finally, at 7am on Friday 8 April, much to the relief of the ship's company, all the squadron aircraft were launched to Hal Far and by noon that day the *Ark Royal* was secured to buoys in Malta's Grand Harbour.

During the stay in Malta the C-in-C Mediterranean, Admiral Sir Alexander Bingley, visited the ship and addressed the ship's company and the personnel of the two helicopter squadrons which had been dispatched to Hal Far. After an 11-day maintenance period in Grand Harbour the *Ark Royal* put to sea at 6.15pm on Tuesday 19 April, and next morning two Whirlwind helicopters arrived, carrying the Governor of Malta and other guests who were to witness an air defence exercise, where the *Ark Royal's* squadrons had to intercept aircraft from HMS *Centaur,* which was on passage between Port Said and Gibraltar. The VIPs left the *Ark Royal* in the evening and she then steamed east to the area off Cyprus to exercise with the destroyer *Scorpion* and the frigate *Eastbourne.* In early May she headed west again for a dry docking in Gibraltar, and by 10.30am on Wednesday 4 May she was secured in the Prince of Wales dry dock in the colony and had been taken over by Gibraltar Dockyard. For two weeks the *Ark Royal* remained in dry dock where, in addition to work on her propeller shafts, the ship's underwater hull was completely scraped and repainted. This provided an excellent opportunity for the ship's company to enjoy the pleasures of 'The Rock' and the nearby Spanish towns of La Linea and Algeciras.

The *Ark Royal* left Gibraltar on Friday 20 May and steamed east again to Malta where, after embarking her squadrons, she prepared for another day entertaining VIPs. On the morning of Tuesday 24 May, with the carrier anchored in Marsaxlokk Bay, a number of senior British Government and military personnel, including the First Lord of the Admiralty, the Chief of the NATO Staff and the GOC Malta, were embarked. After getting under way the carrier rendezvoused with the cruiser HMS *Tiger* and an escort screen for a 'Shop Window' display which served as a rehearsal for a forthcoming visit to Barcelona. That evening, after disembarking the VIPs, the *Ark Royal* set course for a courtesy visit to Toulon where she arrived three days later. After leaving the French naval base on Monday 30 May, the *Ark Royal* rendezvoused with the cruiser *Tiger,* the destroyer *Scorpion,* the experimental guided missile ship *Girdle Ness,* the depot ship and ex-Cunard liner *Ausonia,* and three RFAs, for a well-publicized visit to Barcelona. It was the most powerful force to have visited the Spanish port for many years and it had been arranged to coincide with the annual Barcelona Trade Fair, and particularly with British Day. The force arrived off Barcelona on the morning of Friday 3 June, and after embarking 150 guests just outside the port, the *Ark Royal* and *Tiger* put to sea where they staged a spectacular flying and gunnery display about 20 miles offshore. Following the display the *Tiger* entered the port while the *Ark Royal* anchored just outside the main mole. On British Day the Royal Marines Band from the *Ark Royal* played at the hoisting of the Union Flag, and the Royal Marines detachment gave an exhibition of marching and countermarching before a very enthusiastic holiday crowd. On Whit Monday, 6 June, the

A Sea Vixen about to take the barrier, and . . .

. . . untangling a Scimitar. (K. Smith)

Launching a Scimitar while moored in Grand Harbour.

Royal Marines Band put on a magnificent evening performance of Beating Retreat in the city's vast central square, the Plaza Cataluna. The Barcelona Trade Fair was a major event in Europe, occupying 65 acres, with 10,200 exhibitors and providing a major exporting opportunity for Britain at which the ships' companies of the *Ark Royal* and the other ships conducted themselves as excellent ambassadors for their country.

Following the visit both the *Ark Royal* and the *Tiger* carried out exercises with the French Navy and the USS *Forrestal*, before the two British ships went their separate ways, with the *Tiger* returning to Malta and the *Ark Royal* steaming for Gibraltar, where she arrived on Monday 20 June to carry out a 14-day self-maintenance period. It was Monday 4 July when the carrier left Gibraltar once again, and after recovering her aircraft she set course for Malta. At about 12.30pm next day one of the *Ark Royal's* Whirlwind helicopters ditched in the sea, but the carrier was on the scene and two members of the crew were rescued by the SAR helicopter, the third being picked up by the seaboat. After exercising in the Malta and Cyprus areas with the

Hermes, the *Ark Royal* paid a four-day visit to Piraeus where Admiral Smeeton struck his flag and left by air for the Far East, and the ship's company were able to take time out to enjoy Athens. After leaving the Greek port on the morning of Saturday 23 July, and exercising off Malta with the *Scorpion,* the *Ark Royal* entered Grand Harbour on Friday 29 July, where she remained for 11 days.

The carrier left Malta on Tuesday 9 August, and after recovering her squadrons she rendezvoused with the *Hermes* once again before joining the *Tiger* and the USS *Forrestal* for 'Exercise Royal Flush III'. At the end of the exercise the *Ark Royal* set course west with the *Hermes,* although they parted company for the *Ark Royal* to pay a short visit to Palma while the *Hermes* went down to Algiers, before they resumed their homeward passage together on Tuesday 23 August. Three days later the *Ark Royal* anchored in Portland Harbour, before she steamed north for Lossiemouth where, once again, she joined the *Hermes.* Together the two carriers undertook flying operations in preparation for NATO's 'Exercise Swordthrust' and it was during this period, at 10.12pm on Saturday 17 September, when the *Ark Royal* was 50 miles north of the Shetlands and executing night-flying operations, that Sea Vixen XJ 575 crashed on landing. As it toppled over the port side of the ship, it burst into flames and the planeguard destroyer HMS *Camperdown* immediately started a search of the area. Seaboats from both the *Camperdown* and the *Ark Royal* were slipped, but apart from a very strong smell of kerosene, there was no sign of the aircraft or its crew. Aided by searchlights from the *Ark Royal,* the cruiser *Gambia* and the destroyers *Camperdown* and *Defender* continued to search the area until well after daylight next morning but, apart from a few pieces of wreckage, nothing was found. At 10.33am on the morning of Sunday 18 September a memorial service was held to the memory of the pilot, Lt H. Bond RN and the observer, Lt M. Barnes RN.

The exercise itself began on Wednesday 28 September and the *Ark Royal* got off to a good start by establishing a new record for the highest number of daily sorties from a British carrier since the introduction into squadron service of the Scimitar and Sea Vixen. Most of these sorties were achieved by Scimitars making simulated nuclear attacks against land targets and 'enemy' shipping. In addition helicopters from both the *Ark Royal* and the *Hermes* flew on continuous anti-submarine patrols during daylight hours, which proved a great success when they located and held the nuclear-powered submarine USS *Triton,* playing an 'enemy' role, for so long that it was agreed that under wartime conditions the submarine would have been destroyed. During the exercise the force operated nearly 200 miles inside the Arctic Circle, and 130 miles off the Norwegian coast. Two-thirds of the 855 sorties made by the British carrier aircraft were flown from the *Ark Royal,* using for the first time in a major NATO exercise the fast strike interceptor, Scimitar, and the all-weather fighter, the Sea Vixen. However, on the air direction side the *Hermes'* new 984 radar provided an at-a-glance air picture on a huge plan position indicator in the Operations Room, which was the most significant radar development for many years, but one which would unfortunately never be installed in the *Ark Royal.* After a short stopover of just 16 hours in the Clyde the *Ark Royal* steamed south to Devonport where she docked at 5pm on Monday 3 October.

During her three weeks alongside, which provided a welcome break for her ship's company, the dockyard assisted with the task of essential maintenance. In the ten months since she had recommissioned, the *Ark Royal* had steamed 50,000 miles and her engineers estimated that they had carried out enough repairs to keep 17 large garages in business for a year or make 20,500 saloon cars roadworthy. The pay office staff had paid out £400,000 to the ship's company who, in their turn, had spent £21,000 on postage stamps and postal orders. In the galley the ship's bakery had produced 95 tons of bread and, it was said, her 2,000 officers and men had eaten 700 head of cattle. On the flight deck the carrier's aircraft had flown 6,000 sorties, 300 of them at night, and the steam catapults had worked overtime shooting 1,900 Scimitars, 800 Sea Vixens and 300 Gannets into the air. In addition, the helicopters on board had made over 1,000 flights.

Nevertheless, the commission was far from over and on Wednesday 26 October, after a very early reveille, the families of 170 officers and men were embarked and 20 minutes later, at 8.20am, the ship left her berth to steam into the Channel where the guests were treated to a flying display as the squadrons were re-embarked and put through their paces. At 2.30pm, after an enjoyable but very tiring day, the families were disembarked in Plymouth Sound, after which the *Ark Royal* weighed anchor and set course once again for the Mediterranean. On her arrival at Malta on Friday 4 November she joined HMS *Victorious* in Bighi Bay and 11 days later both carriers left the port to carry out flying operations in the area, following which the *Ark Royal* undertook landing and launching trials with the new Blackburn Buccaneer S1 low-level strike aircraft which continued through to Wednesday 23 November, when the Buccaneer trials party disembarked. The ship's flying exercises had continued meanwhile, and in early December she took part in 'Exercise Pink Gin', with the *Albion* and *Victorious,* finally returning to Gibraltar on Tuesday 13 December, where she secured alongside the South Mole for two days before steaming east to Malta for the Christmas and New Year festivities. On Wednesday 28 December a mammoth children's party was held in the upper hangar for 2,000 youngsters who had been invited on board for one of the biggest tea parties ever held on one of HM ships. On the stroke of midnight, Saturday 31 December 1960, the New Year was welcomed in by Junior Seaman Austin, the youngest member of the ship's company, ringing 16 bells.

A few days later, on Wednesday 4 January 1961, the Admiralty announced that in late February, just before the end of her commission, the *Ark Royal* would make a four-day goodwill visit to New York. But first she was scheduled to carry out more flying operations and at 8.50am on Friday 6 January she left Malta to embark her squadrons for exercises south-east of the island. Later that day, at 6.15pm, in a position Lat 35° - 40' N/Long 14° - 37'E, a Sea Vixen crashed into the sea, and although a thorough search was made of the area by both the carrier and the destroyer *Broadsword,* only an oil slick and small pieces of wreckage could be found. The search continued all through the night before being called off at 8am on Saturday 7 January, and soon afterwards a memorial service was held in memory of the lost aircrew, Lt Dudgeon RN and Sub-Lt Russell RN. The *Ark Royal's* last day with the Mediterranean Fleet was Saturday 14 January, when the C-in-C Mediterranean paid a farewell visit. Next morning course was set for Lisbon, where the carrier and the frigate *Londonderry* were to make a five-day courtesy visit from the

A cold, snowswept flight deck as the *Ark Royal* carries out cold weather flying trials in the Davis Strait between Greenland and Baffin Island. *(Fleet Air Arm Museum)*

afternoon of Wednesday 18 to Monday 23 February.

On leaving Lisbon the *Ark Royal* steamed across the Atlantic to the cold, bleak, storm-swept waters of the Davis Strait, between the west coast of Greenland and the east coast of Baffin Island. Here she carried out cold weather flying trials, and parties of flight deck personnel had to wield picks and axes in the constant battle against snow and ice in order to keep the planes flying. At times, the severe snowstorms reduced visibility to just a few hundred yards, and there was much relief all round when, on Thursday 9 February, course was set south for the port of New York with more exercises en route. Seven days after leaving the Davis Strait the carrier anchored in Block Island Sound, off Rhode Island, where, after the buffeting she had received off Greenland, she was spruced up for her entry into New York Harbour. During the afternoon of Friday 17 February the carrier weighed anchor and made an overnight passage to the entrance of the Hudson River, which she reached at 6am the next morning. The exchange

of official courtesies started early on the Saturday morning when the *Ark Royal* fired a 21-gun salute as she entered harbour and in return she received a similar salute from the First Army Headquarters at Fort Jay on Governors Island. The crashing of the saluting guns woke up many residents of Lower Manhattan and Brooklyn, and generated hundreds of calls to the police from startled householders. New York's welcome for the *Ark Royal*, the *Londonderry* and RFA *Tidesurge* was overwhelming, with both official and private hospitality being shown on a lavish scale. The citizens of New York offered the visiting seamen facilities to tour the city, go dancing and dining, and to take part in a variety of sports. In return the *Ark Royal* hosted a series of parties at which several hundred guests were entertained, and when the ship was opened to the public thousands of New Yorkers took the opportunity to go on board and look round the carrier. However, all too soon the visit came to an end, and at 11am on Wednesday 22 February the *Ark Royal* left Cunard's Pier 90 and steamed out of the harbour,

On Saturday 24 March 1962 the *Ark Royal* steamed south through the Suez Canal, on her way to take up duties on the Far East Station. *(Imperial War Museum HU75009)*

heading into severe Atlantic weather at the start of her passage to Devonport, where she arrived during the afternoon of Tuesday 28 February.

Two weeks after arriving alongside 6 and 7 wharves at Devonport came the final event of the commission when, at noon on Tuesday 14 March, Her Majesty Queen Elizabeth The Queen Mother arrived on board by helicopter and was met by Vice-Admiral Sir Charles Madden, the C-in-C Plymouth. After reviewing Divisions from the ship's Land Rover, the Queen Mother went down to the upper hangar where she spoke to the ship's company, who on this occasion were accompanied by 200 wives and sweethearts. The Queen Mother remarked to her audience: '*Ark Royal* has a very special place in my heart, and it is with constant pleasure when I visit her during her commissions, to find each time the same happy atmosphere, efficiency and comradeship. This ship's company has carried on the tradition of their predecessors in maintaining a high standard.' She then presented the Kelly Memorial Prize, the award for the best ex-Dartmouth

aviator to qualify for wings, to Lt M. K. Johnson of 800 Squadron. Captain Hill-Norton told the Queen Mother that the ship's company appreciated her visit, and he presented her with a leather-bound commission book which as he said, '...contains photographs of nearly everyone on board, as well as giving an account of the ship's activities during the commission.' Afterwards the Queen Mother was the captain's guest for lunch, together with other senior officers, following which, at 3.30pm, the royal visitor left the ship by helicopter.

All that remained was to destore and deammunition the ship, before she was taken in hand by Devonport Dockyard for a refit which would last for six months. It was the end of another successful commission.

During the *Ark Royal's* refit, which lasted from April to September 1961, her starboard catapult was adapted to give the same boost as that on the port side, which at that time had the most powerful thrust of any British aircraft carrier. This was the only major work carried out during the period between commissions, and during the August Bank Holiday weekend the Admiralty departed from their usual custom of allowing no visits to ships undergoing refit, and opened the *Ark Royal* to the public. During the 1950s and 1960s, with plenty of ships to show off, Navy Days were very popular and as well as the *Ark Royal,* 11 other warships, including the cruiser HMS *Tiger,* were opened to visitors.

On Monday 14 August 1961, Captain D. C. E. F. Gibson DSC RN succeeded Captain Hill-Norton as the commanding officer of the *Ark Royal* and soon afterwards the new ship's company joined the carrier. Captain Gibson had been connected with the Fleet Air Arm for most of his service life, although he had first gone to sea in 1933 as a cadet with the venerable British India Steam Navigation Company. He had transferred to the Royal Navy in 1937 and in the following year had trained as a pilot. During the Second World War he had flown Skuas from the previous *Ark Royal,* as well as from the *Formidable* and the *Audacity.* After the war he had served in the aircraft carriers *Theseus, Illustrious, Indomitable* and *Glory,* and he had held the appointments of Commander (Air) at RNAS Culdrose and Commanding Officer of RNAS Brawdy. With over 3,000 flying hours to his credit, he was the ideal officer to command HMS *Ark Royal,* one of the Navy's most powerful aircraft carriers.

Four weeks after Captain Gibson joined the ship, on Tuesday 12 September, the *Ark Royal* recommissioned for further service with the fleet and once again the ceremony was televised. The guests assembled at 2.50pm and half an hour later the guest of honour, the C-in-C Plymouth, Vice-Admiral Sir Charles Madden, arrived on board. The ceremony was held in the upper hangar, with the ship's chaplain, the Rev K. P. Evans, conducting the religious service. Addressing the ship's company, Captain Gibson referred to the spirit which the fourth commission had inherited with the name *Ark Royal* and he declared that the new commission had a duty to enhance the reputation of the ship in order to pass it on to their successors. Following the formalities, commissioning cakes were cut by Captain and Mrs Gibson, Lt-Cdr Skinner (CO 815 Squadron) and Mrs Skinner, Master-at-Arms Roberts and Mrs Roberts, and Chief Air Artificer Prynn and Mrs Prynn. At the close of the ceremony the guests adjourned to the forward end of the hangar for tea, and by 5pm when they had left the ship, all that remained was to prepare the *Ark Royal* for sea.

On Thursday 5 October Rear-Admiral (E) D. J. Hoare inspected the engine room departments and two days later, at 4pm, the pilot was embarked. Twenty minutes later the mooring ropes were slipped and the *Ark Royal* slowly pulled away from 5 and 6 wharves and steamed down the harbour where she secured to C buoy in Plymouth Sound to carry out the final chores before her post-refit inspection. The great event took place during the morning of Monday 9 October when Vice-Admiral Madden toured all departments of the ship; he was obviously pleased with

what he saw, for next morning the carrier left Plymouth Sound and put to sea for her main machinery trials. For most of the day the engineers sweated in the engine and boiler rooms as the ship steamed at full power in the Channel, but by 7pm that evening she had returned to Plymouth Sound for the night. The main propulsion machinery trials continued over two more days before, on Friday 13 October, the carrier steamed east to Portland where she embarked the trials party. After a weekend at anchor in Weymouth Bay the *Ark Royal* was under way again on Monday 16 October, and forty-eight hours later her flying trials started. During the next eight days an assortment of Sea Vixens, Scimitars and Gannets executed deck landings and launchings from the carrier's flight deck, on the conclusion of which she berthed alongside Devonport's No 6 wharf on the morning of Friday 27 October in order to make some final adjustments and to embark the squadron personnel. On the evening of Monday 30 October Rear-Admiral R. M. Smeeton, the FOAC, embarked and next morning he hoisted his flag in the *Ark Royal.*

It was at 8am on the morning of Monday 13 November that the *Ark Royal* left Devonport and steamed out into the Channel to embark the Scimitars of 800 Squadron, the Wessex HAS Mk I helicopters of 815 Squadron and the four AEW Gannets of 849C Flight. 815 Squadron was the first front-line squadron to be equipped with the Wessex HAS Mk I helicopters, which had pioneered the techniques of all-weather and night anti-submarine helicopter operations, contributing a vital role in developing night anti-submarine tactics in the fleet. They had also established the capability of the Wessex in night search and rescue operations, which was to prove extremely valuable later in the commission. After safely embarking the squadrons the *Ark Royal* set course for Gibraltar, and although routine flying operations were carried out during the passage, a sudden deterioration in the weather on Friday 17 November necessitated six aircraft being diverted to North Front and next day the *Ark Royal* herself secured alongside Gibraltar's South Mole. This time it was only a weekend break, however, and on Monday 20 November the carrier left for Malta to begin phase one of her work-up. During exercises and manoeuvres off Malta the *Ark Royal* and the *Centaur,* which was en route to the Far East Station, operated together. On Friday 1 December, in company with the cruiser *Tiger,* the *Ark Royal* moored in Naples for a four-day visit and a well-earned break for the ship's company. The pleasures of the city were sufficient enjoyment for some, but in addition the ship's chaplain organized a number of coach trips to tourist attractions further afield, including Pompeii and even Rome, while a few hardy souls ventured right onto the inhospitable summit of Mount Vesuvius. Finally, on Tuesday 5 December the *Ark Royal* put to sea again in preparation for the second phase of her work-up.

After four days of intensive flying, which took in the NATO exercise 'Royal Flush V' with the *Victorious,* (returning to the UK at the time), the cruiser *Tiger* and the destroyers *Battleaxe* and *Crossbow,* the *Ark Royal* put into Grand Harbour for a weekend break. During the exercises Rear-Admiral Smeeton had transferred his flag to the *Victorious* and on Monday 11 December the *Ark Royal* left harbour to continue phase two of her work-up off the Libyan coast. The exercises were all completed by Saturday 16 December, whereupon the carrier returned to Grand Harbour to undergo a three-week self-maintenance period. On Christmas Eve, Sunday 24 December, the C-in-C Mediterranean, Admiral Sir Deric Holland-Martin, inspected Divisions and attended a church service on board. Although for many this was their first Christmas away from home, there was at least the knowledge that the initial work-up was almost over and the mess decks were decorated festively with streamers, balloons and Christmas cards. In the galley, the cooks turned to with a will and excelled themselves with a magnificent offering of traditional fare.

Just five days after the New Year celebrations, on Friday 5 January 1962, the *Ark Royal* left Malta to implement phase three of her work-up, and to undertake a 52-hour continuous exercise code-named 'Arkex 2'. Once these two tasks had been completed successfully, the carrier was able to set course for home four days later. The only halt on the fast passage to Devonport was a six-hour stop in Gibraltar Bay, and on Monday 15 January the *Ark Royal* entered Plymouth Sound where, as she steamed up harbour, her propellers struck rocks, causing considerable damage to the blades. As a result of this she went straight into No 10 dry dock where the damaged propellers could be inspected, while the officers and men could look forward to long leave. The carrier remained in dry dock during the whole of February 1962, and was finally moved out to No 5 basin on the morning of Friday 2 March. Three days later she was moved to 5 and 6 wharves where preparations were made to get everything ready for sea. She was due to sail for the Far East Station on Friday 9 March, and on the day before her departure there was a 'bomb scare' on board, when an anonymous telephone caller alleged that a device had been planted in B boiler room. Although this type of malicious telephone call is more common today, in the early 1960s it was quite an unusual occurrence, and three senior police officers from Plymouth went on board to initiate a search. It was strongly suspected that a member of the ship's company who was not looking forward to nine months in the Far East was responsible but, if this was the case, then he failed miserably, for at just after 7am on Friday 9 March the *Ark Royal* steamed out of the harbour into the Sound, where she moored at C buoy while the Wessex helicopters of 815 Squadron were embarked. Next

day the carrier steamed out into the Channel where she was joined by 800, 890 and C Flight of 849 Squadron. In addition the Gannets of 831 Squadron, which were engaged in electronic counter-measures trials, were landed on, before the carrier set course for the Mediterranean. After a fast five-day passage to Malta, the *Ark Royal* remained in the area for a few days while conducting flying operations. It was during this period, at 5.30pm on Monday 19 March, that a Wessex helicopter of 815 Squadron ditched in the sea several miles from the ship, but fortunately the crew were rescued by the SAR helicopter and another Wessex of 815 Squadron. Next day the ship set course for Port Said and at 3.50pm on Thursday 22 March she anchored off the port. To manoeuvre a ship the size of the *Ark Royal* through the Suez Canal was no mean feat, for with her wide beam and deep draught there was little room for error. That evening as she lay off Port Said, other vessels which would form part of the southbound convoy began to assemble, and as darkness fell all along the coast, the lights of the towns became visible. Eventually, at just after midnight on the morning of Saturday 24 March, the carrier weighed anchor and steamed into Port Said Harbour where, suddenly, brightly lit streets appeared and the strains of local music drifted out over the harbour. At 3am the *Ark Royal* entered the canal and at first light those up on deck could see that the ship was travelling along the narrow strip of water which stretched in a long, thin line to the horizon. The eastern shore on the port side was an endless, deserted wasteland of sand, but on the western bank there was more of interest, with a good road and groves of trees at intervals. With very little room to spare in the canal, and to ensure that the passage passed off without incident, an officer was stationed at the forward end of the flight deck and another at the after end, in order to check that the carrier held her course and did not swing onto one of the canal banks. During the morning the ship's company discovered that while at Port Said in the early hours, a number of traders had been embarked and they had spread out their wares on the flight deck. Soon there was a brisk trade as wooden camels, Egyptian slippers and even carpets found their way onto the mess decks. Then there was the Gully-Gully man, dressed in his long flowing robe who, to his frequent cries of 'gully-gully-gully-gully-gully', produced tiny, bewildered, squeaking day-old chicks from the most unlikely places. As always he could bewilder everyone with his tricks performed with cards, string, coins and scarves, and eventually he would bring forth loose cash from the pockets of even the most reluctant onlookers as his fez was passed round the audience. Finally, at just before 4pm, after a 13-hour passage, the *Ark Royal* cleared the Suez Canal, and with the ship's company having changed into white uniforms for the first time in the commission, the carrier steamed into the Red Sea and set course for Aden.

The *Ark Royal* enters
Port Everglades during
the summer of 1976
during America's
celebrations of its
200th Anniversary of
Independence.
*(Fleet Air Arm
Museum)*

Below:
An impressive view of
the *Ark Royal* on
exercises in the
Mediterranean.
(L. Fleming)

The *Ark Royal* at Spithead and dressed overall for the 1977 Silver Jubilee Fleet Review. *(D. Smith)*

The Silver Jubilee Fleet Review at Spithead. HMY *Britannia* steams past the *Ark Royal*. *(L. Fleming)*

A Phantom is launched.

(L. Fleming)

The *Ark Royal* leaving Devonport and steaming past her older sister *Eagle* which was awaiting her final voyage to the breaker's yard.

(Fleet Air Arm Museum)

The impressive sight of HMS *Ark Royal* demonstrating the Royal Navy's air power during the 1970s.
(Fleet Air Arm Museum)

(Fleet Air Arm Museum)

A very busy flight deck.

Alongside her fitting-out berth on the River Tyne. *(Fleet Air Arm*

The *Ark Royal* at sea in the autumn of 1984 for her contractor's sea trials. *(Fleet Air Arm Museum)*

The *Ark Royal* leaves the River Tyne in April 1985 for her final machinery trials.   *(Fleet Air Arm Museum)*

With a Sea Harrier and a Swordfish on deck, the *Ark Royal* entered Portsmouth Harbour for the first time on 1 June 1985.   *(Fleet Air Arm Museum)*

The *Ark,* with her aircraft ranged and flight deck manned, prepares to enter Sydney Harbour during her 'Outback 88' deployment. *(Royal Australian Navy)*

Escorted by a flotilla of small ships, the *Ark Royal* sails through Sydney Harbour in October 1988.

(D. Smith)

The *Ark Royal* off Gibraltar in 1989.

(Fleet Air Arm Museum)

During the tedious three-day passage down the Red Sea, with the temperature and humidity steadily increasing, life became ever more uncomfortable on board and eventually, at 10.40am on Tuesday 27 March, the *Ark Royal* anchored off the barren rocks of Elephant's Back Hill in Aden's outer harbour. Keenly awaiting her arrival was HMS *Centaur* which was being relieved by the *Ark Royal* as the operational aircraft carrier east of Suez. Whichever view one takes of Aden there is very little to attract the visitor, but MFVs from the shore base HMS *Sheba* laid on a ferry service for those who wished to go into Steamer Point where the shops on The Crescent were stacked with an Aladdin's Cave of cheap electrical goods, and many members of the ship's company were able to perfect the art of bartering with the local traders. On Wednesday 28 March, in company with the destroyer *Cavalier,* the *Ark Royal* left Aden and after three days of flying exercises off the colony she set course for the Strait of Malacca and the cooler breezes of the Indian Ocean. Arriving off the island of Penang on Sunday 8 April, the squadrons participated in flying exercises with the RAF, using their airfield at Butterworth as a diversionary runway, then four days later, at 4pm on Thursday 12 April, the *Ark Royal* secured alongside No 8 berth in the Singapore Naval Base and officially joined the Far East Station. Shortly after her arrival on station the Flag Officer, Second in Command, Far East Station (FO2 FES), Rear-Admiral J. B. Frewen, hoisted his flag in the *Ark Royal*. Admiral Frewen would have felt very much at home in the carrier for only three years previously he had commanded her older sister, HMS *Eagle.*

After 12 days of rest and recuperation in Singapore, the *Ark Royal* was at sea again when, at 4.26pm on Tuesday 24 April, only five hours after leaving the naval base, a Gannet crashed into the sea close to the Horsburgh Light while the squadrons were being embarked. The carrier stopped at once and launched her seaboat, but despite the efforts of the rescuers, sadly only two survivors were found, and the next day a memorial service was held for the lost crewman, Lt B. T. Jones RN. On the following day, with the ship off the east coast of Malaya in the vicinity of Pulau Tioman,

On Friday 8 February 1963 the prototype P1127, which later became the Sea Harrier, made its first deck landing on an aircraft carrier. Here the aircraft approaches the *Ark Royal's* flight deck.

(Imperial War Museum HU75008)

the *Ark Royal* took part in 'Exercise Fantail', before sailing for Manila where she joined HMAS *Melbourne* and USS *Bennington* for the SEATO exercise 'Sea Devil'. The exercise was designed to strengthen the defensive capability of the six SEATO navies, but it was marred by a series of accidents. One man fell overboard from the destroyer HMAS *Vendetta,* and the American aircrew of a Skyraider, which crashed on take-off from the USS *Bennington,* had to be picked up from the sea. Finally, a Sea Vixen from the *Ark Royal* crashed into the sea, but fortunately the aircrew managed to eject from the crippled aircraft which sank rapidly before they too were rescued from the sea. The exercise reached its final stage on the morning of

The landing of the P1127 on 8 February 1963 created a great deal of interest on board, with goofers out in force to witness this landmark in naval aviation history.
(Imperial War Museum A34713)

Wednesday 2 May, when a column of 34 warships, 14 miles long, steamed into Manila Bay, led by the aircraft carriers *Melbourne, Bennington,* and *Ark Royal.* It was the largest fleet to have visited Manila and when leave was granted that afternoon the bars of the city were swamped with sailors from six nations. After three days off Manila the *Ark Royal* steamed round the coast of the Bataan Peninsular to Olongapo, where she went alongside the US Naval Base at Subic Bay for a 'never to be forgotten' four-day visit.

Following her departure from Subic Bay there were further exercises with US units in the local exercise areas, but even as these were under way, Communist Pathet Lao forces were mounting an offensive into Laos very near to the border with Thailand, as a result of which a US force of 5,000 soldiers and marines, together with RAF fighters from Singapore, were sent to Thailand in a move which was designed to reassure the Siamese that they had the full weight of SEATO behind them in an emergency. These measures also reflected President Kennedy's determination

to hold the line against communism in Thailand and South Vietnam. As units of the United States Seventh Fleet, including the aircraft carrier *Coral Sea,* steamed towards the area there was a great deal of speculation about the *Ark Royal's* movements, fuelled by the cancellation of a proposed visit to Japan. No information was forthcoming from the Admiralty, but in the event, after leaving the Philippines area the *Ark Royal* steamed north to Hong Kong where she anchored four miles out off Green Island at the eastern side of Victoria on Thursday 17 May. Fortunately, large ferries were laid on to carry liberty men ashore. Unfortunately, Susie Wong was nowhere to be found, but the floating restaurants at Aberdeen, the Tiger Balm Gardens and the magnificent view over the harbour from the Peak were more than adequate compensation for the ship's company. After nine days in the port she put to sea to carry out flying exercises in the area during which, on the morning of Tuesday 29 May, a Wessex helicopter of 815 Squadron ditched close to the ship, but fortunately the four crew members were rescued by another helicopter from the squadron, and the SAR helicopter. On conclusion of the exercises the *Ark Royal* returned to Hong Kong for a further four-day stay in the harbour, before leaving for Okinawa with HM Ships *Carysfort*, *Cavalier* and *Eastbourne* and USS *Hancock*. During the passage, at just after midday on Thursday 7 June, a report was received from a USAF Super Sabre that it was out of fuel and ditching in the sea in a position Lat 22° - 12'N/Long 128° - 03'E, quite close to the *Ark Royal's* position, and she started to search the area. However, about an hour later there was a fire in B boiler room which took 15 minutes to extinguish, but even as the fire parties were mustering, another signal was received with the welcome news that the US pilot had been rescued. Two days later the *Ark Royal* anchored in Buckner Bay, Okinawa, where leave was granted and the United States Marine Corps put on an impressive display of marching and countermarching on the flight deck. Perhaps the most popular events were two shows staged by a US theatre company in the upper hangar, with glamorous singers and dancers who were much appreciated by the massive audiences.

On Wednesday 13 June the *Ark Royal* and her escorts left Buckner Bay for six days of exercises with the US Navy, after which she departed for the seven-day return passage to Singapore. On Thursday 28 June the squadrons were flown off to the RN Aircraft Holding Unit RAF Tengah in Singapore, and next day the carrier moored alongside No 8 berth of the naval base in Singapore's Johore Strait. During the stay in Singapore the ship's drama society put on a very creditable performance of the play 'The Long, The Short and The Tall', FO2 FES transferred his flag to the cruiser HMS *Tiger* and the FOAC, Rear-Admiral F. H. E. Hopkins, hoisted his flag in the carrier. After a 13-day maintenance period in Singapore the *Ark Royal*, together with HM Ships *Bulwark*, *Tiger*, *Carysfort*, *Cavalier*, *Cassandra*, *Plymouth* and *Eastbourne* and the Australian and New Zealand frigates *Parramata*, *Yarra* and *Tarranaki*, sailed for 'Exercise Fotex 62' in the South China Sea off Pulau Tioman. During the exercise a Gannet of 849C Flight made the 3,000th deck landing of the commission, and the C-in-C Far East Station, Admiral Sir David Luce, paid a visit to the ship. As always the most popular spell of any 'Fotex' exercise were the days spent anchored off Pulau Tioman, when recreational leave was granted. However, to the relief of most on board, the exercises ended on Thursday 26 July with the C-in-C FES being dispatched back to Singapore in one of the *Ark Royal's* Gannets, and next morning the carrier berthed at the Singapore Naval Base for a ten-day break before exercises got under way again, this time for the benefit of representatives of the Malayan Armed Forces.

On the morning of Monday 6 August the *Ark Royal* left Singapore Dockyard to embark the squadrons and to hold the first rehearsal of 'Exercise Showboat' off Singapore's south coast. The exercise, like the 'Shop Window' displays which were carried out from time to time, was a unique opportunity for the Royal Navy to sell itself in front of distinguished guests, and in addition approximately 150 spectators had been invited by FO2 FES to watch the proceedings at the rehearsals. 'Showboat' itself was staged on Thursday 9 August when, at 8.15am, the C-in-C FES embarked, followed by the Malayan Head of State, Inche Yusof bin Ishak, the Yang de Pertuan Negara, several VIPs from the legislature of Malaya, members of the Consular Corps and business leaders. At 9am the *Ark Royal* left her anchorage in Singapore's Outer Roads and during the day the guests were shown every aspect of life in an operational carrier, with both static and flying displays. There were also synchronized attacks by the aircraft and the ship's armament, which emphasized the deadly efficiency of the carrier. With negotiations under way for the merger of Malaya, Sarawak, Sabah and Singapore to form the state of Malaysia, towards which Indonesia was extremely hostile, it is no wonder that one newspaper reported thus the great interest shown by Malaya's Head of State: 'For more than three hours he stood on the bridge and trained his cine-camera at the thick of the mock battle as jet aircraft roared in the sky and bombs hit their target in the sea.' On completion of the exercises, after disembarking the guests into launches in the Singapore Roads, the *Ark Royal* set course for Fremantle in Western Australia, for a visit which everyone was eagerly anticipating.

The carrier's passage to Australia took her through the Karimata Strait between Borneo and Sumatra, along the Gaspar Strait close to Bangka Island, then through the Sunda Strait and past the island of Krakatau. She then steamed across the Timor Sea and into the Indian Ocean. On Saturday 11 August, shortly after crossing the equator, as the *Ark Royal* steamed through the Gaspar Strait, the flight deck was the setting for a scene of what was described as 'near-medieval pomp and splendour'. At 9.30am His Majesty 'Neptunus Rex' emerged from the depths of the after lift well, accompanied by Queen Amphitrite and the royal retinue of barbers, bears, policemen and doctors. At the ducking pool they were met by Captain Gibson, who turned out to be the first 'victim' closely followed by the Executive Officer.

Once into the Indian Ocean and south of Christmas Island, the carrier was subjected to six more days of flying exercises, during which the Scimitars caused the people of the Australian town of Geraldton some surprise when they zoomed in low over their houses. On a sadder note, NA D. M. Eynon lost his life in a flight deck accident and later that day, in a position Lat 24° - 30'S/Long 112° - 00'E, off the coast of Western Australia, his body was committed to the deep. Two days later, at 5.45pm on Saturday 18 August, the alarm bells rang on the bridge signalling a man-overboard alert. In the event the speedy launching of the SAR helicopter ensured that the sailor was rescued within five minutes. Finally, at 9.30am on Monday 20 August, the *Ark Royal* was manoeuvred alongside Fremantle's 7 and 8 wharves for a ten-day visit which Captain Gibson described as, 'a tremendous treat for all aboard.' From first to last there was never a dull moment as the 'pommies' were welcomed ashore, and on board the 'cobbers' were made just as welcome. The Royal Marines Band was kept busy playing at schools, the Wardroom dance, the ship's company dance and appearing on television. Nearly 3,000 people turned up for the ship's dance and one newspaper reported the event thus: 'Girls outnumbered sailors at a dance given by the officers and men of the visiting Royal Navy ships at South Perth last night. Almost 3,000 people attended the dance – probably the biggest held in Perth for several years. Although 1,000 tickets were issued to Western Australian girls, door attendants did not query hundreds of girls who arrived without tickets. Under giant Chinese lanterns – reminiscent of the Far Easern ports of Singapore and Hong Kong recently visited by the Royal Navy ships – the dancers were entertained by a ten-piece Navy band.' Apparently, when the dance ended, fleets of special buses were laid on to run the guests home again. During the stay in Fremantle there was a constant stream of visitors to the ship with reciprocal invitations to visit homes and join in outings. During the four-day period of official visiting, over 15,000 people toured the ship, and despite all the wonderful technical static displays, the most popular 'exhibits' turned out to be two monkeys which belonged to two seamen. They received an enormous amount of publicity and one local lady, distressed to hear that the monkeys were unhappy in Fremantle's moderate temperatures, being used to the heat of Singapore, knitted little woollen sweaters for them. On Monday 27 August, with Force 9 winds and torrential rain lashing the dockside, the police forecast a poor attendance when the ship was opened to the public, but how wrong they were, for with still two hours to go before opening there were already over 2,000 people queuing. That afternoon, when there were over 4,000 people on board, the gale force winds loosened three bollards on the quay and parted nine heavy hawsers, and with very little holding the ship onto the wharf, the engine rooms were brought to four hours' notice for steam. Eventually the ship was made fast again, but not without a few anxious moments. Down in the hangar, meanwhile, unaware of the conditions outside, 300 children were enjoying a magnificent party, quite oblivious to the fact that the duty watch was desperately trying to secure the ship alongside. At the other end of the scale, the official guests included the Prime Minister of Western Australia and other local VIPs, but it was the sheer enthusiasm of the people of Western Australia which ensured that the occasion was a truly memorable one.

Finally, at 9am on Thursday 30 August, the *Ark Royal* was given her biggest send-off ever received as she left Fremantle and set course for Singapore. During the passage, at 1am on Sunday 2 September, there was another fatal accident, as a result of which Lt J. G. Randall RN lost his life. Later that day, at 4.20pm in a position Lat 18° - 27'S/Long 106° - 48'E, a funeral service was held and Lt Randall's body was committed to the deep. Two days later, at 10pm on Tuesday 4 September, during night-flying exercises, a Gannet crashed on landing, hit the port landing mirror and fell into the sea over the port side. However, as it left the flight deck it hit the radar masts, which were in the down position, whereupon the forward half of the Gannet fell into the sea, whilst the after section remained jammed in the aerials. Fortunately, the crew were picked up safely by HMS *Eastbourne*. Just over an hour later a Sea Vixen crashed on landing, but luckily once again there were no casualties. Ten days later, at 1pm on Friday 14 September, the *Ark Royal* secured alongside No 8 berth of Singapore Naval Base.

Shortly after her arrival back in Singapore the lower deck was cleared and a service was held on the flight deck on the morning of 16 September to commemorate the first anniversary of the recommissioning service, but unfortunately this landmark was soon overshadowed by a rather distasteful incident. On 25 September the body of LA J. W. Storey was found in the waters of the Johore Strait, off the dockyard, and following a police investigation an able seaman from the *Ark Royal* was charged with manslaughter. Three days later the carrier was at sea once again, and at 11.47am on Monday 1 October, as the ship was exercising in the South China Sea, NA Sorfleet fell overboard from the flight deck. However, despite a day-long search by the *Ark Royal* and her escorts, no trace was found of the missing man and it was presumed that he had drowned. Four days later the carrier berthed in Hong Kong Harbour for a seven-day visit to the colony, before leaving for Singapore once again, where she arrived during the afternoon of Friday 19 October. With the carrier's first 12 months of the commission having been completed, it was time to steam west once again for a few weeks in the area of the Middle East Station then, to everyone's great relief, head home for Christmas. When the *Ark Royal* left Singapore for Aden at 9am on Thursday 25 October, carrying the troops, transport and equipment of the 34th LAA Regiment, she looked more like a commando carrier and there was much speculation about her destination. Five days after leaving Singapore, when she was in the Indian Ocean, she received an emergency signal from a French steamship, SS *Donai*, which was on fire in a position Lat 09° - 43'N/Long 62° - 37'E, about 70 miles distant. The *Ark Royal* immediately altered course towards the *Donai* and within 20 minutes a Wessex helicopter had been launched. However, at 9.30am, the *Donai* reported

The *Ark Royal* makes a ceremonial entry into Singapore Dockyard on 11 July 1963.

that her engine room fire was under control and that no assistance would be required. Although the Wessex was recalled to the ship, the *Ark Royal* continued to steam towards the *Donai*, which she closed at 11.30am, and after double-checking that all was in fact under control she continued her voyage to Aden, where she arrived on the morning of Sunday 4 November. During the ship's stay in Aden's Outer Harbour the Army Regiment was disembarked and the Steamer Point Light Opera Society offered to stage a performance of Gilbert and Sullivan's 'The Mikado' in the ship's upper hangar. At the best of times such a production is a major undertaking, but to perform in the hangar of one of Her Majesty's aircraft carriers in the sweltering heat of such an inhospitable place deserves the highest praise, particularly as it involved a boat ride of three miles from the colony to the *Ark Royal's* open anchorage. However, despite a very bumpy crossing, the cast of 60, a stage staff of 38 and an orchestra of 28, plus all their scenery, lighting and costumes arrived safely, then from the moment of the opening chorus the ship's company were taken into the wonderful world of Gilbertian fantasy, and the show was much appreciated by everyone in the audience.

During the first three weeks of November the *Ark Royal* remained in the vicinity of Aden carrying out flying exercises before setting course for Mombasa and anchoring in Kilindini Harbour on Thursday 22 November. During the short visit the squadrons made a dramatic fly-past over Mombasa, and Captain Gibson hosted a party for tribal chiefs who travelled all the way from the country's heartland to see the *Ark Royal*. Despite the popularity of Mombasa as a run ashore, everyone was pleased to be leaving the port on Monday 26 November for the fast passage home, and after making her northbound transit of the Suez Canal on 5 December, and a 24-hour stop off Gibraltar on 10/11 December, she launched her squadrons to their respective stations during the morning of Friday 14 December. Later in the day the *Ark Royal* secured to C buoy in Plymouth Sound and despite the fact that Customs clearance had not yet been obtained, night leave was granted. Two days later the carrier steamed up harbour to secure alongside 7 and 8 wharves in Devonport Dockyard in preparation for a refit, and seasonal leave was taken on completion of the first half of a very busy commission.

On Wednesday 23 January 1963, two days after his official appointment, Captain M. P. Pollock MVO DSC RN joined the ship and assumed command of the *Ark Royal* from Rear-Admiral Gibson who had been promoted and appointed to the position of FOAC. However, two days later Admiral Gibson returned to his old command when he hoisted his flag in the carrier. Captain Pollock had entered the Royal Navy in 1930, and by 1941 he was specializing in gunnery. During the Second World War he served in the battleship *Warspite*, the cruisers *Arethusa* and *Norfolk* and the elderly V-class destroyer HMS *Vanessa*, in

the North Atlantic, Mediterranean and the Indian Ocean. After a spell in the Admiralty Captain Pollock took command of the frigate HMS *Vigo*, which had started life as a destroyer, later undergoing conversion to a Type 15 frigate, which altered her appearance completely. On joining the *Ark Royal* Captain Pollock was taking up his first appointment to an aircraft carrier.

On Monday 4 February 1963 the *Ark Royal* put to sea again with a Buccaneer trials party embarked, and next day, at 3.32pm on Tuesday 5 February, a Blackburn Buccaneer S2, a much more powerful aircraft than the S1, landed on board. That evening, in snowstorms and a heavy sea, a Sea Vixen performed a number of touch and go circuits to test new flight deck floodlighting. Later that same evening, at 10.17pm, distress calls were received from a merchantman, the *John Collett*, which was in trouble in heavy seas in the Channel, whereupon the *Ark Royal* headed for the area. On arrival at the scene at 1am the next morning she closed the distressed vessel to find that the South African merchant ship *President Kruger* was also standing by. Soon afterwards a large ocean-going tug also arrived and it took the *John Collett* in tow, following which the *Ark Royal* returned to Lyme Bay where she continued the flying exercises. The highlight of the trials occurred at just after midday on Friday 8 February 1963 when, with the ship off Berry Head, a Hawker P1127 vertical take-off and landing strike fighter made its first deck landing on board an aircraft carrier at sea. The P1127 had been the 'star' of the 1962 Farnborough Air Show and, powered by a single Bristol Siddeley Pegasus engine and with swivelling nozzles which provided thrust for both vertical and horizontal flight, the aircraft could move forwards and backwards, and it could take-off and land vertically. The experimental aircraft, which was one of only six which had been built, was piloted by the late Mr A. W. (Bill) Bedford, Hawker Siddeley's chief test pilot, whose historic achievement held great significance for both the Royal Navy and the US Navy. After making this first successful vertical landing, the aircraft went on to make a number of vertical take-offs and landings. The complete novelty of such an aircraft is reflected in the *Ark Royal's* log which contains the following entries: '13.48 Hawker P1127 approached ship and started flying backwards. 13.51 Hawker P1127 hovered over the ship and landed vertically abreast the island.' The trials continued until 3.30pm that afternoon and next day the *Ark Royal* anchored in Weymouth Bay, but unfortunately shore leave was disrupted when severe gales caused all boat traffic between the ship and the shore to be suspended. That night all liberty men were accommodated ashore at HMS *Osprey*, and next day they were able to return to the ship. On Wednesday 13 February the carrier weighed anchor and put to sea again, and that afternoon she started further trials with the Hawker P1127, this time with the aircraft making short take-offs and landings. Today we take

The *Ark Royal* and *Albion* off Pulau Tioman during 'Exercise Fotex 63'. (*Fleet Air Arm Museum*)

the P1127's successor, the British Aerospace Sea Harrier, for granted, but in the early 1960s the whole idea of vertical take-off and landing was a totally new concept, and there were many senior figures in the Admiralty who were sceptical of the whole idea.

After two more days of flying trials the *Ark Royal* steamed round to Spithead, and at 4.30pm on Friday 15 February she secured alongside Portsmouth Dockyard's South Railway Jetty. Soon after going alongside news came through that, for the second time in the commission, the carrier would be steaming east of Suez. In December 1962 an armed revolt had broken out in the Sultanate of Brunei, a small oil-rich country west of the colony of North Borneo, and although this had been dealt with quickly and efficiently by a force of Royal Marines and Gurkhas, with the help of the commando carrier HMS *Albion,* it was apparent that there were going to be serious problems with Indonesia and her president, Achmed Sukarno. It was strongly suspected that he had been behind the Brunei rebellion, as he was vehemently opposed to the Federation of Malaysia which was being negotiated. The Federation was not a popular idea in Brunei and it was here that

President Sukarno saw an opportunity to foment trouble. Although the rebellion was a failure, in early 1963 groups of Indonesian 'volunteers' began to infiltrate across the border into Sabah and Sarawak, triggering one of Britain's colonial 'bushfire' wars which became known as the 'Confrontation' with Indonesia, and which lasted until August 1966. It was to meet this escalating crisis that the *Ark Royal* was being sent east once again, to join the *Hermes* which was already on the Far East Station, and the *Centaur* which was also being sent east of Suez at short notice.

After leaving Portsmouth on the morning of Tuesday 19 February and re-embarking her squadrons in the Channel, the *Ark Royal* put in to Devonport on the last day of the month for a short break before putting to sea once again on the afternoon of Tuesday 5 March. This time it was to participate in the NATO exercise 'Dawn Breeze VIII', which was plagued by severe weather throughout, and so there was a great deal of relief when, on the morning of Friday 15 March, the carrier returned to Devonport. No sooner was she alongside than the first party to take their foreign service leave left the ship to travel home, having been issued with return air tickets to Gibraltar. After another short break the *Ark Royal* sailed again on Tuesday 19 March, bound for Gibraltar. The passage south across the Bay of Biscay and the Atlantic Ocean was extremely bumpy as the ship steamed into yet more severe gales and heavy seas before arriving at Gibraltar on Friday 22 March where she was manoeuvred into No 1 dry dock for routine hull maintenance. Eight days later, with the ship in dockyard hands, the second long-leave party was flown home in a fleet of Cunard-Eagle Britannias. The remaining members of the ship's company meanwhile were living in dockside accommodation and on 6 April the third leave party flew home from North Front. By 1 May everyone was back on board and the ship was afloat once again and alongside Gibraltar's South Mole.

At 9am on Friday 3 May the *Ark Royal* left Gibraltar to steam east, and an hour and a half later, after embarking her squadrons, a memorial service was held over the position of the wreck of her predecessor. Three days after leaving Gibraltar there was a short stop off the island of Malta, and on Thursday 9 May the carrier anchored off Port Said to await her southbound convoy. It was at just after 1am on the following morning when she weighed anchor and steamed slowly into the approaches to the Suez Canal, and 19 hours later she cleared Port Suez and entered the Gulf of Suez, bound for Aden. After carrying out flying exercises with the Scimitars, the *Ark Royal* anchored off Aden's Outer Harbour and shore leave was granted for those who did not mind the six-mile round trip between the ship and Steamer Point. During the afternoon of Wednesday 22 May the carrier departed to carry out more flying exercises, despite the fact that there was a hurricane to the east of the area. The exercises were relatively trouble-free and on Monday 3 June the *Ark Royal*, in company with the *Corunna* and *Blackpool*, steamed south to Mombasa, where she arrived during the afternoon of Friday 7 June to carry out a period of self-maintenance. As always after the sweltering heat of the Aden area, Mombasa provided welcome relief for the ship's company, but all too soon, during the morning of Wednesday 19 June the *Ark Royal* left the port to carry out flying exercises off Malindi and to make her passage across the Indian Ocean to Gan accompanied by HMS *Cambrian*. After passing the small island on the last day of June, the *Ark Royal* set course for Pulau Langkowi where she was scheduled to join the Far East Station, and at 10am on Tuesday 2 July, when she was in a position Lat 02° - 41'N/Long 82° - 52'E, King Neptune's Court gathered for the traditional Crossing the Line ceremony. Three days later, during the afternoon of Friday 5 July, when the ship was south-west of the Nicobar Islands, one of the Wessex helicopters was dispatched to the Norwegian oil tanker, the MV *Credo*, one of whose crew members was injured; he was taken off the vessel and subsequently flown on to RAF Butterworth in Northern Malaya. Next day, as the ship steamed into the Strait of

Malacca, FOAC carried out his Operational Readiness Inspection, and during the morning of Sunday 7 July the *Ark Royal* anchored off Langkowi Island, where recreational leave was granted. Early next morning, together with HMS *Hermes*, the Australian destroyers *Vampire* and *Voyager* and the frigate *Duncan*, the *Ark Royal* weighed anchor to carry out 'Exercise Birdbarge' in the Andaman Sea, which was a rehearsal for the forthcoming major exercise for the Far East Fleet, 'Fotex 63'. On the conclusion of these practice manoeuvres, during the evening of Wednesday 10 July, the *Ark Royal* set course for Singapore where, after a full ceremonial entry, she secured alongside No 8 berth in the naval dockyard to carry out a 13-day maintenance period.

'Exercise Fotex 63' was the largest such exercise in the Far East for a number of years, and as well as the *Ark Royal*, which was wearing the flag of the C-in-C Far East Station, it involved the commando carrier *Albion*, the cruiser *Lion* (flag of FO2 FES), HM Ships *Cambrian*, *Duchess*, *Duncan*, *Plymouth* and *Salisbury* and the Australian and New Zealand ships *Quiberon*, *Vendetta* and *Otago*. The fleet left Singapore on Thursday 25 July and steamed into the South China Sea to the exercise areas off Malaya. However, it was not long before the *Lion*, suffering from problems with her boilers, was forced to return to Singapore and FO2 transferred his flag to the *Albion*. Much to everyone's relief, Sunday 28 July was spent at anchor off Pulau Tioman where recreational leave was granted, but next day the fleet was at sea again for exercises to begin in earnest. At 10.27am on Wednesday 31 July, Scimitar XD 326, piloted by Lt A. G. Macfee RN, crashed into the sea in a position Lat 02° - 01'N/Long 104° - 35'E while carrying out rocket projectile attacks on splash targets which were being towed by the *Ark Royal* about half a mile astern. The SAR helicopter, with its diver, was immediately diverted to the spot and the carrier herself stopped and lowered the seaboat. However, the pilot had not been able to get clear of his aircraft and the SAR diver was unable to get down to the Scimitar before it sank, taking Lt Macfee with it. At 11.15am, having recovered the seaboat, the *Ark Royal* got under way again in order to land on the aircraft which were still airborne. Next day the carrier began to experience problems with the turbines in Y engine room, and when the fleet anchored off Tioman it became clear that dockyard assistance would be required in effecting permanent repairs. This was the end of the *Ark Royal's* contribution to 'Fotex 63', and on Saturday 3 August, while large numbers of officers and men were enjoying the beaches of Tioman, the C-in-C and the Wessex helicopters of 815 Squadron transferred to the *Albion*. When the fleet left the anchorage during the morning of Monday 5 August the *Ark Royal* did not sail with them, but she remained behind until 4.30am the next morning, when she departed for Singapore Dockyard her 'tail between her legs'.

The breakdown in the *Ark Royal's* main engines had quite

a far-reaching effect within the Navy, for it was decided to send the *Victorious* out to the Far East early, and the departure of the *Hermes* for home was delayed by ten days. All in all, the *Ark* was not popular with the men serving aboard the other two carriers, but when the repairs were completed in mid-August the *Hermes* was allowed to return to Portsmouth for the end of the month. At 11.15am on Thursday 22 August the *Ark Royal* left Singapore for the exercise areas in the South China Sea, where she carried out manoeuvres with the other invalid of 'Fotex 63', HMS *Lion*. At 6.23pm on Thursday 29 August, whilst the two ships were operating off Singapore, a mayday signal was received from one of the Sea Vixens of 890 Squadron, which then ditched into the sea. Although both the *Ark Royal* and *Lion* combed the area for over an hour, they found nothing, and the search was abandoned. However, a Wessex helicopter from 815 Squadron continued to look for the missing aircraft, and the pioneering role they had played in effecting the techniques of all-weather and night anti-submarine duties paid off, for they found and rescued the crew of the Sea Vixen who were in the sea, very close to the beach.

On Saturday 7 September the *Ark Royal* arrived in Hong Kong and anchored in Junk Bay, outside the Lei Yue Mun Narrows and the main harbour, but this did not detract from the enjoyment of the seven-day visit. After leaving Hong Kong on Saturday 14 September the *Ark Royal* returned to Singapore for just three days before leaving at 10am on Monday 23 September, to rendezvous with the *Victorious* in the Strait of Malacca at 11.30am the next day. After operating together for just over two hours the ships parted company and went their separate ways, the *Victorious* to join the Far East Station while the *Ark Royal* set course for the Middle East. In company with the frigate *Plymouth,* the *Ark Royal* steamed into the Gulf of Oman and on Saturday 5 October both vessels anchored off Khor Al Fakkan (Khowr Fakkan), in the United Arab Emirates, for a courtesy visit of just 42 hours. Upon departure at 7am on Monday 7 October the *Ark Royal,* and the frigates *Plymouth* and *Jaguar,* steamed into the Persian Gulf for the six-day exercise 'Biltong', during which the carrier flew the flag of the C-in-C Middle East Station, Rear-Admiral J. E. Scotland. There were sighs of relief all round when the *Ark Royal* left the Persian Gulf on Sunday 13 October and set course for Mombasa. Five days later, after launching all the serviceable aircraft to Embakasi outside Nairobi, the *Ark Royal* moored in Kilindini Harbour to carry out a 14-day self-maintenance period.

During the early afternoon of Friday 1 November the *Ark Royal* and *Plymouth* left Mombasa and set course across the Indian Ocean for Karachi, the former capital of Pakistan. It was on the afternoon of Saturday 9 November when the carrier anchored off the port, which will probably be remembered by most members of the ship's company for the flies and the abject poverty of many of the people. Also anchored off Karachi was the US Navy's aircraft carrier *Essex,* and from Monday 18 to Friday 22 November the two carriers undertook manoeuvres with Pakistani naval units in 'Exercise Midlink', after which the *Ark Royal* steamed south to Zanzibar, where she dropped anchor at 5pm on Wednesday 4 December. This small island situated off the coast of what was at that time Tanganyika (Tanzania), was a Sultanate which had been a British Protectorate since 1890, and at midnight on the evening of Monday 9/Tuesday 10 December it was due to gain independence. During the *Ark Royal's* six-day stay off the island she played host to a number of local dignitaries, including the Prime Minister and the Sultan, and on the evening of Monday 9 December Admiral Scotland and Captain Pollock went ashore to attend the Independence Ceremony and celebrations. At 9.30am on Tuesday 10 December, having seen the island gain its independence, the *Ark Royal* sailed for Mombasa, but before the end of January civil strife and bloodshed would dominate the political scene in Zanzibar and pave the way for a union with the newly independent Tanzania on the East African mainland. The *Ark Royal* put into Mombasa for a three-day visit, after which she set out on a fast passage home, and on Christmas Eve she made her northbound transit of the Suez Canal. Five days later she steamed past Gibraltar's Europa Point and on the morning of Tuesday 31 December all the aircraft were flown to their stations. That evening, at 8.30pm, the carrier secured to C buoy in Plymouth Sound where she had to await Customs clearance, and the ship's company could only observe from a distance the New Year's Eve celebrations which were taking place ashore. It was 7.30am on Friday 3 January 1964 when she weighed anchor and steamed up harbour to secure alongside No 6 and 7 wharves in Devonport Dockyard just over an hour later.

Almost immediately deammunitioning and destoring began and on Wednesday 15 January those members of the ship's company still left aboard moved to shore accommodation in HMS *Drake,* the Royal Naval Barracks, or onto the laid-up cruiser HMS *Blake,* which was moored at No 15 wharf in the inner basin. Nine days later Captain A. T. F. G. Griffin RN assumed command of the *Ark Royal* and Captain Pollock took his departure. By the end of February 1964 the dockyard had taken over the ship for a lengthy refit, marking the end of the fourth commission.

Work on the *Ark Royal's* refit continued throughout 1964 and despite being hindered by an industrial dispute involving boilermakers in the dockyard, by the second week in November the ship was ready to be recommissioned. The carrier's new commanding officer, Captain A. T. F. G. Griffin, was the son of an Army officer and he had been born in India. He had joined the Royal Navy in 1934, and during the Second World War he had served with the East Indies Fleet, in the Mediterranean, the

The *Ark Royal* leaves Portsmouth on 7 December 1964.

(F. S. Stockton)

Heavy seas during the *Ark's* work-up in northern waters in early 1965.

(F. S. Stockton)

North Atlantic and the Far East, during which time he specialized in navigation. After a spell at the Imperial Defence College he took over the command of the *Ark Royal* just prior to her refit. Thursday 12 November was the date of the commissioning ceremony for the fifth commission, which marked the end of her ten-month refit and the start of a busy programme of storing and trials which was scheduled for completion by Christmas that year. The day dawned bright and sunny and the guests, many of whom were relatives and friends of the ship's company, streamed aboard in their hundreds. The VIPs, among them the C-in-C Plymouth, Admiral Sir Nigel Henderson, and the Lord Mayor of Plymouth, arrived at 11am and the ceremony began soon afterwards. The reading of the Commissioning Warrant was followed by a short religious service, after which Captain Griffin gave a welcoming address to the families and friends who had come for the occasion. Then he got the lighter side of the festivities under way by assisting his wife to cut the traditional commissioning cake. A few days later the ship was towed into No 5 basin at the dockyard where tilting trials were held, then, having got the carrier onto an even keel again, she was towed back to No 5 wharf to prepare for sea.

The next few days passed in a flurry of activity while storing and ammunitioning were completed, and on 19 November everyone was reminded of the carrier's real purpose when the two Whirlwind helicopters of the ship's flight landed on board. It was at just after 8am on Tuesday 24 November when the mooring ropes were slipped and the *Ark Royal* steamed slowly down the Hamoaze, into Plymouth Sound and out into the open sea where the engine room department were put through their paces with full-power trials. At just after 8pm on the following day a Sea Vixen aircraft, which had flown out from Yeovilton to inspect the carrier's new flight deck lighting, failed to return to its base in Somerset. That night the *Ark Royal* searched the area for survivors or wreckage and at 2.30am on the morning of Thursday 26 November the seaboat was lowered to investigate a floating object which was thought to be wreckage. In the event it turned out to be just another piece of flotsam littering the English Channel and by mid-morning the search had been called off and the carrier commenced her gunnery trials. That evening the *Ark Royal* moored in Plymouth Sound where 'Jane', a float carrying two rocket-assisted ejection seats, was launched from the catapults. As the float reached the end of the catapult, the seats were fired, throwing the dummies high into the air, after which they then drifted gently down on their parachutes. After a weekend moored at C buoy, the *Ark Royal* put to sea again at 6.50am on Monday 30 November and just over three hours later, at 10am when the ship was in the Channel off Berry Head, Lt-Cdr W. H. Barnard RN, the commanding officer of 849 Squadron, brought his Gannet into land to make the first arrested

landing of the commission. Next day 'Flying Stations' was piped at 10.30am and throughout the day Sea Vixens, Scimitars and Gannets tested the landing gear and catapults. On the following day the Flag Officer Flying Training, Rear-Admiral D. C. E. F. Gibson, landed on the flight deck in a Wasp helicopter to watch the day's flying operations. As the former commanding officer of the *Ark Royal* for the second half of the second commission, Admiral Gibson was no stranger to the carrier and he spent four hours on board. There followed two more days of trials, on completion of which the carrier steamed into the Solent before entering Portsmouth Dockyard and securing alongside South Railway Jetty at 1pm on Friday 4 December.

During the weekend in Portsmouth relatives of ship's company members who lived locally were able to go on board to have a good look over the ship, and the trials teams from Whale Island were embarked. After a pleasant break, the *Ark Royal* departed at 1.30pm on Monday 7 December to steam into the Channel for gunnery trials, to be met by Force 8 gales which luckily subsided in time for the next session of flying trials. On the morning of Friday 11 December the carrier anchored in Weymouth Bay for two hours and after getting under way at just after 6am, the Secretary of State for Defence (Navy), the Rt Hon Christopher Mayhew MP, came on board by helicopter to pay a four and a half hour visit to the ship. Although the minister himself was a great champion of Britain's naval air power, most of his colleagues in the newly elected Labour Government were not, and although he could not but have been impressed by the flying display by the Gannets, Scimitars and Sea Vixens, some uncertain years lay ahead for the Fleet Air Arm at the hands of its political masters. However, having got their sea legs, it was now time for the Christmas break and at 12.45pm on Monday 14 December the *Ark Royal* secured alongside Devonport Dockyard's No 5 wharf.

With Christmas and New Year leave having come and gone, early January 1965 brought the cold reality of further storing and ammunitioning ship on bleak winter evenings, and on Tuesday 12 January Rear-Admiral H. R. B. Janvrin DSC, the FOAC, hoisted his flag in the *Ark Royal*. The ship was to have sailed the next day, but severe gales delayed her departure for 24 hours and it was at 2pm on Thursday 14 January, with the ship's company manning the flight deck, that the *Ark Royal* left her berth and steamed out into the Channel. During the last hours of daylight the Sea Vixens of 890 Squadron and the Gannets of 849C Flight were safely landed on, after which the ship set course up Channel for the Strait of Dover and the North Sea. During the morning of Saturday 16 January, as the *Ark Royal* steamed north, the Scimitars of 803 Squadron and the Wessex helicopters of 819 Squadron landed on to complete the carrier's air strength. At noon the ship moored off Rosyth for what should have been a brief visit, but as she was approaching the buoy, a boat rope

The new Buccaneer Mk II during its deck landing trials in March 1965.

(F. S. Stockton)

but often the MFV which provided a link between the ship and the shore was unable to come alongside in the heavy seas and on more than one occasion visitors were in danger of being stranded on board. Of course, during the work-up, the centre of activity was the flight deck as the pilots practised their landings and launchings in daylight, at dusk and in the dark after nightfall. Finally, during the evening of Monday 25 January, with the first phase of the work-up completed, the *Ark Royal* set course for a four-day visit to Brest. During the passage south the carrier went to the aid of a small Grimsby-based fishing vessel, the MV *Aldersea,* which had been drifting for two days in a storm-lashed North Sea, with no radio and with her engines unserviceable. As they saw the *Ark Royal* approaching, the *Aldersea's* crew lit hand flares and flew their Union Jack upside down as distress signals, and fortunately their plight was spotted. Captain Griffin altered course to close the small vessel, before sending over four engineers, two wireless operators and a doctor in the seaboat. Although the engineers were unable to restart the *Aldersea's* engines and the skipper refused the offer of a tow from the giant carrier, the *Ark* summoned help from Grimsby and as soon as this arrived, in the form of a larger fishing vessel, the carrier was able to resume her passage south.

got entangled with the port outer propeller. However, after a magnificent effort by the ship's diving team in miserable conditions, with high winds, pouring rain and the fast-moving and bitterly cold waters of the Firth of Forth, the offending rope was removed and the *Ark Royal* was under way again at just before 10pm. After steaming north to the cold, grey waters off Lossiemouth, flying operations for the ship's work-up started in earnest, but tragedy struck on the morning of Monday 18 January when, at 8.17am, a Gannet crashed into the sea on take-off. The SAR helicopter was on the scene almost immediately and quickly rescued two crew members, but a third, Sub-Lt D. J. Lowe RN, could not be found, despite a four-hour search. At just after midday the search was called off and Sub-Lt Lowe was posted as 'Missing Presumed Drowned', in the first fatal accident of the commission. During the following week there were fine, cold, dry days; cold days with snowstorms; cold days with gales and, on occasions, just plain cold days. Most evenings, on completion of flying, the carrier would anchor off the Covesea Skerries,

At 1pm on Thursday 28 January, a cold, wet day, the *Ark Royal* approached the French Atlantic port of Brest and at 2.15pm she secured alongside the naval base, astern of the battleship *Richelieu* which, although she had been reduced to the role of an accommodation ship, still looked impressive. She was the *Ark Royal's* host ship for the visit and, despite the fact that that period was overshadowed by the death of Sir Winston Churchill, a great deal of convivial hospitality was offered throughout. In spite of atrocious winter weather the *Ark Royal* was very popular with the local French people, and this became apparent when she was opened to the public. Any ship's company who went ashore were sure to find plenty of good, but expensive food (for the discerning) plus an abundance of cheap, but lethal, wine for the unwise, but local traders did

A Scimitar which almost went over the side.

well with several hundred Breton dolls being bought as souvenirs. These apparently provided a bonanza for the local Customs department when the ship arrived back in Rosyth on 4 May. Following her departure from Brest the *Ark Royal* steamed into strong north-easterly gales, but some flying was achieved as she ploughed north through the Irish Sea, and after the short break at Rosyth she embarked upon the second and third phases of her work-up. On Saturday 13 February, after flying off the aircraft to Lossiemouth, she moored off Rosyth once again, this time to carry out a 12-day self-maintenance period. However, for the ship's company, just getting ashore was a trial since it involved long, dreary boat rides which were often suspended because of high winds. There was, therefore, some relief when on Thursday 25 February the final phase of the work-up got under way. During the flying exercises which followed, at 10.20am on Sunday 28 February a Wessex helicopter crashed into the sea alongside the ship. Fortunately, the seaboat was soon launched and the aircrew were safely rescued. Two days later, at 3.30am, the Operational Readiness Inspection began and continued non-stop for almost 24 hours before FOAC decided that the *Ark Royal* was ready for operational service within the fleet.

The inspection was followed by a 48-hour break in Rosyth, but it was soon 'back to business' once again and on Friday 5 March the *Ark Royal,* together with the cruisers *Lion* and *Tiger,* the destroyer *Cassandra,* the frigates *Brighton* and *Falmouth,* the Dutch aircraft carrier *Karel Doorman,* and units of the Norwegian, American and Canadian Navies, left Rosyth for the NATO exercise 'Pilot Light'. As always when the *Ark Royal* was at sea, Russian trawlers, festooned with radar aerials, were never far away and this occasion proved no different. However, once they were informed that their presence was hazardous to flying operations, they normally kept their distance. The whole exercise came under the general direction of the C-in-C Home Fleet, Admiral Sir Charles Madden, who embarked in *Ark Royal* to join the FOAC who was already flying his flag in the carrier. The exercise was divided into several distinct phases such as anti-submarine defence, mine clearance and air defence, in co-operation with the RAF. Offensive strikes were launched against the Norwegian coast, and both capital ships and their escorts from the different nations carried out joint manoeuvres. The weather varied from flat calm, when the high speeds could be achieved which were needed in order to launch aircraft safely, to howling gales, when the escorts seemed to disappear amidst the enormous waves, and even the *Ark Royal* 'took it green' over the flight deck. There were a number of press reporters on board the carrier and although the broadsheet newspapers reported the events which took place between the fleet, the *Sun* ran an article about what it considered were the poor living conditions on board and the fact that half the ship's company had to 'sling hammocks wherever they can find space.' The article led to questions in Parliament and, having visited the carrier only a few weeks previously, the Navy Minister was in a good position to answer them. In the event Mr Mayhew told Parliament that, 'There is no intention of removing the *Ark Royal* from active service in the present decade'. On conclusion of the exercise the NATO Fleet formed into single line ahead and during the afternoon of Wednesday 10 March steamed into Bergen Harbour where all the ships except the *Ark Royal* were able to get alongside. The carrier anchored in the harbour and once again everyone had to rely on the boat service between ship and shore. The stay in Bergen was the first real 'jolly' of the commission and with make-and-mends being granted every day all personnel enjoyed the break, then during the afternoon of Monday 15 March the *Ark Royal* left the Norwegian port to make a 24-hour passage to Rosyth where, during a brief seven and a half-hour stay, Customs clearance was obtained and the ground parties of 819 Squadron and 849C Flight were disembarked. That evening the carrier weighed anchor and steamed down the North Sea to Spithead, entering Portsmouth Harbour during the early afternoon of Thursday 18 March for a long weekend. During the break a children's party was held in the upper hangar and a large trials team was embarked for the next deployment, the deck landing and launching trials of the Blackburn Buccaneer Mk II. This aircraft was powered by the Rolls-Royce Spey engine in place of the de Havilland Gyron Junior as fitted in the Mark I version. The change of engine was marked by a wider air intake and a much larger engine housing. After leaving Portsmouth during the afternoon of Monday 22 March the *Ark Royal* steamed into the Channel and next day the Chief of the Defence Staff, Field Marshal Sir Richard Hull, embarked by helicopter to watch the new Buccaneer's flying operations. Despite some wet and foggy weather, the Buccaneer Mk II performed well and the *Ark Royal* became the first to launch an aircraft with an all-up weight of 50,000lb. During the trials the opportunity was taken to carry out minimum speed launching trials with the Sea Vixen Mk II, carrying a 37-tube, 2-inch rocket launcher, and the First Sea Lord, Admiral Sir David Luce, also visited the ship and witnessed the 1,000th landing of the commission. At the conclusion of the trials the chief test pilot presented Captain Griffin with a silver trophy of the Buccaneer Mk II, and finally on 1 April the carrier anchored in Plymouth Sound, before steaming up harbour later that day to secure alongside 5 and 6 wharves of Devonport Dockyard.

During the month of April, whilst the ship's company took their Easter leave, the *Ark Royal* lay in No 10 dry dock and it was not until Saturday 8 May that she was shifted back alongside the sea wall of No 5 wharf. At 6.30pm on Monday 17 May the *Ark Royal,* together with the destroyer *Devonshire,* left Devonport for the open sea once again and after embarking the squadrons she carried out eight days of intensive flying operations in the Channel, in the midst of which she also exercised with a squadron of West German fast patrol boats, on 21 May, before mooring in Plymouth Sound early on the morning of Wednesday 26 May. This was to be a very special day for many families of the officers and men of the *Ark Royal* for they were to have the opportunity to go to sea in the carrier and it would prove to be a memorable occasion for them. At about 8.50am Admiralty paddle tugs started to bring the passengers alongside and at 10.30am, with everyone embarked, the carrier slipped her mooring and headed out to sea. The flying programme, with a difference, started at 11am when a Gannet was launched from the port catapult, followed by the launching of two rather elderly motor cars in the same manner. Apparently their owners wished to afford them the dignity of a 'burial at sea' rather than the ignominy of ending up in a scrapyard. Next came a fly-past of the *Ark Royal's* aircraft and a display by the Royal Marines Band, after which a buffet lunch was served in the upper hangar. At 2pm all available hands manned the flight deck and the carrier steamed up harbour to secure alongside 7 and 8

wharves an hour later, when many members of the ship's company left with their families for foreign service leave.

The third week of June 1965 got off to a very dismal and wet start in Devon, and at 7.45am on Thursday 17 June the *Ark Royal* left it all behind as she departed from Devonport bound for Gibraltar and the Far East Station. A few families, friends and well-wishers waved her out of the Sound and during the afternoon the Air Group was landed on, before wet weather returned and the visibility deteriorated. Happily, during the passage south the weather improved, it became sunnier and warmer and, despite a sick plummer block which left one propeller trailing, the carrier arrived off southern Spain on Sunday 20 June to carry out flying exercises. With the ship's company having changed into whites, the *Ark Royal* entered Gibraltar on the morning of Tuesday 22 June, to find HMS *Centaur* already alongside the South Mole. She was in the final weeks of her operational service and on her way home to the UK, by way of Lisbon. Unfortunately, any liberty men who had planned on crossing the border to visit the Spanish towns of Algeciras and La Linea were in for a disappointment, since General Franco of Spain had decided to impose a 'creeping blockade' of Gibraltar designed to force Britain to return 'The Rock' to Spain. Whereas at one time 500 vehicles a day had crossed the border, this number had now been reduced to about a dozen, and it was really only possible to cross over on foot. However, some determined souls managed to make the crossing to sample the dubious pleasures of La Linea. After only a 48-hour break in Gibraltar the *Ark Royal* sailed east, stopping next at the anchorage outside Port Said, where she arrived during the afternoon of Monday 28 June to await a southbound transit of the Suez Canal. She lay outside Port Said for 12 hours whilst the convoy formed up, and at just after 2am she weighed anchor and passed through the harbour then into the canal. Daylight found the *Ark Royal* moving slowly southwards and, as always, the canal transit gave most members of the ship's company the opportunity to relax. A few local traders and their wares had been hoisted inboard and they had set up shop by the island, together with the inevitable and ever-popular Gully-Gully man who never failed to amaze and amuse even the most hardened sailors with his tricks. However many times one has steamed through the Suez Canal, the desert wastes on either side of the ship will always interest the traveller, while the local people on the west bank of the canal seemed just as fascinated by the carrier as she moved slowly southwards. At 8pm that evening, after she had cleared Port Suez, speed was increased and course was set for Aden. At last the *Ark Royal* was east of Suez once again.

However, during her passage the news from Aden was disconcerting, for even the sweltering heat of June and July had not curbed the terrorist activities of the National Liberation Front (NLF) and the Front for the Liberation of

A Sea Vixen lands on – this is the pilot's view of the flight deck runway.

South Yemen (FLOSY). Up until the end of 1964 there had been very few terrorist incidents in Aden State since a bomb blast had claimed the life of a senior government official, and which had almost killed the Governor himself, but Christmas 1964 had seen the start of a terrorist campaign of grenade throwing which was to continue until the colony was handed over in November 1967. It was decided, quite sensibly, by the authorities in the colony that the daily advent of over 1,000 Ark Royal liberty men would be too tempting a target for terrorists and that the security forces would be hard pressed to provide adequate protection so, reluctantly, only one part of one watch was allowed to remain ashore after dark, and all the back streets of Steamer Point and the town of Crater were out of bounds. However, during the carrier's three-day stay in Aden's Outer Harbour, many members of the ship's company did venture ashore and returned on board clutching duty-free electrical goods, cameras, pens and watches, but even so, there were few regrets when, on the morning of Sunday 4 July, the Ark Royal left Aden to rendezvous with the Victorious. This she did in the early

hours of Thursday 8 July, and later that morning the Vic's squadrons made a dramatic fly-past over the Ark, before the former departed for home and the latter set course for Singapore. Replenishment at Sea with a warship on either side of an RFA was a long-established practice in the fleet, but on Sunday 11 July the Ark Royal carried out the reverse evolution with one RFA on either side of her, the RFAs Wave Sovereign and Fort Duquesne, which supplied her with fuel oil and stores respectively. It was the first time that there had been a simultaneous transfer of these commodities. After a further eight days of flying exercises in company with the frigate Chichester, the Ark Royal made a ceremonial entry into the naval base at Singapore during the afternoon on Monday 19 July, to resume her duties as part of the Far East Fleet. After 16 days alongside No 8 berth carrying out self-maintenance, during which the ship's company were able to enjoy the delights of the exotic evergreen island and 'Tiger' beer, the carrier steamed out into the South China Sea. Once the Scimitars, Vixens and Gannets had landed on, she rendezvoused with other units of the Far East Fleet, including the New Zealand cruiser Royalist, and HM Ships

Encore, Falmouth and *Aisne* for the annual Flag Officer's training exercises, 'Fotex 65', off the island of Tioman. During this period the *Ark Royal* flew the flag of Vice-Admiral P. J. Hill-Norton, the FO2 FES, who had, of course, commanded the carrier in 1959/60 during the third commission. On completion of the exercises, which involved several days of day and night flying in the area off Singapore, during which period the island of Singapore became an independent sovereign state, having withdrawn from the Federation of Malaysia, the fleet steamed across the South China Sea and put into the US Naval Base at Subic Bay in the Philippines. Here the ships' companies were free to sample the dubious delights of the nearby town of Olongapo which is noted for its brightly decorated 'jeepneys' – relics of the Second World War – and its two-mile main street flanked by bars, restaurants and cabarets, all of which would offer colourful, exotic and noisy invitations to passers-by. After just two days in Subic Bay, the *Ark Royal,* wearing the flag of Vice-Admiral Hill-Norton, sailed for the first phase of 'Exercise Guardrail', which took her into severe gales and heavy seas in the surrounding exercise areas. During the manoeuvres the CO of 890 Squadron, Lt-Cdr A. M. G. Pearson, made the 2,000th deck landing of the commission, and on Saturday 4 September the *Ark Royal* returned to the naval base at Singapore.

It was on Saturday 18 September that the carrier put to sea again, where she embarked the squadrons for a week's flying, some of it off Vietnam without a diversion airfield. After leaving Singapore the *Ark Royal* steamed up the east coast of Malaya to carry out flying operations close to the area where, 25 years previously, Japanese naval aircraft had destroyed the Royal Navy's capital ships *Prince of Wales* and *Repulse,* left vulnerable because they had no air cover. After five days flying in the South China Sea, the carrier set course for Hong Kong, but her arrival was delayed as she was forced to ride out tropical storm 'Agnes' outside the colony. However, at 10.30am on Tuesday 28 September she finally anchored off Green Island in Hong Kong Harbour, one day later than had been planned. A fleet of ferries had been hired for the eager liberty men, each boat capable of carrying one watch, and they were able to deposit their passengers in the heart of Wanchai, not far from the China Fleet Club and its ice-cold 'San Miguel' beer. However, three days after arriving in the colony the Chinese People's Republic celebrated its National Day and, as civil disorder ashore could not be ruled out, leave was restricted. Nevertheless, those who did remain on board were not left out, and they were entertained by a professional troupe of Chinese dancers. A few days later, on Sunday 10 October, when Nationalist Chinese celebrated their National Day, leave was again restricted, but fortunately an attempted coup in Indonesia did not affect the carrier's stay in Hong Kong. On Tuesday 12 October the *Ark Royal* steamed out of Hong Kong Harbour to return to Singapore where,

eight days later, she started a self-maintenance period which was intended to prepare the ship for her part in a three-nation exercise off the coast of Australia, code-named 'Exercise Warrior'. The *Ark Royal* was scheduled to head a force of seven British ships during joint manoeuvres with units from the United States and Australian Navies. On Friday 29 October 1965, Captain M. F. Fell DSO DSC RN took over command of the carrier and at noon that day Captain Griffin was rowed to the dockyard by the Heads of Department. Captain Fell had joined the Royal Navy in 1938, and he was one of its most distinguished aviators, having won both the DSO and DSC during the Second World War and being involved in one of the Fleet Air Arm's attacks on the German battleship *Tirpitz.*

Two days later, on Sunday 31 October, during the dog watches there was a pipe over the tannoy, 'Fire in B boiler room'. As always, the Fire and Emergency parties responded rapidly, and, supported by the Dockyard Fire Brigade, it seemed that the fire had been extinguished by 9.30pm. However, it soon became clear that this was not the case and that the blaze had taken hold in the funnel uptakes. Frank Stockton recalls that a film show was in progress on the flight deck, with the screen up against the island superstructure, when thick black smoke started to belch from the funnel and fire parties arrived to hose it down to prevent overheating. However, with the film well under way, the audience was in no mood to stop the show and Frank remembers that as the smoke got thicker and the firefighters needed more space, the film show continued with the screen, the projectionist and the audience being slowly forced forwards towards the edge of the island. In order to put the blaze out it was necessary to hose down the hangar bulkheads and the island superstructure and eventually, by 2am on Monday 1 November, the conflagration had finally been extinguished. When daylight came the full extent of the damage, both to the boiler room and the funnel uptakes, could be seen and it was immediately apparent that with essential repairs likely to take three to four weeks, the *Ark Royal* would have to withdraw from 'Exercise Warrior'. Once the decision was taken, FO2 FES transferred his flag to HMS *Devonshire* and three days later, leaving the carrier in dockyard hands, the fleet sailed from Singapore. In the event the *Ark Royal* was still firmly alongside No 8 berth in Singapore Naval Base, when her sister ship HMS *Eagle* arrived on the Far East Station on Friday 12 November and she had to secure on B buoy in the Johore Strait, much to the annoyance of her liberty men. Furthermore, in order to make room for the *Eagle's* squadrons at RAF Changi, the *Ark Royal's* air group were dispatched to RAF Butterworth in northern Malaya, but during November 1965 political events in Africa were about to influence the movements of both the *Eagle* and the *Ark Royal.*

The dissolution of the Central African Federation in

HMS *Eagle* relieves the *Ark Royal* on station in the Mozambique Channel in April 1966.   *(Imperial War Museum A35019)*

1963 had left the British Government with the problem of negotiating the independence of Southern Rhodesia, which the whole of the self-governing colony's European population believed to be overdue. However, the majority African population were naturally hostile to independence being granted to the Rhodesian Front led by Winston Field, and no British Government was prepared to concede to a political party which practised apartheid and which was opposed to any political concessions to the African majority. In April 1964 Field was replaced by Ian Douglas Smith, who had once served as a pilot in the RAF. Six months later, when the Labour Government took office in Britain, any hopes of a reasonable settlement became even more remote and after calling an election, at which the European voters overwhelmingly endorsed Smith's intransigence, on 11 November 1965 he issued a unilateral declaration of independence in language which echoed the famous Independence Speech of 4 July 1776. With the political situation in Rhodesia deteriorating, on Thursday 18 November the *Eagle* left for the Indian Ocean and the waters off Mozambique. There was to be no change of

scenery yet for the *Ark Royal,* however, and it was Tuesday 7 December before the fire damage had been repaired and she was able to put to sea for day and night flying exercises. Two days later the C-in-C British Forces in the Far East, Air Chief Marshal Sir John Grandy, visited the ship, but it was not long before mechanical problems resurfaced – this time in the form of contaminated boiler feed water – and with her visit to Australia in jeopardy, the *Ark Royal* returned to Singapore dockyard on 13 December. Fortunately, a complete change of feed water resolved the problem and four days later she sailed for a fast passage south to Fremantle, Western Australia. That same evening the carrier crossed the equator and next morning, at 9am, the traditional Crossing the Line ceremony was held on the flight deck with Captain Fell being the first 'victim' to be lathered, shaved and thrown to the bears. Four days later the 3,000th arrested deck landing of the commission was recorded, and on Thursday 23 December came the much awaited landfall, as the coast of Western Australia slowly came into view. After checking the ship's draught the harbour pilot was embarked, and with a full 'Alpha' range of aircraft and ceremonial manning parties in position, the *Ark Royal* steamed through the narrow entrance to the port of Fremantle, turned through 180 degrees in order to point her bows toward the harbour entrance, and secured alongside the port's 7 and 8 berths. Astern lay HM Ships *Devonshire* and *Blackpool,* which had both taken part in 'Exercise Warrior'.

Soon after her arrival in Fremantle most of the flight deck, after lift and upper hangar were converted into venues for the official functions, with the aircraft being struck down and moved forward. Ashore the ship's company, after a disappointing start at the Pagoda Ballroom, were overwhelmed with hospitality, whilst on board there was a magnificent children's party and over 6,000 people toured the ship when it was opened to the public. The ship's carol singers were plied with mince pies, washed down by ice-cold lager, and the Royal Marines Band spent a hectic festive season Beating Retreat and playing for official functions on board and ashore, even turning up in full regalia at the local racecourse. Finally, however, on a dull, grey Wednesday 29 December, with large crowds of hosts, friends and well-wishers gathered on the quayside, the *Ark Royal* left harbour after a very successful visit.

After leaving Fremantle there were New Year's Eve flying exercises off the Cocos Islands as well as the Christmas pantomime which was very loosely based on 'A Christmas Carol' by Charles Dickens, but with the addition of an extremely realistic Dalek! On Saturday 8 January 1966 the *Ark Royal* arrived back in Singapore for a 19-day maintenance period, and this was followed by five days of flying exercises during which the FO Naval Air Command, Vice-Admiral D. C. E. F. Gibson, a former commanding officer of the carrier, visited the ship. Then on Tuesday 1 February she set course for Mombasa where she was to relieve HMS *Eagle* in the Indian Ocean, which would allow the latter to return to Singapore to carry out maintenance. During the passage, flying exercises were carried out off the island of Gan, and on Friday 18 February the *Ark Royal* moored in Kilindini Harbour for a 13-day visit to Mombasa before departing on Thursday 3 March, as everyone thought, to return to Gan and Singapore.

On leaving Mombasa Captain Fell announced that the *Ark's* return to Singapore had been delayed and that instead they were to carry out, '...an important operation in support of Her Majesty's Government's policy of economic sanctions directed against Mr Smith's Government in Southern Rhodesia.' The *Ark Royal,* together with the frigates *Rhyl* and *Lowestoft,* was to patrol the Mozambique Channel in order to prevent oil tankers carrying their cargo into the port of Beira, from where it could be pumped to Rhodesia. The primary means of plotting the movement of ships in the Mozambique Channel was to be the Gannet AEW aircraft of 849C Flight, assisted by the Vixens and

Scimitars which could rapidly identify and photograph contacts made by the Gannets. In the event, with the carrier's role having been announced publicly, the Portuguese decided to send an aircraft over daily to keep an eye on the *Ark Royal,* but on Tuesday 15 March the *Eagle* arrived to take over the surveillance task, and after steaming together for a few hours the *Ark* left for Singapore, where she arrived on Friday 25 March.

It had been intended that the *Ark Royal* would return to the Beira Patrol in the third week of April, but mechanical problems delayed her departure from Singapore until Tuesday 26 April, and on the afternoon of Wednesday 4 May she rendezvoused with HMS *Eagle* off Gan to embark three Scimitars and a Gannet in order to make up her aircraft complement. Next day, as the *Ark Royal* continued her westward passage, there were problems with the starboard rudder, but she finally arrived in the Mozambique Channel on Saturday 7 May to begin her second Beira Patrol. Once again the Gannet AEW aircraft of 849C Flight provided day and night surveillance of the Mozambique Channel, with the Scimitars and Vixens rapidly making contact and identifying all vessels in the area, but three days after her arrival on patrol tragedy struck. At 9.25am on Tuesday 10 May 1966, Sea Vixen 014 which was being flown by Lt Alan L. Tarver with Lt John H. Stutchbury as the observer, was on a routine patrol, in a position Lat 20° - 14'S/Long 36° - 24'E, when the aircraft suffered a flame-out to its port engine and an electrical failure. In additon the fuel for the starboard engine was being jettisoned, and unless something was done then the aircraft would quickly run out of fuel altogether. A Scimitar tanker aircraft was quickly launched, but as attempts were made to carry out in-flight refuelling the Vixen's remaining engine failed and the aircraft quickly lost height. At about 6,000 feet, as the plane was losing height, Lt Tarver ordered the observer to eject, but the equipment failed and he then ordered him to climb out of the aircraft, which was, by this time, losing height rapidly; unfortunately, being a very tall man, Lt Stutchbury appeared to be stuck in the narrow hatchway. At about 3,000 feet, with the aircraft's speed down to 200 knots, Lt Tarver rolled the stricken Vixen upside down in an effort to get his observer clear, but again his efforts failed. Finally, with his observer almost out of the hatch and lying prone along the Vixen's fuselage, Lt Tarver tried to free him from the obstruction which was clearly preventing his escape. Overhead in the refuelling Scimitar, the pilot saw these final efforts, before the Vixen rolled over to port and Lt Tarver ejected just seconds before the aircraft hit the water, sending up a fountain of spray. The Scimitar pilot who witnessed the incident did not think Lt Tarver could have survived, so late had he left his own escape, but in fact his parachute had half opened and although badly stunned and shaken, he managed to struggle free from his equipment and get into his dinghy. At 9.57am, just half an hour after his aircraft had first suffered problems, Lt Tarver was picked up by a helicopter and eight minutes later he was back on board. Despite searching until almost noon, there was no trace of Lt Stutchbury, or of any wreckage, and the *Ark Royal* was obliged to continue her flying operations. That evening, at 8pm, a sick man was transferred from HMS *Leander* by helicopter for treatment aboard the carrier and at 9.41pm Gannet 036 ditched over the side on take-off, but happily the crew members were rescued by the seaboat and the SAR helicopter. Six months later, on Tuesday 1 November, Lt Tarver went to Buckingham Palace where, for his conspicuous courage in delaying his own escape from his stricken Sea Vixen in an attempt to save the life of his observer, Her Majesty the Queen presented him with the George Medal.

The *Ark Royal* remained in the Mozambique Channel until Wednesday 25 May, when she left the area to return to Devonport. During her second patrol her aircraft had surveyed over 12 million square miles of ocean, locating and identifying 500 ships, and in the month of May alone the carrier had steamed some 12,000 nautical miles. Five days later, at 10pm on Monday 30 May, she anchored off Aden for 16 hours and on Saturday 4 June she made her northbound transit of the Suez Canal. It was Monday 13 June when the carrier returned to Devonport, having spent 12 months away from her home port, and hundreds of families, friends and well-wishers gave her a warm welcome

when she secured alongside in the dockyard, having steamed 65,000 miles east of Suez. The whole ship's company could now look forward to some very welcome leave before embarking on the final leg of the commission with the Home Fleet, not in the blue spiced waters of the Indian Ocean, but in the cold, grey, North Sea.

By August the *Ark Royal* was operating in northern waters and taking part in NATO's 'Exercise Straight Lace'. On Tuesday 20 September 1966 the Queen Mother visited the ship when she was at sea about 20 miles east of Girdleness, Aberdeenshire. Also present to watch the royal visitor's arrival in a helicopter of the Queen's Flight was a Soviet tug of the Okhterskiy class, which had stationed itself within two miles of the *Ark Royal,* and shortly before the carrier's aircraft began a display using high explosive bombs, Captain Fell signalled by aldis lamp in Russian: 'You are in a dangerous position. My aircraft will be carrying out firings on my port side and astern of me. Keep outside four miles' range from me.' Wisely the tug's skipper slipped eight miles astern while Scimitars and Vixens from the carrier used 500lb bombs, rocket projectiles and 30mm cannon in their display. However, when the show was over the tug closed once again to within two miles of the carrier.

Fourteen days later, with her squadrons having left for their respective shore stations, the *Ark Royal* returned to Devonport on Tuesday 4 October 1966 to undergo a three-year, £30 million modernization refit similar to that which her sister *Eagle* had undergone between 1959 and 1964.

HMS *Ark Royal* refuels from RFA *Tidesurge* in the Beira Strait.   *(Fleet Air Arm Museum)*

Chapter Seven

The Final Years 1970-1979

In 1957 the Admiralty had outline drawings produced of a new aircraft carrier for the Royal Navy, and this design eventually became the ill-fated CVA 01 of the 1960s. The proposed new carrier was to have a displacement of 54,650 tons, with a length overall of 963 feet, and in June 1964 it was announced that bids from shipbuilders would be requested in April 1966. The new type of carrier was to have replaced the ageing *Victorious* in 1972, and the *Ark Royal* in 1974, and so even in the early weeks of 1965 it was accepted that the *Ark's* days were numbered. However, in the General Election of October 1964 a Labour Government led by Harold Wilson was elected and it was clear that their approach to Defence matters would be very different from that of their predecessors. Following a Defence Review in 1965, the proposed new aircraft carrier, CVA 01, was cancelled in February 1966 and it was announced that instead, '...the existing carriers will be refitted continually over the next ten years to keep them in service. The process will start with a £30 million refit for the *Ark Royal* to equip her to take Phantoms and Buccaneers.' The announcement was a great blow to the Navy and to the Fleet Air Arm in particular, for it meant the rundown of fixed-wing flying in the Royal Navy, which was to coincide with the withdrawal of British forces from east of Suez in the early 1970s. Apparently the powers-that-be seemed to equate the retention of the aircraft carrier with Britain's presence east of Suez, as the Government White Paper stated: 'Experience and study have shown that only one type of operation exists for which carriers and carrier-borne aircraft would be indispensable. That is the landing or withdrawal of troops against sophisticated opposition ouside the range of land-based air cover.' Obviously no one envisaged such a scenario taking place in the western hemisphere. However, despite the announcement and the obvious economic savings which would result, it was decided that the *Ark Royal's* £30 million three-year refit would still go ahead and, in fact, work commenced at the end of 1966.

The modernization of the *Eagle* and the *Ark Royal* were the largest single

A completely new look for the *Ark Royal*, post 1970.   *(Fleet Air Arm Museum)*

The Royal Navy's biggest and most powerful warship during the 1970s. *(Fleet Air Arm Museum)*

Phantoms parked on the new flight deck space aft.

(Fleet Air Arm Museum)

tasks to be undertaken by any of the naval dockyards, and the *Ark*, with ten decks below the flight deck and four more in the island superstructure itself, represented a huge undertaking for Devonport Dockyard. The major part of the modernization was the fitting of the fully-angled 8½° flight deck, which entailed the removal of the gun sponsons on the port side. The flight deck itself was also enlarged on both sides aft, in order to provide more parking space. Two long steam catapults were fitted, one on the angled deck and the other on the port side of the flight deck, extending back past the forward lift. New direct-acting arrester gear was installed to handle the Phantom aircraft which were on order for the Royal Navy and the RAF. All the ship's armament was removed and in place of the Type 984 radar two Type 965, two-dimensional air-search radar sets were installed, with the existing Type 983 height-finders being retained. In all this meant that some 3,000 tons of new structure, which included 5,000 feet of bulkheads, 50 miles of piping and 1,200 miles of electrical cable, were installed. The 'minor' electrical work included the changing of 25,000 light fittings, 11,000 switches and sockets, 600

changeover switches and 750 emergency lanterns. Perhaps, most important of all for the ship's company were the improvements to the living accommodation in the ship. Over three-quarters of the ratings on board would be in one of the 26 entirely new messes, or one of the fully refurbished mess decks, all of which were fitted with bunks. The senior rates' messes were all refurbished and the entire living accommodation was air-conditioned; unlike the *Eagle*, the *Ark Royal's* wardroom was left in its original position below the lower hangar.

The modernization refit was lengthy and, inevitably, there were a number of frustrating delays. However, in late 1967 and the early days of 1968 there came rumours that, with the Government needing to make large cuts in spending, they were intending to accelerate the withdrawal of British forces from east of Suez and disband the Royal Navy's aircraft carrier force by the end of 1969. By mid-January 1968 the rumours were largely substantiated, although it was officially announced that the withdrawal from Singapore would be in December 1971 and the aircraft carriers would be phased out during the following

HMS *Ark Royal* approaches Gibraltar in October 1970. *(Imperial War Museum HU75013)*

year, three years ahead of the original schedule. This was a terrific blow to the Fleet Air Arm, and the only ray of light was the fact that the *Ark Royal* was to complete her three-year modernization refit as scheduled. However, the only reason for the reprieve was the fact that £10 million had already been spent on the ship and the cancellation of work on her would have resulted in a saving of only £7 million, in addition to which she would have to be withdrawn from service immediately. Two major casualties of the defence cuts were the aircraft carrier *Eagle*, which would not undergo the necessary modernization to allow her to operate Phantom aircraft, and the cruiser HMS *Lion* which would not be converted to a helicopter carrier. Thus, not only was the *Ark Royal* to be the Royal Navy's last aircraft carrier, but she was to be the only vessel able to operate the Navy's 48 Phantom jets which were due for delivery in April 1968. With only the *Eagle* and the *Hermes* in commission, and the *Ark Royal* in refit, the late 1960s were deeply depressing days for the Fleet Air Arm, particularly when the Minister of Defence, Denis Healey, announced in Parliament, 'The position after the carriers have been

phased out in 1972 is that there will be no carriers in the Mediterranean after that date. Amphibious forces will be permanently stationed in the area.' As to the *Ark Royal's* role during what was thought to be her final commission from 1970 to 1972, he told Parliament, 'The aircraft carrier *(Ark Royal)* will not be continuously in the Mediterranean when the assault ship or command ship is not able to be there. When the carrier will be in the Mediterranean, it will be there for comparatively short periods.' His words, and the full implication of the Government's defence policy, were obviously not lost on the military planners in Argentina.

On Monday 31 March 1969 at Yeovilton, No 892 Naval Air Squadron, which was thought at the time to be the Royal Navy's last fixed-wing air squadron, was commissioned with their newly delivered Phantom FK4 all-weather fighters which were capable of speeds greater than Mach 2. In its air defence role the aircraft could carry four sidewinder and four sparrow missiles or, in its strike role, it would be armed with a variety of air to ground weapons including 20-inch rockets and 540lb bombs. The two Rolls-Royce Spey engines which powered the aircraft could deliver 12,250lb of thrust each, or 20,515lb each with reheat engaged, giving the aircraft its high rate of climb and maximum speed of Mach 2.1 at sea level, and a cruising speed of about 500 knots. So, while the *Ark Royal* was in dockyard hands, her main fighter squadron was working up to prepare it for operational service. Meanwhile, in the summer of 1969, as the *Ark Royal's* refit neared completion, the Government's attitude towards the Fleet Air Arm remained unchanged. During Parliamentary Questions, Mr Healey confirmed his policy when, in answer to a question he replied: 'The Government's plans for aircraft carriers remain unchanged - that is to say they will be phased out of their present fixed-wing flying task after the withdrawals from Malaysia, Singapore and the Persian Gulf have been completed in December 1971.' In reply to a question as to whether, after having spent over £32 million on the *Ark Royal's* modernization refit, it would be unwise to get rid of her before 1975, Mr Healey commented: 'I do not believe that is the case. When the Government decided not to continue the carrier force it was because the running costs annually and the costs of replacing carriers as they become obsolescent were out of all proportion to the military value which could be obtained, particularly once we have decided to leave our bases east of Suez.' Needless to say there was a great deal of opposition to this policy, but the Government was adamant, and it appeared that after her modernization the *Ark Royal's* career would be limited to just one full commission. Meanwhile, on Thursday 12 June 1969, as the refit proceeded, fire broke out in the *Ark Royal's* boiler uptake shaft, but although firemen had to work in very cramped conditions, they soon had the blaze under control. Later Rear-Admiral D. B. Wildish, the Admiral Superintendent at Devonport, described the fire as, 'short, hot and local', and he praised the speed and efficiency of the fire brigade.

On 17 July 1969 the *Ark Royal's* new commanding officer, Captain R. D. Lygo RN, was appointed to the ship, although it would be December that year before he actually joined her at Devonport. His first recollections of the *Ark Royal* make interesting reading: '...when I got out of my car alongside I was immediately dwarfed and humbled. Was I really supposed to get this mass of steel, covered in scaffolding and brown with maties, and attached to the jetty with wires and pipes like the oars of a galley, out of "Guzz" and on her way? I picked my way up the gangway and was piped on board midst a bustle of activity, the din of windy hammers and the whine of metal grinders. Life for me, then, was spent in a Portakabin alongside. For the ship's company, it was in the old wooden hutted accommodation in *Drake*. By the time the ship's company rose to 1,000 the problem of getting back and forth, often in pouring rain, was becoming obsessive. Not enough

Pusser's transport we were told. We solved that by hiring corporation buses.'

Captain Lygo had joined the RNVR in 1942 and soon afterwards he was flying Seafires from the *Indefatigable* and *Implacable*. In 1945 he received a permanent commission in the Royal Navy, and in the late 1940s and early 1950s he flew jet fighters in liaison with the US Navy from the USS *Franklin D. Roosevelt*, the USS *Coral Sea* and the USS *Philippine Sea*. He commanded 759 Naval Air Squadron in 1951 and two years later he was appointed to command the frigate HMS *Veryan Bay*. Following this Commander Lygo commanded 800 Naval Air Squadron of Seahawks during the *Ark Royal's* first commission. Between 1961 and 1963 he commanded the frigate *Lowestoft*, and after two years in the Admiralty with the Deputy Director of Naval Air Warfare, he was appointed to command the brand new Leander-class frigate HMS *Juno*, which had been built at Southampton. It was from the *Juno* that Captain Lygo was appointed to the *Ark Royal*.

Following the completion of most of the dockyard's work, the *Ark Royal* was due to leave Devonport at first light on Saturday 13 December 1969 to carry out her preliminary sea trials. Although there were some who considered the 13th a somewhat unlucky day for sailing, particularly after more than two and a half years alongside, nevertheless Captain Lygo had chosen that day because it was the first time that there were favourable tides during daylight hours. However, in the event, severe gales twice prevented the ship from sailing and it was the morning of Monday 15 December before the *Ark Royal* slipped her moorings and put to sea for four days of sea trials. These were conducted with only three boiler rooms working, and with some 600 dockyard personnel embarked, and on their completion, on Friday 19 December, the carrier returned to Devonport Dockyard for the final touches to her refit and to prepare for sea. Since entering Devonport Dockyard in October 1966 the ship had gained thousands of tons in weight, and she was now the heaviest and largest warship in the Royal Navy. With Christmas and New Year leave having been taken, and with the ship's company up to full strength, Commissioning Day finally arrived on Tuesday 24 February 1970. The Queen Mother who, as Her Majesty Queen Elizabeth, had launched the ship some 20 years previously, agreed to attend the ceremony at Devonport Dockyard and altogether some 4,000 people packed into the upper hangar for the occasion. It was the Queen Mother's sixth visit to the ship and for five hours she toured the various departments before wishing the ship's company well and delivering the traditional, and always very welcome, naval message, 'Splice the Main Brace'. Following this she cut the 410lb commissioning cake, the largest ever cooked in a British warship. Before leaving, the Queen Mother attended the christening ceremony for the nine-week-old son of Ldg Steward Jim

The *Ark Royal* moors in Kalkara Creek, Grand Harbour, Malta, in October 1970. *(Imperial War Museum FL5663)*

Marshall, for whom she brought a christening gift of a knife, fork and spoon.

The *Ark Royal* sailed for her extensive post-refit trials on Wednesday 4 March 1970 and during this period the new waist catapult was tested by two Phantoms which were successfully launched from the ship in almost 'nil wind' conditions. This was also a good test of the strengthened deck panels and jet blast deflectors that had been fitted against the fierce heat of the Phantom's jet exhausts, and the bridle catchers, which were first employed in HMS *Victorious* during the early 1960s. The *Ark Royal* also rendezvoused with her sister ship *Eagle* in Lyme Bay, where the Hawker Harrier aircraft, first seen as the P1127 in February 1963, made an appearance and flew between the carriers, afterwards landing on both of them. After almost three weeks at sea the *Ark Royal* returned to Plymouth

Sound to carry out heeling trials, before going back into Devonport Dockyard for rectification work and for the ship's company to take some leave. Finally, on Monday 20 April the *Ark Royal* sailed from Devonport to undergo the final stage of her post-refit trials in the Channel off Plymouth and Portland. These were broken up by a long weekend at Rotterdam where the carrier had an excellent berth in the heart of the city for what proved to be a highly successful visit; a new tulip was even named 'Ark Royal' in honour of the ship. After leaving the Dutch port on Monday 27 April, the carrier returned to the Lyme Bay and Plymouth areas for flying trials which began on 1 May. On the third day of the trials, at about 8.25am on Sunday 3 May, there was tragedy when a Phantom F4K of 892 Squadron, which was one of the three aircraft that had embarked to prepare the carrier for Phantom operations, disappeared from the radar screens while operating some 20 miles from the carrier, about 40 miles off St Alban's Head. Sadly, despite an extensive sea and air search, no trace could be found of the pilot or the observer.

During the trials some problems arose with the jet blast deflectors, the bow catapult and the arrester gear and so, on Friday 15 May, the *Ark Royal* returned to Devonport where the faults could be rectified. The *Ark Royal's* spell in dock coincided with a General Election and, much to everyone's surprise, the Conservatives led by Edward Heath were elected to office with a majority of 37, which gave rise to hopes of a major change in Defence policy. However, there would be no sudden change to the *Ark Royal's* immediate schedule and on Friday 12 June she left Devonport for the Moray Firth to begin the first phase of her work-up. Everything went smoothly right up to 25 June when another defect occurred on the arrester gear and, as the ship was due to spend the last weekend of the month at Liverpool, it was decided to go ahead with the visit and to carry out repairs there. So during the morning of Saturday 27 June the carrier, which had been built on the River Mersey, steamed upriver and berthed alongside Princes Pier to an enthusiastic welcome from the local population. Surprisingly, it was the ship's first visit to the Mersey since her departure on Friday 25 February 1955, three days after her commissioning at Cammell Laird's shipyard. However, it was clear that Merseysiders had not forgotten her and when the ship was opened to the public, some 8,000 visitors went on board in the space of five hours. The second phase of the work-up was completed in the Irish Sea in appalling weather during the first nine days of July, and with thick fog affecting flying operations, the Phantoms were lucky to at least try their hand at missile firings on the range in Cardigan Bay, off Aberporth. By this time the Sea King helicopters of 824 Squadron, the Buccaneer Mk IIs of 809 Squadron and the Gannet AEW

A very impressive view of HMS *Ark Royal* at sea, with a Buccaneer being launched from the waist catapult.

(*Fleet Air Arm Museum*)

3s of 849 B flight had joined the ship, and after a short self-maintenance period at Devonport the third phase of the work-up got under way, this time in the Bristol Channel. Finally, on 28 and 29 July it was time for the Operational Readiness Inspection, on conclusion of which the *Ark Royal* returned to Devonport on the last day of the month for leave and a period of maintenance.

By this time the new Conservative Government had had an opportunity to review the Defence Policy which had been set by the previous administration, and with the redundancy programme for Fleet Air Arm fixed-wing pilots and ground crews having been put into abeyance temporarily, there was some hope that both the *Eagle* and the *Ark Royal* would be retained at least until the end of the 1970s. What was clear was that without seaborne air power the Royal Navy would have to bow out of any maritime confrontation unless, of course, its adversary was thoughtful enough to stay within 800 miles of one of the RAF's bases.

During the August Bank Holiday of 1970 the *Ark Royal*

was the major attraction at Navy Days, then three days later, on Thursday 3 September, she sailed for two days of flying exercises in the Channel. Saturday 5 September had been set aside as 'Families Day' and so the carrier returned to C buoy in Plymouth Sound where over 2,000 relatives of the ship's company were embarked from tugs, before the *Ark Royal* sailed out to sea where the squadrons staged a full programme of flying and armament demonstrations. That afternoon, as the ship was returning to Plymouth Sound, the guests witnessed a dramatic real-life rescue operation when a rating who had been working on one of the ship's boats slipped and fell 40 feet into the sea. In less than four minutes the SAR helicopter retrieved the man from the water and landed him safely back on board. So smooth and efficient was the rescue that many of the guests assembled on the flight deck thought it was merely another demonstration. Just for the day the lower hangar was converted into a huge restaurant to feed the 2,000 guests, amongst them a Birmingham family who had mistaken one of the tenders carrying families to the *Ark Royal* for the

Torpoint Ferry; instead of crossing the Hamoaze they found themselves on board the aircraft carrier in Plymouth Sound, but apparently they enjoyed the day in spite of the mix-up. After all the passengers had been disembarked in Plymouth Sound later that afternoon, the *Ark Royal* steamed round to the Bristol Channel for more flying exercises. That weekend the Ministry of Defence announced that Captain Lygo had been appointed the key post of Director of Public Relations for the Royal Navy, which was very appropriate for a man who had started his working life in 1940 as a 16-year-old office boy with *The Times* newspaper. The appointment certainly augured well regarding publicity for the *Ark Royal*, although he was not due to leave the ship until March 1971.

During the second and third weeks of September the *Ark Royal* completed a fourth work-up phase prior to joining the NATO striking fleet in 'Exercise Northern Wedding' and once again the work-up was bedevilled by bad weather conditions in the Irish Sea and Bristol Channel. In fact, on the night of Tuesday 8 September she stood by the coaster MV *St Brenden*, which was on fire off Lundy in the Bristol Channel, until the arrival of the destroyer HMS *Cavalier* which towed the stricken ship to Milford Haven. 'Exercise Northern Wedding' was scheduled for the end of the month, when the strike fleet steamed through the Faroes-Shetland gap from the Atlantic to the operating area in the North Sea, and this was followed by a NATO visit to Oslo for four days from Monday 28 September. On leaving the Norwegian port on Friday 2 October, the *Ark Royal* steamed into Force 9 north-easterly gales as she headed south in the North Sea. The 44-knot winds and huge waves caused problems for a number of small ships and during the passage a distress call was intercepted from a German coaster, MV *Leda*, which was wallowing in the heavy seas after her deck cargo of wood had shifted, causing a 45° list to port which had flooded her engine room. All but three of her crew had been taken off safely, and as conditions worsened it was decided that her master, first mate and another crew member, all of whom had hoped that they could save their stricken vessel, should also leave. A Sea King helicopter of 824 Squadron, flown by Lt Barry Randle, was dispatched immediately to the *Leda* and, in very difficult and hazardous conditions, the three men were airlifted to safety and cared for in the carrier's sickbay before being landed at

Plymouth when the *Ark Royal* arrived there. Subsequently the squadron received a citation and an award from the German Government. Initially, when the *Ark Royal* had sailed from Devonport following 'Families Day' it was thought that she would not return until just before Christmas, but in the event mechanical faults in the catapult and arrester gear machinery meant that, much to the delight of the ship's company, she was recalled early for urgent repairs and she arrived at Devonport on Sunday 4 October.

After six days alongside, the *Ark Royal* sailed for Lyme Bay to test the catapult and arrester gear before she left for the Mediterranean on Wednesday 14 October, arriving in Malta's Grand Harbour five days later to undergo a short self-maintenance period. It was whilst she was in Malta that the Government announced a change to the previous administration's plan to phase out the Royal Navy's aircraft

An excellent view which shows the bridle catchers, which had first been used on HMS *Victorious* in 1961. *(Fleet Air Arm Museum)*

On 28 July 1971 the former paratrooper Chay Blyth received a warm welcome from the *Ark's* ship's company as he neared the end of the first solo non-stop world voyage by the east to west route in the 17-ton yacht *British Steel*. He had left England on 18 October 1970.

(Imperial War Museum A35365)

carriers in 1972. Quite rightly it had been accepted that their withdrawal would leave a serious gap in the capability of the Navy's fleet, and two options were put forward for avoiding such a situation. The first was to introduce the Exocet anti-ship guided missile system which would improve the strike capability of surface ships, and the second was to retain the *Ark Royal* in service until the late 1970s. Although this decision would mean a reprieve for the *Ark Royal* there was to be no stay of execution for the *Eagle*, and unless new 'through deck cruisers', as the next generation of small aircraft carriers were known, came into service with their STOVL aircraft, then the future for the Fleet Air Arm still looked bleak. Although there would be times during the 1970s when the Navy would have no operational carrier, the *Ark's* refits would be arranged to provide the best possible value, to the great relief of both the Ministry of Defence and the NATO planners.

During her passage south from Devonport, as far as the Strait of Gibraltar, both radio and radar silence had been maintained which had succeeded in keeping at bay the ever-present Soviet shadowing ships, in the form of radar-festooned trawlers or destroyers, and this had allowed for some rather more private than usual flying exercises off Sardinia. However, this state of affairs would not last for long. After leaving Malta on Thursday 29 October the *Ark Royal* took part in 'Exercise Lime Jug 70', and operations were made easier when a fault which had dogged the bow catapult was finally rectified, while the arrester gear continued to behave itself after the problems which had been experienced the previous month. With the exercise scheduled to last for just over two weeks the carrier was able, for the first time since her modernization refit, to operate her aircraft at full intensity during both day and night flying operations. Predictably, the Soviet Navy had sent along an uninvited guest in the form of the Kotlin-class destroyer *Bravyy* and during Monday 9 November she stuck close to the *Ark Royal*. From dawn it had been a normal flying day for the fixed-wing operations of the

The *Ark's* upper and lower hangars, with Phantoms and Buccaneers. *(Fleet Air Arm Museum)*

Phantoms, Buccaneers and Gannets as well as the Sea King helicopters, and at one stage the SAR Wessex had delivered fresh bread, mail and newspapers to the accompanying frigates *Yarmouth* and *Exmouth*. The presence of the *Bravyy* was not at all unusual, for both NATO and Soviet warships had, for a number of years, observed each other's naval exercises in the never-ending quest for intelligence.

The *Ark's* Engineer Officer recalls the events which occurred at 6.40pm, when the carrier was some 100 miles south of Cape Matapan: 'After a long dog watch break, a fresh flight deck crew was ready, the night flying aircrews were briefed and the aircraft manned. All the ship required was the captain's permission to alter course into the wind and to increase speed. The first Phantom was ready to load on the steam catapult. Below decks, the ship's company, some with work finished for the day or off watch for a period, were relaxing, perhaps watching closed-circuit TV, writing letters, chatting, or sleeping. In the wardroom, the majority of officers had finished their evening meal, although some late arrivals were about to get their coffee.

Unconsciously each man on board noted the alteration of course and the increased tempo of the main engines as they were adjusted to the higher revs. The reverberations of the first Phantom's engines on reheat permeated the ship's ventilation systems and faded as the aircraft left the flight deck. The ship shuddered as the catapult pistons were retarded at the end of the launch stroke. Everything was set for some good night flying. There was enough wind, not too much swell, and sufficient visibility to see the horizon and the clear navigation lights of the planeguard in station on the port quarter. However, before the night was over the airborne Phantom was to be diverted ashore.' No second launch ensued, for even as the Phantom was being ranged, the *Bravyy* approached the *Ark Royal* on her starboard side and crossed the carrier's bows. As the Soviet destroyer turned to port, and was only a mile away from the carrier, Captain Lygo signalled: 'You are standing into danger.' The story is taken up once again by the Engineer Officer: 'The noise of the second night launch never came. Instead, the vibration aft changed suddenly and it became clear that the

On 1 May 1974, as the *Ark Royal* entered Plymouth Sound, the Fleet Air Arm's historic flight of a Swordfish, Sea Fury and Firefly made a fly-past over the ship. *(Fleet Air Arm Museum)*

ship was no longer steaming ahead but was actually working up to a fast "full astern". Had the first Phantom ditched ahead of the ship? No one below could tell. Inquiring glances were answered by the strident call of the alarm rattler for Emergency Stations. Clearly something serious had happened. Mess decks emptied and passageways filled as everyone not on watch made his way to his Emergency Station where he would report and remain ready. The two hangars and the flight deck were thronged with Fleet Air Arm officers and ratings, and others with no responsibility for ship safety and damage control.'

Unfortunately, despite going 'full astern' for at least two minutes, as the *Bravyy* cut across the *Ark Royal's* bows, the carrier's stem collided with the destroyer's port side and seven Russian seamen were seen to either jump or be thrown overboard by the force of the collision. On board the *Ark Royal* the damage control parties immediately began checking the forward bulkheads and compartments for damage and flooding, and checks were made to ascertain whether anyone was injured or missing.

Simultaneously, a search for the Russian seamen began, with Sea King helicopters from the *Ark Royal* being joined by the seaboats from the carrier and the *Yarmouth*. It was these boats which picked up five of the seven Russian seamen and returned them to the *Bravyy*, but as darkness fell two men were still missing and it had to be assumed that they had drowned. Fortunately there were no casualties on board the *Ark Royal* and the damage was limited to a jagged 3ft by 4ft gash in the ship's stem, about 4ft above the waterline, but luckily very little water had entered the hole. The shipwrights got to work immediately and constructed a 'cement box' and a watertight cofferdam which rendered the carrier seaworthy again at about 4am the following morning, although she remained in the area until after daybreak.

Although the full extent of the damage to the Soviet destroyer will probably never be known, a study of the photographs taken and of damage to the *Ark Royal's* paintwork indicated that there were many points of contact. It seemed that the carrier's starboard anchor had

A weatherbeaten *Ark Royal* returns to Devonport in April 1975.

(Fleet Air Arm Museum)

embedded itself deep into the deckhouse below the destroyer's SAM missile launcher which was situated abaft the after funnel, and there was severe damage to the destroyer's port quarter. Before the *Ark Royal* had stopped, the *Bravyy* appears to have heeled over heavily to starboard, and then pivoted upright and to port beneath the carrier's overhanging flight deck, resulting in her propeller guard cutting open the hole in the carrier's stem with an action like a tin opener. Fortunately quick action by those on the *Ark Royal's* bridge, and the immediate reaction of those on watch in the engine rooms, had prevented a terrible tragedy such as that which had taken place on the night of 9/10 February 1964 when the aircraft carrier HMAS *Melbourne* sliced the destroyer *Voyager* in half, with the loss of 85 lives. At first light helicopter searches were resumed for the two missing Russian seamen and these continued all day without any success. Despite the fact that the International Regulations for Prevention of Collision at Sea are quite definite in stating that ships must keep clear of an aircraft carrier when aircraft are being operated, it was not long before the unhappy incident became a full-scale diplomatic

row and despite the fact that the *Ark Royal* was steaming a straight course during her flying operations, and she was showing appropriate signal lights meaning 'hampered vessel', the Soviet Government blamed the *Ark Royal* for the collision. Captain Lygo, describing the incident later, said that the carrier was launching aircraft, with the Russian ship in her 'usual position on the starboard quarter' three miles away. He made it clear that the Russian destroyer was visible in the darkness, and that visibility was enhanced by the incandescence of the Phantoms' exhausts. He went on to say that the impression in the carrier was that the Soviet destroyer had meant to steam starboard astern of the *Ark Royal*, but when she came to within half a mile she turned parallel with the *Ark Royal* and then came up on the bow - 'a difficult situation' given the fact that a carrier turns in a mile and a destroyer in 300 to 400 yards. Captain Lygo said that he had stopped launching the Phantoms, flashed the signal 'You are standing into danger' and ordered a midshipman to call out the destroyer's range in cable lengths. Then, about two minutes before impact, he ordered all the engines half astern, and almost

immediately full astern and hard to port in order to lessen the blow. When the destroyer disappeared from view directly beneath the *Ark Royal's* bows, the carrier was doing just three to four knots. As a Member of Parliament commented in the House of Commons: '...an incident of this sort had become inevitable in the long run.'

Once the search and rescue operations had been called off 'Exercise Lime Jug' resumed, and on its conclusion the *Ark Royal* set course for Malta where more permanent repairs to her stem could be carried out. During the afternoon of Saturday 14 November she stood by HMS *Fife* when the destroyer suffered a major fire in her main gas turbine room, and the Sea King helicopters airlifted foam and fire-fighting equipment to the *Fife*. Two days later the *Ark Royal* arrived in Grand Harbour to carry out a nine-day maintenance period, having been shadowed yet again, this time by two Soviet destroyers which stuck with her until she was about ten miles off Malta where they anchored just outside territorial waters, ready to take up the trail the moment she left Malta. After her self-maintenance period in Malta the carrier left Grand Harbour on Wednesday 25 November for five days of flying exercises off the island. During this period two

notable events took place; the first, on 28 November was the 'Malta Sea Day' when flying displays were arranged for local dignitaries who had been invited on board. The following day was 'Hot-Air Balloon Day' when an unusual addition to the carrier's flying strength became airborne while the carrier was near the southern coast of Malta. The hot-air balloon, named *Bristol Belle*, carried Lts Terry Adams and Howard Draper on a flight from the ship to Malta, lasting just 30 minutes. Initially the course taken by the balloon seemed to indicate that it would miss the island and land in the sea, but a judicious application of heat took it up to 2,000 feet where the winds blew it inshore. As it was the first time that a hot-air balloon had been launched from a ship at sea, a special one-day cover was designed which helped to raise £1,000 for the ship's welfare funds.

After further exercises in the area the *Ark Royal* put into Naples on Thursday 3 December for a five-day stay, her only real 'foreign' visit during the first leg of the commission. Having been able to berth alongside, the time spent in the city was a great success, with trips being organized to Rome, Pompeii and other places of interest. Leaving Naples on Tuesday 8 December there was time to fit in a 48-hour flying exercise off Sardinia, before course was set for home. The passage was broken by a 24-hour stopover in Gibraltar, when there was a last-minute opportunity to buy Christmas presents, and after flying off the serviceable aircraft to their stations, the *Ark Royal* docked alongside at Devonport on Friday 18 December 1970, to carry out a three-month Docking & Essential Defects (DED) period and, even more importantly, for her officers and men to take their Christmas leave.

During the time that the *Ark Royal* spent under refit at Devonport during the early months of 1971, there were two notable events. The first was the announcement from the Government that the Board of Inquiry into the collision between the *Ark Royal* and the *Bravyy* had come to the conclusion that no blame attached to any Royal Naval personnel. The second, on Tuesday 9 March 1971, was a change of command for the *Ark Royal*, when Captain Lygo was relieved by Captain J. O. Roberts RN. During the Second World War the carrier's new commanding officer had served as a midshipman in HM Ships *Renown* and *Tartar*, and as a sub lieutenant in the destroyer HMS *Serapis*. In 1944 he trained as a pilot and following this he served in HMS *Triumph*, HMAS *Vengeance* and HMAS *Melbourne*. As the commanding officer of 803 Squadron he served in HMS *Eagle*, flying Sea Hawks during that carrier's third commission. In 1960 he was appointed commanding officer of the frigate HMS *St Bride's Bay* and after serving in the Admiralty, in 1964 he was appointed as the commanding officer of the brand new Leander-class frigate HMS *Galatea*. Following this he served a further spell in the Admiralty before being appointed to the *Ark Royal*.

On Thursday 15 April 1971 the *Ark Royal* left Devonport to carry out her post-refit trials in the Channel, before steaming north to the Clyde and round to the Moray Firth where her work-up and flying trials were completed, after which she took a three-day break at Rosyth in early May. After leaving Rosyth the *Ark Royal* carried out trials with RAF Harrier aircraft and, in fact, it was the first time an RAF fighter squadron had taken off from a carrier since the Second World War. More significantly, perhaps, the ten days of trials previewed what would become a new era of carrier-borne flying in the Royal Navy during the 1980s and into the 21st century. Despite the *Ark Royal's* reprieve, the axing of CVA 01 and the imminent withdrawal of the fixed-wing aircraft carriers was a great blow to the Fleet Air Arm and the plans drawn up in the late 1960s and early 1970s for what were described as 'through deck cruisers' appeared to hold out hope for fixed-wing flying with the Hawker Harrier. It was a project which the First Sea Lord, Admiral Sir Michael Le Fanu, supported vigorously and it is reported that he kept a model Harrier on his desk at the Ministry of Defence. Exercises had shown that the RAF could not provide adequate protection for the fleet at sea, even in home waters, and it had not been forgotten how in December 1941, contrary to all their promises, the RAF

had failed to provide protection for the ill-fated *Prince of Wales* and *Repulse* off the east coast of Malaya. However, despite this clear deficiency in their capabilities, the RAF were vehemently opposed to any long-term resurrection of naval fixed-wing aviation, and Admiral Le Fanu had both politicians and RAF chiefs to contend with in his battle for what eventually became a new generation of light fleet aircraft carriers. Nevertheless, the trials with the *Ark Royal* in early 1971 were carried out by four Harriers and their pilots from No 1 Squadron, RAF Wittering, in Cambridgeshire. The pilots there had been training for some time on an area which had been marked out on their runway as a deck area measuring 560 feet by 160 feet. Some minor modifications had been made to the four Harriers, including the addition of clamps and outriggers for deck lashing, the marking of the tailplane angle for precise take-off settings, and some changes to the navigation systems. The pilots also underwent instruction from the Navy in underwater escape techniques. As Hawker had already supplied 60 Harriers to the United States which were specially modified for flying on and off the decks of ships, the Fleet Air Arm could clearly be optimistic, intending as they were to operate the Harriers from a short ramp on the flight deck of the through deck cruisers, thereby improving the aircraft's capabilities. Meanwhile, on board the *Ark Royal* the ten days of trials were keenly observed by Government ministers, the Vice-Chiefs of both the Air Staff and the Naval Staff and nine other navies, including the US Navy, which had already spent £50 million on the aircraft. The trials were interrupted for a short period when the carrier anchored off Lossiemouth, and on Friday 21 May the *Ark Royal* returned to Devonport for a short maintenance period.

It was on Wednesday 2 June when the ship next left Plymouth Sound, and after landing on her Air Group she sailed south-west, bound for the Caribbean. Three days into the passage she was off the Azores where, with a diversionary airfield available, the opportunity was taken to carry out flying exercises. Soon afterwards, when the *Ark Royal* was some 360 miles south-west of the Azores, Phantom 007 which had refused to take off from Yeovilton the previous week, was landed on, making its 1,700-mile flight something of a record. It was not long before the temperatures were such that pale white skins became red and sunburned and goofing became a very popular occupation indeed. On Friday 11 June the carrier anchored off Puerto Rico for a pre-exercise briefing which was held on board the giant US Navy carrier USS *America*. Next day the *Ark Royal* weighed anchor to take part in missile firing and carrier exercises, code-named 'Rimex' and 'Barex', in the US Navy's Atlantic Fleet Weapons Range. Four days of these were immediately followed by 'Exercise Opredex', which was, in fact, the *America's* Operational Readiness Inspection which terminated in a passage northwards for a

The *Ark Royal* paves the way for her successor as she carries out trials with the Sea Harrier.

(Fleet Air Arm Museum)

maximum air strike on military installations on the island of Bermuda. Finally, after flying off most of the embarked Air Group to the US Navy's air station at Cecil Field, Jacksonville, the *Ark Royal* steamed south and, at 7am on Tuesday 22 June, she entered Port Everglades Harbor, Fort Lauderdale, Florida. With the decks manned for a full ceremonial 'Procedure Alpha', and aircraft ranged on the flight deck, the *Ark Royal* was an impressive sight as she berthed on the landward side of the Intercoastal Waterway, just inland from the coast. The berth was close to where, until only four months previously, the old Cunard liner *Queen Elizabeth* had been moored during her unsuccessful two-year career as a showpiece. As such the area was part of a fresh, clean port complex which was in stark contrast to Devonport Dockyard. As is always the case when HM Ships visit US ports, the hospitality ashore was both spontaneous and magnificent, and nearby Miami also proved very popular. When the ships left the port a week later there were some very sad faces both on board and on the quayside, and next day when the carrier berthed at the US Naval Base of Mayport, 300 miles north of Fort Lauderdale, for a seven-day self-maintenance period, several enthusiastic souls actually made the journey back south for a long weekend. However, during the stay at Mayport staff of the depot ship USS *Yosemite*, which was acting as the host ship, worked very hard on behalf of the *Ark Royal's* ship's company. They advertised in the press and on radio and television, for girls to attend the ship's company dance which was held at Jacksonville Beach, and also arranged coach tours to the Space Centre at Cape Canaveral and other places of interest, as well as putting on a full sporting programme. As so often happened, when the visit came to an end on Wednesday 7 July there were sad faces on board and tears on the quayside as the *Ark Royal* set course for the Caribbean once again.

Four days after leaving Mayport, on Sunday 11 July, the carrier was once again in the waters off Puerto Rico and carrying out Phantom hot weather trials in the US Navy's exercise areas. These concluded with 48 hours at anchor off the island of St Thomas in the US Virgin Islands, where recreational leave was granted, and the idyllic beaches provided the venue for two banyans and barbeques, followed by a 'Sods Opera' in the upper hangar, which were enjoyed by all who took part. On Wednesday 21 July the *Ark Royal* set course for Devonport and seven days later, on 28 July, when she was some 300 miles south-west of Land's End, she met the renowned yachtsman, Chay Blyth, who was nearing the end of his epic single-handed circumnavigation of the world, travelling against the prevailing westerlies.

Two days after flying off the Air Group, the carrier secured to C buoy in Plymouth Sound, where the weekend was spent embarking an enormous amount of equipment for a BBC Television team who were to trasnmit a live broadcast from the ship. The end result was 'Exercise Lymelight' which involved live transmissions from the flight deck, in Flyco, from a Sea King, from the frigates *Eurylas* and *Galatea*, the submarine *Sealion* and the RFAs *Olmeda* and *Regent*. The whole exercise took place in Lyme Bay, about 30 miles off the Dorset coast, and viewers ashore could watch an anti-submarine search by a frigate and helicopter, catapult launches from the *Ark Royal*, air-to-surface rocket firing and arrested recoveries of the carrier's Phantoms and Buccaneers. At the end of the exercise the carrier returned to Plymouth Sound where, on Sunday 5 September, 1,500 relatives of the officers and men were embarked for a 'Families Day', where flying displays were staged in the Channel off the Eddystone Light. As a bonus there were photographic displays, a cinema show for the children, and the Royal Marines Band Beat Retreat on the flight deck. The finale was the passage up harbour into Devonport Dockyard with a commentator describing all the features of interest. Before they left the ship the BBC TV team were presented with a magnificent giant 'oggie' for their filming of the programme, 'At Sea With the Navy'. Once alongside, the ship went into dockyard hands for a 30-day assisted maintenance period, during which the annual Navy Days event was held and, as always, Devonport had a formidable flotilla on show led by the *Ark Royal* and the commando carrier, HMS *Bulwark*.

The refit came to an end on Tuesday 14 September 1971 when the *Ark Royal* sailed for the Moray Firth to embark her Air Group and to take part in 'Exercise Royal Knight' in the traditional hunting grounds of the Western Fleet, in the North Sea and up into the Arctic Ocean in the cold waters off the North Cape, where Russian Tupolev TU-16 (Badger) aircraft were able to get some close-up shots of the *Ark Royal*, which would have been of great interest to them as the Soviet Navy was building its own Kiev class of aircraft carriers. During this exercise the *Ark Royal* operated as part of a NATO strike fleet which included other Royal Navy ships as well as American, Dutch, German and Norwegian units, and on conclusion of the manoeuvres the 'wash-up' was held at Rosyth, following which the carrier joined a 48-hour exercise 'Magic Sword IV' in the North Sea. On this occasion the *Ark Royal* flew the flag of the new C-in-C Western Fleet, Admiral Sir Edward Ashmore, while she operated in close liaison with the USS *Independence* before steaming south to Portsmouth where, on Saturday 9 October, the families of the Pompey men were embarked at Spithead for the passage up harbour. It was the *Ark Royal's* first visit to Portsmouth since March 1965, and her presence drew large crowds onto the Southsea seafront to watch her enter harbour. During the three-week stay alongside Middle Slip Jetty there was some unwelcome publicity when fires broke out, and on one occasion firemen toiled for six hours to extinguish the blaze. It was later established that none of

The ship's company man ship for the Queen's Silver Jubilee Fleet Review.   (L. Fleming)

them had been started deliberately, then in the final week of her stay a call was received stating that there was a bomb on board which led to a full-scale alert, although it turned out to be a hoax.

Saturday 30 October saw the *Ark Royal* departing from Portsmouth to land on the Air Group in preparation for flying exercises in the South-Western Approaches before steaming south for the Mediterranean. After passing through the Strait of Gibraltar early on Thursday 4 November, during the forenoon the engines were stopped in the approximate position of the sinking of her predecessor almost 30 years previously and a memorial service was held on the flight deck. Next day the *Ark Royal* docked in Palma, Majorca, where the large port facilities were able to accommodate the carrier as well as two cruise ships. It was one of those rare occasions when the *Ark Royal* was able to go alongside which made for a more convenient and enjoyable stay. Prominent among the out-of-season tourists on the island were a large number of Blackpool landladies, who were enjoying their own seaside holiday, and when the ship was opened to the public thousands of

local people went on board. During the weekend the Royal Marines Band gave open-air concerts in the gardens of the cathedral at Palma which were attended by large crowds, whilst the ship's company enjoyed a splendid run ashore. Four days in the port were followed by 'Exercise Med Passex' with the USS *Independence*, which involved a period of cross-operating aircraft in the Ionian Sea. After two more days of independent exercises off Malta, the *Ark Royal* steamed into Grand Harbour and secured to head and stern buoys in Bighi Bay, abreast Gun Wharf Jetty. Much to the disappointment of the ship's company, the stay in Malta was limited to just five days and it was then followed by some hectic flying exercises, first off Decimomannu, Sardinia, where the weather conditions were poor, and then in the Alboran Channel, east of Gibraltar, where visibility was so good that the Sierra Nevada mountains in Spain could be seen, 60 miles away, as well as the Rif Mountains of Morocco. Finally, in early December the *Ark Royal* berthed alongside Gibraltar's South Mole for two days, in time for the ship's company to take part in the 'Top of the Rock' race. In the event the carrier entered 300 runners,

The *Ark Royal* and her ship's company looking very smart as they await the Queen at Spithead. *(M. Lennon)*

plus a giant teddy bear which raised £20 for charity. After leaving Gibraltar the *Ark Royal* steamed out into the Atlantic Ocean and set course for Devonport, where she arrived on Tuesday 7 December for a dockyard assisted maintenance period while the officers and men took their Christmas and New Year leave.

It was on a bleak Thursday in the third week of January 1972 that the *Ark Royal* left Devonport once again to set course west for a transatlantic crossing to the Virginia Capes area for joint exercises with the US Navy. Six days into the passage an order was received diverting the carrier into the Caribbean, following reports that Guatemalan troops were being massed on the frontier with British Honduras (Belize). British Honduras was a coastal strip of land in Central America, next to Guatemala, to which British pioneers had gone in the 17th century to cut timber, and even in the 20th century the hardwood timber trade was still the mainstay of this small colony's economy. The land area of the colony, which incuded swamps, was 8,600 square miles and its population of 90,000 was a mix of American Indians, Negroes and Europeans. The main political problem which dogged the colony was caused by sporadic claims to British Honduras by Guatemala, and mid-January 1972 had seen the Guatemalan Army being sent to the province of Petan, which bordered both British

Honduras and Mexico, ostensibly to hunt down a group of rebels in the area. Although there was no direct evidence to suggest the Guatemalan Army was going to invade, it was clear that they were testing British resolve to defend the self-governing colony and, in the event, the British Government acted swiftly and decisively. As well as dispatching the *Ark Royal* to the area, the County-class destroyer HMS *London* and the Leander-class frigates *Dido* and *Phoebe* were sent into the Caribbean from the Atlantic Ocean, and troops of the Grenadier Guards and the Army's 24th Airportable Brigade were also flown into the colony. As the *Ark Royal* headed for the area, by way of the Florida Strait and the Yucutan, revolutions were increased and she steamed at speed into a head sea, with a heavy swell and a wind speed of 70 knots blowing over the flight deck. Fortunately, structural damage was limited to a buckled 3T starboard boat deck, plus some broken whip aerials and guard rails. On Friday 28 January, when the *Ark Royal* was south-west of Bermuda, two Buccaneers of 809 Squadron were launched for Belize to overfly the capital and to reassure the residents of Britain's resolve to defend them. In addition two tankers were launched so that the 'strike' pair could be refuelled in mid-air on both the outward and homeward flights. The mission entailed six hours of continuous flying and a round trip of 2,600 miles, for which the crews were awarded the Boyd Trophy in recognition of a fine demonstration of naval air power. It was also, however, a sober reminder that, once again, the RAF were unable to cover the air defence of the colony and ironically, back home in Portsmouth, the events in British Honduras coincided with the final homecoming and decommissioning of the *Ark Royal's* older sister, HMS *Eagle*.

During the evening of Saturday 29 January the *Ark Royal* was ordered to proceed to the US Navy's exercise areas off Florida's Key West Naval Base, to carry out flying exercises and await developments in the political situation with Guatemala. Happily by Wednesday 2 February, with the crisis over, the carrier was able to set course for New York to keep her schedule for a seven-day visit to the city. After the tropical climes of the Caribbean, the morning of Friday 4 February was bitterly cold with a wind of 20 knots blowing over the flight deck and the air temperature well below freezing as the *Ark Royal* entered the Hudson River, but she looked a magnificent sight as she steamed under Verrazaro Narrows Bridge and through Upper New York Bay. Originally it had been intended that the ship would secure to head and stern buoys which had been specially laid for her alongside the centre of Manhattan, about a mile and a half from the Cunard Pier to which the ship's boat service would run. On her previous visit to the city she had actually berthed alongside the Cunard Pier, but with the withdrawal from service of the liners *Queen Mary* and *Queen Elizabeth*, the mooring had silted up and it could not provide the 40 feet of water the *Ark Royal* needed. Although he would have preferred calmer conditions, Captain Roberts was confident that the carrier could be successfully moored at buoys. With the help of six tugs the *Ark Royal* was manoeuvred into position, but suddenly, just as it seemed the operation had been a success, a shackle securing the head buoy to its mooring broke and the ship's bow swung free with the buoy attached to it. As the carrier was abeam the main stream of the Hudson, immediate action was needed and fortunately, with steam on the main engines and with tugs assisting, she was soon under way once again - but without a berth. Initially she anchored off Staten Island in the Quarantine Anchorage, and that evening only those with wives and relatives ashore were granted leave. Next day she moved to a permanent anchorage about a mile off St George's Coastguard Base at Staten Island, and the base soon became swamped with the *Ark's* liberty men as they made use of the landing and shore facilities there. Although it was a last-minute arrangement, the coastguard personnel went out of their way to ensure that all amenities were available to the *Ark Royal*, and the boats' crews were also worthy of praise, for in the freezing weather the sea spray washing over them froze as soon as it hit the launches. Nevertheless, despite the cold weather, the customary warm welcome from the New Yorkers made for another very successful visit, even though the bright lights of Manhattan were some six miles away and it meant a long boat ride, a half-mile walk and a 30-minute ferry trip to get there.

After leaving a very cold New York Harbor on Friday 11 February 1972, the *Ark Royal* steamed south to warmer waters once again to carry out flying exercises off Puerto Rico, during which, on 15 February, a Buccaneer was lost over the side when it broke free of its lashings. That weekend the carrier anchored off Virgin Gordo, one of the larger of the British Virgin Islands, which is approximately eight miles square and with only about 1,200 inhabitants. Here the unspoilt beaches with beautiful clear water and the hot, sunny weather provided ideal conditions for banyan parties with barbeques laid on by the supply department. The Royal Marines Band gave a concert for the residents of the nearby island of Tortola, whose cricket team beat the ship's eleven by nine wickets, but luckily the *Ark's* football team subsequently salvaged some pride by beating the Tortola team 6 - 3. Back on board 809 Squadron arranged an evening's entertainment of 'horse racing', otherwise known as 'Royal Arskot', and a fancy dress competition. With everyone having recharged their batteries it was time for 'Exercise Lantreadex', which was the Operational Readiness Inspection for the modernized aircraft carrier USS *Franklin D. Roosevelt*. The exercise took place in the Atlantic Fleet Weapons Range north of Puerto Rico and among the operations were missile firing, a tactical 'war at sea' and for the grand finale, a 'sinkex', in which a decommissioned US Navy destroyer was used as a target for live missiles, shells and bombs. First of all the unfortunate target was attacked by American and British guided missile destroyers and then the *Franklin D. Roosevelt* kindly allowed the *Ark Royal's* Air Group to have first go at bombing the concrete-filled former destroyer. Attacked by 809 Squadron carrying four 1,000lb bombs and 892 Squadron with ten 540lb bombs, the target ship received ten direct hits and it was sent to the bottom before the *FDR's* Air Group had a chance to drop their bombs. During the exercise the *Ark's* Buccaneers cross-operated with the American carrier, with two of them being landed on and catapulted off again. On conclusion of the exercise the *Ark Royal* anchored off Roosevelt Roads, Puerto Rico, on the last day of February, and the sports teams managed to get ashore before the carrier left for home on Wednesday 1 March. The transatlantic passage was one of extremes, ranging from flat calm seas which allowed flight deck athletics and a Royal Marines Band ceremony of Beating Retreat to take place on 4 March, to storm force winds only two days later, when 38ft waves lashed the flight deck with sheets of spray which drenched the parked aircraft and generally gave the ship quite a battering. Seven days after leaving Puerto Rico, on Wednesday 8 March when the ship was off the Scilly Islands, the squadrons were flown off to their respective stations and next day the *Ark Royal* berthed at Devonport

The *Ark Royal* leaves Malta on 12 November 1977.

(M. Cassar)

to begin a three-month assisted maintenance period.

It was Tuesday 6 June 1972 when the *Ark Royal* sailed for her post-refit trials, shakedown and work-up. By now it was becoming more and more difficult to tell when one commission ended and the next started, for there was virtually a continuous commission system operating with what was known as 'trickle drafting'. This meant that on this occasion there were 500 new members of the ship's company embarked, and their training programme had to be combined with machinery and systems trials. During the first few days of the work-up the ship anchored for periods in Weymouth Bay and Torbay, and during one of the days at sea a group of Wrens were flown out to the carrier from RNAS Culdrose. Four of the Wrens were married to members of the ship's company, and this gave them the opportunity of seeing where their husbands lived and worked. Four days of trials in the Channel were followed by the first phase of the flying work-up in the South-Western Approaches, then on Saturday 17 June the *Ark Royal* appeared in the Firth of Clyde to carry out main propulsion machinery trials on the Arran Measured Mile,

where conditions were more sheltered than in the choppy waters of the Atlantic Ocean. The second phase of the work-up was completed as the ship steamed around Cape Wrath, past the Old Man of Hoy and through the Pentland Firth to Scotland's east coast. One of the highlights of this period was a four-day visit by the late Sir Bernard Miles, the distinguished actor and founder of the Mermaid Theatre. During his visit Sir Bernard charmed and amused everyone, entertaining the officers and the men, as well as appearing on the *Ark Royal's* closed-circuit television, but unfortunately he had to make an unscheduled visit to the sickbay after cutting his head on a hatch coaming and needing stitches to the wound. After this he was presented with a special 'Sir Bernie' hard hat for the rest of his stay.

Following the final phase of the work-up, which was also carried out in the South-Western Approaches, the *Ark Royal* put into Portsmouth on Friday 30 June as part of a series of ship visits to various UK ports for a 'Meet The Navy' recruiting drive. During the nine-day stay more than 1,000 schoolchildren, head teachers and careers advisers from dozens of schools and colleges in the south of

HMS *Ark Royal* with RFA *Olmeda* during her last WESTLANT deployment in April 1978.

(Fleet Air Arm Museum)

Below:
The *Ark Royal* sails from Port Everglades, Florida, in June 1978 after a two-week visit to the USA. *(Imperial War Museum MH25105)*

England were welcomed on board. It was also a period for departmental inspections, self-maintenance and Admiral's Divisions, and the Prime Minister, Edward Heath, also visited the carrier at this time, flying in direct from the Wimbledon Tennis Championships. The departmental inspections were part of an overall ship inspection which would culminate in the Operational Readiness Inspection, but prior to this there was a three-day exercise, 'West Hoe', which took place between 13 and 16 July, off the west coast of Ireland. Fog hampered much of the exercise which involved a strong fleet of ships including, in addition to the *Ark Royal*, the commando carrier *Bulwark*, the cruiser *Blake*, the destroyer *Caprice* and the frigates *Achilles*, *Jaguar* and *Lynx*. The *Ark Royal's* 24-hour Operational Readiness Inspection commenced at midnight on 16/17 July and most of the evolutions, including the disembarkation of the Air Group, went smoothly. On its conclusion the carrier anchored in Torbay, although problems were encountered when the time came to weigh anchor and she arrived at Devonport later than scheduled on Tuesday 18 July to carry out essential maintenance.

During the stay alongside there was a change of command on Tuesday 22 August, when Captain A. D. Cassidi RN took over from Rear-Admiral Roberts, who had been promoted and appointed Flag Officer Sea Training. Captain Cassidi had joined the Royal Navy as a cadet during the Second World War and he had qualified as a pilot in 1945. Following this he served in a number of squadrons and in 1955 he was appointed as the commanding officer of 820 (Gannet) Squadron. He served as the First Lieutenant of HMS *Protector* and he had commanded the frigate HMS *Whitby* and the destroyer *Undaunted* as Captain (D) at Portland.

On the last day of August 1972 the *Ark Royal* sailed from Devonport to take a westabout route by way of the Irish Sea to the Moray Firth, where the Air Group was embarked for seven days of flying exercises prior to a NATO show of strength, 'Exercise Strong Express', which got under way on Thursday 14 September in the North Sea and off the North Cape. It was the biggest NATO exercise ever held, involving 300 ships and 64,000 men, and the Royal Navy's contingent was headed by the *Ark Royal* with HM Ships *Albion*, *Blake*, *Fearless*, *Fife*, *Juno*, *Norfolk*, *Achilles* and *Arethusa* also participating, as well as minesweepers and the submarines *Conqueror*, *Dreadnought*, *Alliance*, *Oberon*, *Grampus*, *Rorqual* and *Walrus*. Representing the US Navy were the aircraft carriers *John F. Kennedy* and *Intrepid*. During the manoeuvres the men were testing methods of anti-submarine warfare, minelaying and the control of merchant shipping, as well as practising the landing of 3,000 British, US and Dutch marines in Norway, who were 'opposed' by 4,000 Norwegian troops. The *Ark Royal's* fighters, which were providing CAP cover for the fleet, were presented with an

excellent opportunity for training by the large numbers of Russian long-range maritime patrol aircraft which maintained strict surveillance of the activities. Their presence also provided ample justification for the retention of a fixed-wing capability for the Fleet Air Arm. On completion of the exercise a six-day 'wash-up' was held at Rosyth, following which the carrier undertook flying exercises in the North Sea in some very inclement weather before she steamed up the picturesque Oslo Fjord on the beautifully clear morning of Thursday 12 October to anchor at the head of the fjord, about a mile from the City Hall. The five days spent in the Norwegian capital proved highly enjoyable, if somewhat expensive, and for the Royal Marines detachment it was a busy few days with the band playing at an official reception on the first night as well as putting on two concerts ashore. On Sunday 15 October the band and detachment were landed at the City Hall from where they marched to the city's university to give a concert and perform the ever-popular ceremony of Beating Retreat. Next day the musicians played in the grounds of Ulleval Hospital, to the great delight of the patients there, and some of the youngsters from the adjoining children's hospital even joined in with the entertainment.

After leaving Oslo on Monday 16 October, the *Ark Royal* steamed south, back to the UK and Portsmouth where, after disembarking the squadrons, she arrived on the morning of Friday 20 October, to begin an 18-day self-maintenance period. Flying off the aircraft was another milestone in Fleet Air Arm history, with the eight Buccaneers of 809 Squadron joining their new base, RAF Honington, for the first time, while the Phantoms of 892 Squadron proceeded to RAF Leuchars. During the stay in Portsmouth there was a very nostalgic reunion for 250 survivors of the third *Ark Royal*, in their first meeting on board their old ship's successor. There were many stories to tell, including the seaman who still kept the key to his old kit locker in the hope that, one day, he would be able to recover his belongings. After the veterans had toured the *Ark Royal* they were served refreshments before attending the nostalgic Sunset ceremony, played as only the Royal Marines Band can play it. That evening the reunion adjourned to Southsea's Royal Beach Hotel where, no doubt, many more reminiscences were shared.

With her maintenance period completed, the *Ark Royal* left Portsmouth on Tuesday 7 November to recover her Air Group for a week's flying in the South-Western Approaches, which included trials of a new Martel missile by two Buccaneers from Boscombe Down, before leaving UK shores for the Mediterranean. During the voyage south she operated with French naval aircraft off the coast of Portugal, when she acted as a target for strikes by them and by Royal Navy submarines. Ten days after leaving Portsmouth the carrier arrived at Barcelona, which provided a welcome break for the ship's company, even

A US Navy Phantom lands on the *Ark Royal*.

(Imperial War Museum HU75012)

though they were anchored a mile off the end of the port's mile-long breakwater, which itself was two miles from the city. However, despite this handicap, the charming port with its wide streets, colourful shops, bars and restaurants provided something for everyone, with more favourable prices than those encountered in Oslo, and warm, sunny weather into the bargain. After leaving Barcelona on Wednesday 22 November the *Ark Royal* steamed north-east to French waters off the Cote d' Azur where, in the French Navy's exercise area around the island of Hyeres, she carried out flying exercises before taking part in a Royal Naval exercise, 'Corsica 72', an amphibious landing on Corsica's west coast. The Royal Navy's 'heavies' included the *Ark Royal, Bulwark, Fearless* and *Intrepid,* as well as the frigate *Arethusa* and the RFAs *Lyness, Regent, Resource* and *Olwen.* The other ships of the 'invasion' fleet had sailed from Malta for the assault on the beaches, and the *Ark Royal* rendezvoused with them to provide air support from the Buccaneers of 809 Squadron. Opposing the landings were the Second Parachute Regiment of the French Foreign Legion and aircraft from the French Air Force. Towards the

end of the exercise the mistral came whistling down the Rhone Valley generating Force 11 winds and heavy seas around the coastal areas, but by then it was time for the *Ark Royal* to move on to the area off Decimomannu, Sardinia, where for two days she cross-operated with the USS *Forrestal* and exchanged Buccaneers and Phantoms for some A7 Corsairs, A6 Intruders and US Navy style F4B Phantoms. Finally, on Wednesday 6 December she docked alongside Gibraltar's South Mole for two days, which was a good opportunity for last-minute Christmas shopping. Once again the ship's athletes broke all records for the fastest time in the 'Top of the Rock' race and, after taking the Fleet Trophy, the *Ark Royal* left the colony for a choppy passage to Devonport, where she arrived on Tuesday 12 December for seasonal leave and an assisted maintenance period.

The New Year of 1973 saw Britain inextricably linked to Europe when she joined the EEC, along with Ireland and Denmark. It was a clear sign that the country was turning away from the Commonwealth in favour of much closer ties with her European neighbours which for centuries had been rivals, both politically and economically. As for the

Ark Royal, the new year signified her forthcoming spring deployment, the first part of which began on Thursday 25 January when she left Devonport for flying operations in the South-Western Approaches, but bad weather in the area and the lack of diversionary airfields anywhere in south-west England hampered the proceedings and on Friday 2 February she turned south to take part in a medium-scale NATO exercise, 'Sunny Seas', off the coast of Portugal. Here she was joined by NATO's Standing Force North Atlantic which consisted of Dutch, Canadian, Norwegian, US and RN vessels. Seven days later she joined some 27 other Royal Navy units at Gibraltar which had assembled to take part in a series of exercises in the Mediterranean, code-named 'Medtrain 73'. Although these exercises were regular occurrences, it was unusual to see such a concentration of naval ships and the sheer number of liberty men ashore strained to the limit the facilities which Gibraltar could offer. During the three days in the colony the C-in-C Fleet, Admiral Sir Edward Ashmore, paid a visit and spent some time on board the *Ark Royal*. Also taking part in the exercises were the cruiser *Tiger*, the destroyers *Glamorgan* and *Norfolk*, the nuclear-powered submarines *Dreadnought* and *Conqueror*, plus frigates and RFAs. The comprehensive series of weapon training exercises started on Wednesday 14 February with an anti-submarine phase, 'Sardex', which took place off Sardinia, and with the USS *Forrestal* in the vicinity, the two carriers cross-operated and exchanged Phantoms. The operations were wound up on 22 February and next day the *Ark Royal* put into Malta for an assisted maintenance period, aided by part of the Fleet Maintenance Group who were flown out from the UK. The Maltese people gave the *Ark Royal* a warm welcome when she arrived and berthed in Kalkara Creek, between Fort St Angelo and the old Bighi Hospital. For a number of reasons the carrier had to be moored with her stern tucked well into the creek, and this involved some cautious manoeuvring just inside the harbour entrance while she was swung round and pushed back into her berth. It had been intended to provide a pontoon walkway from the ship to St Angelo, but strong winds and a swell inside the harbour made the plan impractical - much to the relief of the local dghaisamen. Among the events during the eight-day stay was a visit by Admiral of the Fleet Lord Mountbatten, Ceremonial Divisions, and a group of the ship's company undertook the renovation of an orphanage at Zetjun, between Valletta and Marsaxlokk. On Tuesday 6 March the *Ark Royal* left Malta to participate in 'Exercise Ruler', which took her on a roundabout passage out of the Mediterranean by way of the Strait of Messina, the Bonifacio Strait between Sardinia and Corsica, and then between the Balearic Islands. Embarked for the passage was a film crew who were making a documentary titled 'Bequest to the Nation', about life in the *Ark Royal*, and on leaving the Mediterranean the carrier headed home. Whilst off the Portuguese coast a number of aircraft were flown off, and next day whilst crossing the Bay of Biscay two of the Buccaneers returned to the ship, one of them bearing a Government minister. Finally, on Thursday 15 March the *Ark Royal* steamed up harbour to berth alongside 5 and 6 wharves of Devonport Dockyard for leave and maintenance.

The final deployment of the commission would follow a similar pattern to that of June 1971 and would in fact be the longest, which meant that her long refit would be delayed by several months. After leaving Devonport on Monday 30 April the squadrons were embarked for five days of flying exercises in the Channel, following which the carrier set course for Puerto Rico in company with HM Ships *Devonshire*, *Diomede* and *Rothesay*. Whilst on passage, advantage was taken of the presence of a French naval force, including the aircraft carrier *Foch*, to carry out 'Exercise Passex', and on Monday 14 May the *Ark Royal* arrived at her destination of Roosevelt Roads, Puerto Rico. However, less than 24 hours later she was at sea once again and carrying out intensive flying operations in the Atlantic Fleet's Weapons Range. It was during this period that the *Ark Royal* and *Devonshire*, the night planeguard, were involved in a highly efficient night sea rescue when Gannet 043 of 849B Flight suffered an engine failure after launching from the carrier. Although his crew baled out, the pilot was unable to get clear, but he managed to ditch the aircraft about four miles from the ship where he was picked up by one of 824 Squadron's Sea Kings. Meanwhile, the two observers were rescued by the seaboats from the *Devonshire* and the *Ark Royal*, with the entire operation taking only 29 minutes from the first distress call being made.

During this period the C-in-C Fleet visited the ship, as did HRH The Prince of Wales, then a lieutenant, who arrived by jackstay with other officers of similar seniority to spend a busy day on board broadening their knowledge of naval operations. The final phases of the exercises were carried out with only three of the carrier's main engines operational, then, in near windless conditions, flying was curtailed and the ship anchored in Magers Bay, St Thomas, for two days of weekend banyans.

The main event of the deployment was 'Exercise Lantreadex' which started on the last day of May. The *Ark Royal* and her escorts rendezvoused with a US Navy task force 700 miles north-west of the Puerto Rican exercise areas, off the northern Bahamas, then the whole group, consisting of four RN units, three RFAs and two US naval units, made an 'opposed' passage back to the area off Puerto Rico. The exercise was primarily intended as the work-up of the USS *Franklin D. Roosevelt* and it took the form of the familiar 'war at sea' phase, a missile firing exercise and a 'sinkex'. On Friday 8 June, much to everyone's relief in the hot weather, the *Ark Royal* steamed into Port Everglades, Fort Lauderdale, Florida, where the local population made the ship's company very welcome

Replenishment at sea during 1978.

(L. Fleming)

during their six-day visit. There then followed a further four days of flying in the area off Jacksonville, where the delay in starting her long refit made itself felt in the form of machinery defects, with only three main engines serviceable and problems with the fresh water evaporators and the waist catapult. Fortunately a call at Mayport allowed for some maintenance, and some enjoyable runs ashore where many new friends were made and old haunts revisited during the 11-day stay. The return transatlantic passage was beset with mechanical problems, including the evaporators playing up again, but it did not prevent flying exercises and a Grand Charity Fete being held before the carrier arrived off Cape Wrath on Monday 9 July. Over the next two weeks she took part in the exercises 'JMC 168' and 'Sally Forth 73', both of which were watched closely by Soviet warships. No one really missed a cancelled weekend at Scapa Flow, and at Rosyth, where the fleet had gathered, liberty men were restricted during the six days by a long boat ride to the shore. Finally, in the third week of July came the day which everyone had been looking forward to when, in the early hours of a summer morning, the *Ark Royal* secured to C buoy in Plymouth Sound. The day had been set aside for families and the first of 1,600 guests embarked at 7.40am for a day at sea with the Air Group putting on a fine display. Flying from their shore bases, the aircraft included the Sea Kings of 824 Squadron and the SAR Wessex, out of which 'fell' a well-disguised ship's diver, fooling many of the spectators who thought it was a 'lucky Granny' taking the flight as a raffle prize. Needless to say, he was swiftly and efficiently recovered. One of the Gannets demonstrated flare dropping, after which the Phantoms and Buccaneers of 892 and 809 Squadrons performed devastating rocketry on smoke floats, followed by a low-level fly-past and seamen demonstrating a jackstay transfer with RFA *Resource*. The outing was brought to a close by a leisurely transit of the Sound while the Royal Marines Band entertained everyone with their playing.

That afternoon the *Ark Royal* tied up to her berth in Devonport Dockyard at the end of a long commission to undergo a much needed refit, and for a ceremony at which her officers and men received the Freedom of the City of Leeds.

The association between the City of Leeds and HMS *Ark Royal* dates back to the Second World War when, during the dark days of November 1941, a Government sponsored scheme aimed at encouraging people to save for the war effort, called 'Warship Week', was launched. The city of Leeds decided, through its National Savings Committee, to adopt the very high-profile aircraft carrier *Ark Royal* and a target of £3 million was set. Sadly, just days after the decision was made the *Ark Royal* was sunk, but such was the enthusiasm in the city that over £9 million was raised, which was a staggering amount of money in those days. Although an order had been placed for the aircraft carrier which was to become the fourth *Ark Royal*,

in September 1942 it was still planned to call the vessel *Irresistible*, but such was the reputation of the third *Ark Royal* that the city formally adopted the name at a ceremony held in Leeds Civic Hall on 19 September 1942, when the ship's crest was presented to the Lord Mayor. It was then some years before the adoption became a reality, but in May 1950, when the *Ark Royal* was launched, the City of Leeds was well represented, as it was at the official commissioning ceremony on 22 February 1955. Over the years the ties had grown even stronger, and to honour 'their' warship the citizens of Leeds granted the freedom of the city to their ship. For operational reasons the ceremony could not take place until after her refit had started, with Thursday 25 October 1973 being chosen as the day. The ceremony was attended by Her Majesty Queen Elizabeth The Queen Mother, and the people of Leeds turned out in force, emphasizing their remarkable loyalty towards the ship despite the fact that the nearest port in which the *Ark Royal* could berth was Liverpool. In her speech the Queen Mother mentioned the special place which the *Ark Royal* held in her heart, and the fact that she had visited the great ship during all but one of her commissions. As Captain Cassidi put his signature to the Roll of Freedom he remarked that the £9.3 million which had been raised by Leeds 'when our fortunes at sea were at a low ebb' would have been worth £31 million at 1973 values. Finally the Queen Mother inspected a Royal Guard from the ship and after the ceremony 400 representatives of the ship's company marched through the streets with Colours flying, drums beating, and with bayonets fixed. Overhead the carrier's Wessex and Sea King helicopters staged a fly-past, two of them trailing White Ensigns, and they were followed by Gannets and formations of Buccaneer and Phantom jets. As well as the official ceremonies there were other events to mark the occasion and at a luncheon in Leeds Civic Hall, the even earlier *Ark Royal* – the seaplane carrier purchased by the Admiralty in 1914 – was represented by 65-year-old Mr Joseph Ware who had served as a stoker in the old ship for two years, during which time he had witnessed some early naval aviation trials. Another celebratory gesture was the recording of a special programme of hymns for a Remembrance Sunday broadcast by 250 members of the ship's company and the Royal Marines Band at the Yorkshire Television Studios.

Meanwhile, back on board the *Ark Royal* at Devonport the aircraft hangars had been converted into giant stores complexes teeming with brown-overalled dockyard workmen, while on the flight deck the Portakabins had assumed an almost permanent air. In the passageways countless air, water and steam hoses made getting around more like an obstacle course, but in spite of the chaos the carrier retained her identity with the ship's sports teams and the Royal Marines Band much in evidence. On 27 November 1973 Captain Cassidi relinquished command of the carrier and Captain J. R. S. Gerard-Pearse RN took over as the new commanding officer. Captain Gerard-Pearse had joined the Royal Navy in 1943 and his commands included the destroyer *Tumult*, the Blackwood-class frigate *Grafton*, the Daring-class destroyer *Defender* and the assault ship HMS *Fearless*.

Owing to a number of delays due to machinery defects, it was the late spring of 1974 before the *Ark Royal* had completed her sea trials and was ready to embark her squadrons once again. In April there was a dramatic moment when an old Buccaneer went to a watery grave after being pushed off the stern round-down whilst the ship was under way, and on 1 May, as the carrier entered Plymouth Sound, three veteran aircraft from the Fleet Air Arm Historic Flight performed a fly-past over the carrier. A Swordfish flown by Lt-Cdr J. Frost, a Sea Fury piloted by Lt-Cdr K. Harris (the CO of 849B Flight) and a Firefly flown by Cdr John Rawlins made the flight from RNAS Yeovilton on their first joint flight of 1974, which was, in fact, the year of the Diamond Jubilee of Naval Aviation. In early July the *Ark Royal* began her post-refit work-up and no sooner had she left Devonport than a Soviet spy trawler took up position astern of her, and a W-class submarine was also traced close to the carrier. Some cynics on board were heard to remark that the Soviet Government appeared to be taking more interest than the British Government in the Fleet Air Arm. The return of a Labour Administration in February 1974 had virtually ruled out any hope of a further reprieve for the *Ark Royal*, and it was generally accepted that the decision to phase out the carrier in 1978 was irrevocable. One of the very visible signs of the effects of the rundown in naval fixed-wing aviation could be seen in the wardroom, where there were many RAF uniforms in evidence. The general opinion on board, from the wardroom down to the junior rates mess decks, was that the true relative costs of operating aircraft carriers as opposed to land bases had not been adequately assessed. There was also a feeling that the fleet aircraft carrier's potential as a 'presence' to damp down trouble anywhere in the world had been underestimated. However, in the short term the main task was to work up to peak efficiency which would allow her to land on her 24-ton Buccaneers and Phantoms at the rate of one every 30 seconds, in time for NATO's autumn exercises. On 14 June, whilst the *Ark Royal* and the RFA *Resource* were carrying out manoeuvres, the Soviet submarine which was shadowing the carrier sent the signal, 'We congratulate you with Queen's birthday' to which Captain Gerard-Pearse replied, 'Thank you for your good wishes. I hope we are not delaying your arrival home.' During the work-up periods the carrier received a number of visitors, including Rear-Admiral Cassidi who was now the Flag Officer Carriers and Amphibious Ships (the successor to FOAC).

In the second week of July 1974 the *Ark Royal* steamed south for the Mediterranean, and during the passage came the news that an IRA bomb had exploded at the Tower of London, in the heart of the capital, killing one person and injuring 41, including young children. It was one of a series of IRA bomb outrages in major British cities, including one in the Palace of Westminster. On board the *Ark Royal* many of the ship's company were moved by the plight of the young victims and within 24 hours almost £900 had been raised for St Bartholemew's Hospital where the children were being treated.

Following her sojourn in the Mediterranean the *Ark* returned to home waters and on 7 September she was riding out gales which were sweeping the south coast, when a distress call was received from a coaster, the *Greta C*, which was on passage from Falmouth to the Isle of Wight with a cargo of stone which had shifted, causing the vessel to list severely. With the coaster sinking rapidly, the *Ark Royal* immediately turned downwind, and in storm force winds with speeds of up to 55 knots and a heavy tumbling sea, launched two Sea Kings of 824 Squadron. About one and a half hours later the helicopters sighted two dinghies, in one of which were four survivors from the *Greta C*. After winching one of the men to safety the first helicopter on the scene returned to refuel, while the second crew took over the rescue and picked up the other three men. Sadly the coaster's master had last been seen clinging to a hatch cover on his doomed ship, and his body was later recovered from the sea and flown to Portland. The two helicopters which had taken part in the rescue were Sea King 053 flown by Lt John Passmore and Lt Barry Hill, with their crew Lt Paddy Healey, Chief Aircrewman Hall and Ldg Aircrewman Christopher Bond, who was lowered into the sea to help the first survivor into the rescue strop, and Sea King 050 piloted by Lt John Eacott and Lt Bill Shurey (both RAN pilots) and crewed by Sub-Lt Gordon Hall, PO Aircrewman Fowles and Aircrewman Allen Ottaway, who was responsible for bringing the remaining three men to safety.

Just a few weeks later, when the carrier was in the Mediterranean, the helicopters of 824 Squadron were again involved in a dramatic rescue at sea. This time it was an Italian freighter, the *Giovanna Assenso*, that was in trouble, and a Gannet of 849B Flight spotted red flares being fired from the vessel, about 150 miles from the *Ark Royal*. On closer inspection it could be seen that the freighter had a 30° list to starboard and that she was wallowing badly in a heavy sea. Once again two Sea Kings of 824 Squadron were scrambled and the first helicopter on the scene, piloted by Lt Richard Pharoah and Lt Vincent Ratcliffe, with crewmen Sub-Lt Raymond Dogget and Ldg Aircrewmen Christopher Bond and Kenneth Winter, winched four of the Italian sailors to safety, leaving behind Ken Winter. The second Sea King flown by Lt John Passmore and Lt William Harper, with Lt John Eacott, CPO William Hall, PO Raymond Higginson and LA (Phot) Larry McKenzie,

'David and Goliath' – the *Ark Royal* and USS *Nimitz* at Norfolk, Virginia, USA.

rescued the two remaining crewmen from the freighter, along with Aircrewman Winter, and as they left the *Giovanna Assenso* she was still making way with her engines running, but with an ever-increasing list.

During the autumn of 1974 the *Ark Royal* remained in the Mediterranean, but she was back at Devonport by Christmas for leave and maintenance. In the New Year of 1975 the engineers were able to assist their colleagues in the commando carrier HMS *Bulwark*, which was just completing a 12-month refit, when JMEM Ian Nicholson carried an Olympic-style flame from one of the *Ark's* boiler rooms to the *Bulwark's* A boiler room, to flash up her rather elderly Admiralty three-drum boilers. By the first week in February 1975 the *Ark Royal* was back at sea in the Channel and demonstrating the new Harrier STOVL aircraft to Roy Mason, the Minister of Defence. The trials were of great importance to the Fleet Air Arm, for once again the future development of the aircraft was in doubt and it would not be long before the minister had to finally decide whether a maritime version of the Harrier was to get the go-ahead.

Soon after the trials were completed the *Ark Royal*, together with the destroyer *Hampshire* and RFA *Resource*, was crossing the Atlantic to take part in what had become an annual event, exercises with the US Navy in the area of their Atlantic Fleet Weapons Range off Puerto Rico. During the transatlantic crossing a mid-Atlantic search and rescue competition was held between helicopter crews from the *Ark Royal*, *Hampshire* and the *Resource*, which involved precision winching, a man overboard exercise and a high-line transfer, the difficult manoeuvre which allows a casualty to be lifted from the bottom of a cliff. In the event the winning crew were from the *Ark Royal*, led by Lt David George. Soon after her arrival in US waters the carrier was visited by the chairman of the US Joint Chiefs of Staff Committee and other American Service Chiefs, who were shown how the *Ark Royal* and her escort made use of the US weapons range. Following these exercises the carrier anchored off Virgin Gorda Island for recreational leave and banyans. During exercises with the USS *Independence* the two carriers cross-operated their aircraft and at one stage the *Ark Royal's* flight deck took on the appearance of a US Navy carrier, with very little parking space to spare. The final phases of the exercises were completed on the Atlantic Fleet Weapon Range along with HMS *Fearless* and, as before, the operations were concluded with a visit to Mayport, Florida, for self-maintenance. Among the tourist attractions which the ship's company could visit were Disneyworld, Marineland and the Kennedy Space Centre, while Captain Gerard-Pearse was invited to open a display commemorating the 200 years of British rule in Florida which had ended in 1784.

Following the WESTLANT deployment off the USA, the *Ark Royal*, *Hampshire* and the RFA steamed south to join the helicopter cruiser *Blake*, the frigates *Falmouth*, *Leander* and *Achilles*, and the nuclear-powered submarine *Warspite*, to carry out weapons training exercises with the Brazilian naval units *Mariz E. Barras*, *Espirito Santo* and *Maranhao*. During the exercises the *Ark Royal* embarked a squadron of Brazilian Sea King helicopters, and afterwards the carrier, together with the *Blake*, *Hampshire* and *Falmouth*, put into Rio de Janeiro, which proved very popular with the ships' companies. Other Royal Navy units were visiting Salvador and Santos, making a total of 15 British warships in Brazilian ports, a gathering brought about by the linking of the *Ark Royal's* force and that led by Flag Officer First Flotilla, Vice-Admiral H. C. Leach, in the *Blake*. They had steamed across the Indian Ocean from a Far Eastern deployment to call at Cape Town before crossing the Atlantic. Following the departure of the ships from the South American ports, more exercises were held with the Brazilian Navy before the whole force steamed back home again. The *Ark Royal* arrived at Devonport on 12 June 1975 to undergo a short refit and also to welcome a new captain. The carrier's new commanding officer was Captain W. J. Graham RN, who had joined the Royal Navy during the Second World War, specializing in gunnery.

It was the autumn of 1975 when the carrier left Devonport once again, steaming past the sad sight of her sister ship HMS *Eagle* laid up off Cremyll and awaiting disposal. Her final duty was to provide spare parts for the *Ark Royal*. During the *Ark's* trials at this time, further operating tests were undertaken with the Harrier GR3, in the Portland and Bristol Channel areas. Soon afterwards, when the *Ark Royal* was carrying out work-up exercises off the east coast of Scotland, Her Majesty Queen Elizabeth The Queen Mother visited the ship to watch flying operations. She witnessed catapult launches and recoveries, and she was given an impressive demonstration of the strike power of the *Ark Royal's* aircraft, with Phantoms of 982 Squadron firing rockets and Buccaneers of 809 Squadron performing bombing runs, as well as displays by 848B Flight of Gannets and 824 Squadron's Sea Kings. After lunch the Queen Mother viewed displays by the ship's departments, before having tea with the CPOs of 4D Mess. Before she left the ship Captain Graham presented Her Majesty with a framed lithograph of the *Ark Royal*, and she addressed the assembled ship's company in the hangar. After taking off from the deck, the royal helicopter made a final circuit of the ship and the Queen Mother sent the signal, 'Please convey to the officers and all ranks my sincere thanks for a most wonderful day.'

The *Ark Royal's* final deployment of 1975 was the major NATO maritime exercise code-named 'Ocean Safari' which took place in the Eastern Atlantic and the Norwegian Sea in November. The exercise involved 75 ships and 17,000 men from the UK, USA, Canada, Denmark, West Germany, Norway and the Netherlands and it was designed

Another view of the *Ark Royal* and USS *Nimitz* together at Norfolk, Virginia.　　　　　　　　　(*L. Fleming*)

to provide the NATO navies with realistic training in maritime operations under the adverse conditions found in the Norwegian Sea in winter. As well as the *Ark Royal*, the Royal Navy's representatives included HM Ships *Hermes*, *Blake*, *Devonshire*, *Danae*, *Bacchante*, *Eskimo* and *Tartar*, as well as the submarines *Finwhale*, *Osiris*, *Otter* and *Sovereign*, and seven RFAs. Needless to say this impressive presence attracted great interest from Soviet forces and right from the start it was a case of, 'We're watching you watching us.' Two Phantoms from the *Ark Royal* were the first to intercept Tupolev TU-95 (Bear) reconnaissance aircraft over the fleet, and during the exercise many long-range and medium-range strike aircraft were sighted. Conditions on the flight deck of the *Ark Royal* were cold and wet and the crews there worked hard to keep the Buccaneers airborne as they made simulated attacks on radar installations along the Norwegian coast. Meanwhile, F104 aircraft of the Norwegian Air Force 'attacked' the NATO fleet, which kept the early warning Gannets of 849 Squadron fully occupied.

Following Christmas and New Year leave, and a maintenance period at Devonport, the *Ark Royal* started 1976 by taking part in exercises off Gibraltar with HMS *Antrim*. The two ships rendezvoused in the Bristol Channel in early February, and after the *Ark* had played host to a number of VIPs they were joined by the *Blake* and two RFAs for the passage south to warmer waters. After taking part in 'Exercise Springtrain' the *Ark Royal* set course west to make what had become her annual voyage to the Caribbean for the WESTLANT deployment with the US Navy. This time she had travelling with her a BBC film crew who were on board to film a documentary which became a big hit on BBC television, the series 'Sailor'. On Monday 23 February, whilst the *Ark Royal* was on passage to Puerto Rico, she was diverted from her course to airlift a sick US Navy seaman from the submarine USS *Bergall*. Two Sea King helicopters flew on ahead of the carrier to a point about 300 miles west of the Azores where, early in the morning, in a 30-knot wind and with a 12ft swell, the transfer took place. CPO Aircrewman Roy Withell was

A Buccaneer is launched from the waist catapult.

(L. Fleming)

lowered with a stretcher onto the submarine's casing where he detached himself from the winch hook so that the helicopter could stand off safely. CPO Withell takes up the story: 'At this time there were two US Navy personnel on the casing, attached to lifelines, who were to assist me with the stretcher. I grabbed one of the lifelines with one hand, holding the stretcher with the other. When the sick man came up onto the casing I began to strap him in. I had already got my feet wet with the occasional wave washing over the deck, and while I was strapping him into the stretcher, the two men held onto it and onto me. Then it happened! Every now and again you get a big wave – we got one. The stretcher was lifted and thrown sideways from the casing. I held on as I presumed the two guys were holding onto the stretcher, but they couldn't hold it, so over we went, the sick man and me. We drifted aft rather quickly and we were lucky not to get eaten by the propeller,

which was just breaking the surface of the water. If the captain of the submarine hadn't put on full starboard rudder I dare not think what might have happened. Almost immediately we had cleared the stern, the winch hook was lowered to us and I hooked both of us to it and we were winched up into the helicopter.' Later in the year the whole nation would see the drama of the rescue on television, but in the meantime the patient was rushed to hospital in the Azores where he made a good recovery.

The transatlantic passage also coincided with the 21st anniversary of the carrier's first commissioning and a signal was received on board from the Queen Mother, which read: 'My thoughts are with you on this historic occasion and I send to all members of the ship's company my warmest good wishes for the years ahead.' Captain Graham replied: 'All of us in *Ark Royal* now in mid-Atlantic were greatly honoured to receive your 21st anniversary greetings. We remember your visit to us last year with great affection and wish to offer you our loyal greetings.' Once again the WESTLANT deployment was a great success, but after eight weeks at sea the ship's company were relieved to put into Mayport for a three-week assisted maintenance period. Although there was plenty of work to be done, every opportunity was taken to get away from the ship for 'rest and recreation'. One indication of how air travel was rapidly reducing distances between continents and becoming available to more and more people was the fact that over 100 wives, children and girlfriends flew out from Heathrow to Jacksonville on a specially chartered aircraft. As always the local people displayed the wonderful hospitality which is typical of the United States, and there were countless invitations to visit homes and attend barbeques etc. With America celebrating 200 years of independence, the country was in a truly festive mood and the ship's company were cordially invited to take part in the celebrations.

After leaving Mayport and recovering her Air Group from the shore bases where they had been operating, the *Ark Royal* steamed north to Norfolk, Virginia, to enable repairs to be carried out to her steam catapults. During the stay in Norfolk the aircraft carriers USS *Iwo Jima* and USS *Independence* played host to the *Ark Royal* and the carrier received a visit from the city's Azalea Queen, Miss Susan Ford, daughter of the President. After the three-week unscheduled stop in Norfolk, the *Ark Royal* carried out a week's flying operations before she began a scheduled visit to the Florida holiday resort of Fort Lauderdale, after which she continued with the task of operating her Air Group using the facilities of the Atlantic Fleet Weapons Range off Puerto Rico. During these exercises programmes of bombing, rocketing, missile firing and torpedo dropping proceeded for two weeks, with the frigate HMS *Eskimo* joining the carrier as planeguard escort. Following this, and much to the delight of the ship's company, the *Ark* headed for Norfolk, Virginia, once again, but this time for a ten-day official visit which had been planned for some time. En route to Norfolk, the flight deck was the venue for a 'garden fete' where stands included 'Smash-a-Crab' and 'Guess the Weight' of the PMO's family. The event raised over £800 for the Cookridge Hospital Cancer Fund for Children, which was a vast amount of money in the mid-1970s. After her stay in Norfolk the carrier embarked upon another busy programme of flying, including an Operational Readiness Inspection by the Flag Officer Carriers and Amphibious Ships, Rear-Admiral J. H. F. Eberle. The deployment ended on Friday 16 July 1976, when the *Ark Royal* returned to Devonport for summer leave and for maintenance.

It was in early September that the *Ark Royal* left Devonport to steam out into the Atlantic and round Ireland's west coast and the north of Scotland into the North Sea to embark her squadrons and to carry out flying exercises in the area. These were interrupted by a five-day spell anchored off Leith in the Firth of Forth, but by Monday 20 September she was steaming off Scotland's east coast and carrying out flying operations. It was, by now, even more difficult to say when one commission ended and the next one started, but it could be said that the final commission started on 25 September 1976, for that was the day that her last commanding officer, Captain E. R. Anson RN, arrived on board. Three days later he relieved Captain Graham, who would soon leave the ship to take up his new appointment as Flag Officer, Portsmouth. After completing the NATO exercise 'Teamwork' the carrier, accompanied by a large force of RN ships, including the destroyers *Antrim* and *Devonshire* and the frigates *Andromeda*, *Naiad*, *Bacchante*, *Yarmouth* and *Charybdis*, set course for warmer climes and a four-day visit to the Portuguese capital, Lisbon. During the stay in the River Tagus Rear-Admiral Graham left the ship and he was given a rousing send-off at a ship's company concert. The *Ark Royal's* final commanding officer, Captain E. R. Anson RN, was a former Buccaneer pilot and one of his first official duties was to inspect full Ceremonial Divisions, which were held on the flight deck and in tropical rig - an unusual event with the ship in European waters. While the *Ark Royal* was in Lisbon a Sea King helicopter of 824 Squadron, flown by Lt David Goodall, flew 75 miles to airlift a sick sailor from the Portuguese submarine *Barracuda*. Despite the choppy Atlantic seas the mission went smoothly and the man was transferred to hospital in Lisbon. Following her departure during Saturday 2 October, the *Ark Royal* and her escort force, minus HMS *Devonshire*, which had returned to Portsmouth with boiler trouble, sailed south past Gibraltar and into the Mediterranean where a fleet of 60 NATO ships were gathering for 'Exercise Display Determination'. The force included ships from the USA, Portugal, France, Italy and Turkey, and the *Ark Royal* was one of four aircraft carriers taking part, the others being the US Ships *Nimitz* and *America,* and the French carrier *Clemenceau*. The *Ark Royal* and America operated off the coast of Sardinia where the opportunity was taken for the interchange of squadron personnel and aircraft, with the US Navy's Tomcats attracting more than their fair share of goofers to the island superstructure. On Wednesday 13 October, with the exercise completed, the *Ark Royal* put into the southern French port and naval base of Toulon for a five-day visit, during which a team of planners from Devonport Dockyard flew out to prepare the ship for her seventh, and last, long refit. After bidding farewell to Toulon on 18 October, despite unfavourable weather and minor mechanical problems with the catapults, all the fixed-wing aircraft were successfully launched to their various shore stations during the day. Finally, after a popular overnight stop at Gibraltar on 20/21 October, the *Ark Royal* set off

The *Ark* on exercises in the
final weeks of her operational
life.

(L. Fleming)

on the final leg of the passage home and en route a large quantity of ammunition, fuel and stores was transferred to accompanying RFAs. The carrier entered Plymouth Sound in the early hours of Monday 25 October and steamed up harbour in the dark to secure alongside before daylight, much to the surprise of morning commuters on the Torpoint Ferry.

Although the *Ark Royal's* refit had been scheduled to last from November 1976 to June 1977, preparations had started earlier in the year with the drawing up of defect lists, and work was planned around these. The dockyard personnel who had flown out to Toulon got down to work on the catapults as soon as the last Buccaneers and Phantoms had been launched, while inside the ship large sheets of hardboard began to cover passageways and mess decks in readiness for the onslaught by the dockyard workers. Once alongside an initial four-week programme began, during which tank cleaning vessels and lighters were constantly in attendance as fuel was pumped out, causing the *Ark Royal* to rise higher in the water. At the pre-refit conference it was stressed that the ship must be ready for sea again within 28 weeks, so that she could take her place as the flagship at the Queen's Silver Jubilee Fleet Review at Spithead in June 1977. Members of the ship's company who remained on board enjoyed some light-hearted moments in November 1976 when the BBC returned on board to make a recording of them singing Rod Stewart's song 'Sailing' which had become a chart hit following its use as the theme tune for the highly successful documentary series 'Sailor'. The empty hangar was transformed into a recording studio, complete with a beer bar which, it was claimed, helped to lubricate the vocal chords. Initially the BBC had asked for 200 volunteer vocalists, but nearly 450 turned up and, together with the Royal Marines Band, they recorded 'Sailing' on the A-side and 'The Wombles Song' on the B-side of the record. The audience in the hangar included the Womble 'Great Uncle Bulgaria' and the author of the Wombles stories, Elizabeth Beresford, who presented Captain Anson with an 'Orinoco' mascot. In mid-November the ship's company moved into RNB Devonport, and a few weeks later the *Ark* herself was shifted into No 10 dry dock where fortunately the condition of the hull was found to be better than had been expected.

On the last day of February 1977, with all the necessary dry dock work having been completed ahead of schedule, the *Ark Royal* was refloated and shifted back alongside her outer sea wall berth again. By Wednesday 13 April the accommodation and galleys were ready for use and the ship's company moved back on board. Soon afterwards the first puffs of black smoke from the funnel indicated that the ship was coming back to life and on Wednesday 1 June 1977 the Flag Officer Plymouth, Vice-Admiral J. M. Forbes, made his Completion Day Inspection, declaring himself well pleased with the result. All that remained was to prepare the ship for sea.

The *Ark Royal's* post-refit acceptance trials began at 11.45am on Thursday 9 June, when the great ship slipped her moorings and steamed slowly down the Hamoaze, into Plymouth Sound and out into the Channel. Initially there were problems with a propeller shaft stern gland, which necessitated an unexpected C buoy day in Cawsand Bay, but unfortunately no leave was allowed. In mid-June the first Sea Kings of 824 Squadron were embarked and these were closely followed by the fixed-wing squadrons of Phantoms (892), Buccaneers (809) and Gannets (849B Flight), all of them leaving tyre marks on what had been a spotlessly clean flight deck. During the trials the new Flag Officer Carriers and Amphibious Ships, Rear-Admiral W. D. M. Staveley, spent a day aboard touring mess decks and machinery spaces, and making a number of presentations to the ship's company. The initial trials were concluded by the carrier steaming up and down the measured mile off Looe, during which there was a 'potted sports' tournament on the flight deck, and finally, after disembarking dockyard working parties in Plymouth Sound, the *Ark Royal* set course for Portsmouth to head the Silver Jubilee Fleet Review.

The Fleet Review of 1977 was the first to be held at Spithead since the Queen's Coronation Review of 1953, and for the first time the memory of the battleship had been laid to rest. The fleet which was to assemble in 1977 had some of its origins in the 1966 decision to abandon plans for the new class of fleet aircraft carriers and the sole representative of these leviathans was to be the *Ark Royal*, flying the flag of C-in-C Fleet, Admiral Sir Henry Leach. She would, however, be accompanied by the amphibious assault ship and former aircraft carrier, HMS *Hermes*, the Flagship of Rear-Admiral Staveley, and the Australian light fleet carrier HMAS *Melbourne*. The *Ark Royal* arrived alongside Portsmouth's Middle Slip Jetty during the afternoon of Monday 20 June, to make the final preparations for the Review, which included cleaning, painting and what seemed to be endless rehearsals for the 'man and cheer ship' procedures. As the Fleet Flagship the *Ark Royal* was involved with ceremonial duties on a grand scale and during the build-up to the Review there were countless gun salutes, bugle alerts, parading of the Guard and Band and the playing of National Anthems as ships of the Royal and Commonwealth Navies and vessels from other nations arrived in Portsmouth Harbour. On the afternoon of Thursday 23 June the C-in-C embarked by helicopter before the *Ark Royal* slipped from her berth and steamed out to Spithead, where the navigator found the spot marked 'HMS *Ark Royal*' on a specially produced chart of the Solent, and the ship dropped anchor. It was here that she would remain for the next few days, swinging with the tides and continuing the never-ending process of painting and cleaning ship. There was time for some relaxation on Sunday 26 June when various official

On 20 September 1978, Her Majesty Queen Elizabeth The Queen Mother paid a final visit to 'her' ship and Captain Anson presented her with a miniature of the ship's silver bell, mounted in a small wooden tabernacle.
(L. Fleming)

receptions took place, and families of the ship's company had the opportunity to visit the ship and view the lines of warships from the flight deck. That weekend literally hundreds of pleasure craft, among them even tiny canoes, came to see the ships at anchor and, as always, Spithead was a magnificent sight with all the smart grey hulls of the warships towering above the sightseers. Monday 27 June was taken up with the final rehearsals and the ship's company 'manned and cheered ship' yet again before the RFA *Engadine* took the role of the royal yacht *Britannia* and led the review column of warships. Overhead 154 aircraft, including 110 from the Fleet Air Arm, rehearsed their fly-past in an 'ER' and anchor formation. Shortly afterwards the pride of Britain's merchant fleet, the *QE2*, passed through the review lines as she steamed out of the

Solent on a voyage from Southampton to Cherbourg. During the day there were two live television broadcasts from the *Ark Royal's* flight deck, with the *Blue Peter* programme introducing a special feature and the Illumination of the Fleet presented by Richard Baker. That evening the Queen embarked in the *Britannia* in Portsmouth Harbour, whilst in the Solent the fleet remained lit up for two hours.

Although everyone had hoped for a warm, sunny day, Tuesday 28 June dawned distinctly chilly and blustery, with a wind that at times reached Force 4, but at least the threatened rain held off. Despite the weather the ceremony lacked none of the panache it had acquired since it was first performed in 1773, the year of the Boston Tea Party, and the Review got under way with a 21-gun salute fired from seven warships as the *Britannia,* led by the Trinity House Vessel *Patricia,* left harbour. Unfortunately, the cold weather kept many of the expected crowds away from Southsea seafront, but for two hours the royal yacht, dressed overall, cruised at eight knots down the 15-mile circuit of 180 ships from Britain and 17 other nations, while 30,000 sailors who were lining the decks snapped to attention, raised their caps and cheered as the *Britannia* passed by. Ironically, the largest ship present was the 227,000-ton oil tanker, *British Respect,* while the smallest warships were the tiny minesweepers. Representing the Royal Navy, in addition to the *Ark Royal* and *Hermes,* were the helicopter cruisers *Tiger* and *Blake,* the destroyers *Antrim, Devonshire, Fife, Glamorgan, Sheffield* and *Birmingham,* as well as frigates and nuclear-powered submarines. Unfortunately the Fleet Air Arm fly-past had to be significantly reduced because of the weather conditions, and only 90 helicopters took part. Finally over 200 ratings from the Royal and Commonwealth Navies, who had assembled on board the *Ark Royal,* were conveyed to the *Britannia* to attend a reception, and to complete the celebrations the Queen was the guest of honour at a banquet given by the Flag and Commanding Officers of the Fleet in the upper hangar of the *Ark Royal,* which had been transformed into a festive dining hall with highly polished decking and colourful bunting. To round off the occasion the following signals were sent: 'From the Lord High Admiral, Her Majesty The Queen, to C-in-C Fleet. It gave me great pleasure to review all these ships assembled at Spithead today for my Silver Jubilee Review and to receive the salute of the Fleet Air Arm. I was deeply impressed by the splendid sight of all the vessels in their lines. The smart appearance of the ships and their companies and the precision of the fly-past were in the finest traditions of the sea. I send my congratulations to all who planned and took part in the Review. The Duke of Edinburgh joins me in sending our wishes to you all as you disperse.' The second signal, from the Ministry of Defence read: 'Her Majesty The Queen has requested the Admiralty Board to promulgate the following message: "To the Royal Navy and to the Flag and Senior Officers of the Commonwealth ships at Spithead:- In celebration of my Silver Jubilee and with the Royal and Commonwealth ships assembled at Spithead, Splice the Main Brace – Elizabeth R".' It was the signal that everyone had been hoping for.

Next day, as the ships left Spithead, the *Ark Royal* weighed anchor and headed for the southern side of the Isle of Wight where she led a steam past of 61 warships to acknowledge the retirement of the Chief of the Defence Staff, Admiral of the Fleet Sir Edward Ashmore, who was embarked in the destroyer HMS *Birmingham.* Once this duty had been performed, the *Ark Royal* resumed the role of a fleet carrier undergoing post-refit trials.

As the *Ark Royal* steamed back to Plymouth, pre-wetting trials were carried out, and on the last day of June she embarked her trials teams in Cawsand Bay. Soon afterwards the first aircraft arrived on board in the form of three Phantoms, three Buccaneers and three Gannets, and in early July the flying trials began in earnest. During this period, in the early hours of 1 July, the ship went to the aid of the yacht *Pegasa* which appeared to be taking on water. However, an inspection by the Chief Shipwright revealed that the water was coming from the yacht's own fresh water tanks and her crew were able to continue their voyage. Four days later the carrier was asked to keep a lookout for the MV *Albatross* which had broken down in the Channel. It was soon located, but engineers from the *Ark* were unable to carry out repairs at sea and so another merchant ship towed the *Albatross* to Falmouth. The third incident occurred on 7 July, when the *Ark Royal* was 30 miles south-east of Plymouth and a request came for help in clearing a fouled anchor on the oil rig *Zephyr One*, which was the first exploration rig in the Plymouth area. A seven-man diving team led by Lt Stuart McClelland was flown to the rig and within three hours they had completed the job, which involved unshackling a tug's five-inch mooring pendant and attaching a new one. Not only was the exercise useful for the ship's divers, but the Navy was able to claim reimbursement from the oil rig's owners at the standard rate for the divers' services.

Throughout all this time the flying trials continued uninterruptedly and they were completed ahead of schedule, although hopes of an early arrival in Devonport were dashed by bad weather and it was Tuesday 12 July when the carrier finally berthed alongside for leave and for post-sea trial rectifications and modifications. During the August Bank Holiday all departments put on a good show for Navy Days and 31,648 visitors enjoyed a visit to the Navy's last big aircraft carrier. The seven weeks alongside passed far too quickly for most people on board, and on Thursday 1 September the *Ark Royal* sailed once again to start the first phase of the work-up which would bring the ship to a state of operational readiness. Drama soon raised its head when, during the first RAS with the RFAs *Olmeda* and *Lyness,* two members of the ship's company were swept overboard by a large wave. The SAR helicopter was scrambled and happily they were back on board, none the worse for the experience, within ten minutes. Following this incident the carrier continued her passage up the west coast of Ireland, and Sunday 4 September saw the ship at the southern end of the Minches for her cruise northwards through the Western Isles. Next day she arrived off the Moray Firth where the squadrons were embarked safely and the ship once more took on her role of a busy, noisy and exciting floating airfield. As a break from the flying operations the *Ark Royal* moored in the Firth of Forth, some six miles from Leith, on Thursday 18 September, which presented a welcome opportunity for a long weekend at home for local men, but for anyone who wanted some time ashore there was a long boat ride there and back. The second phase of the work-up got under way in earnest on 20 September and it coincided with a stream of visits from VIPs, including the First Sea Lord, Admiral Sir Terence Lewin, and Commander HRH The Prince of Wales, who arrived on Wednesday 21 September. Prince Charles flew on board in a Buccaneer of 809 Squadron for a visit intended to widen his experience of fixed-wing carrier operations, and during his four-hour visit he toured various parts of the ship. Another new experience for the Prince was to be launched in a Buccaneer flown by Lt-Cdr Tony Mason, the CO of 809 Squadron, from the steam catapult. After a successful launch at 3.45pm that afternoon, watched by a larger than usual contingent of goofers and representatives of the world's press, the aircraft made a low-level pass down the *Ark Royal's* port side before leaving the area. Other visitors to the ship at this time included the Minister of Defence, the Lord Mayor of Leeds and a NATO Defence Review Committee. The next interlude which the ship's company were eagerly anticipating was a four-day visit to Hamburg, always a popular port of call.

On completion of a night flying programme on Wednesday 28 September the ship headed south from the Moray Firth, and on the morning of Friday 30 September she arrived off the Elbe estuary, for the start of a 70-mile passage of the river which signalled a long day for the Special Sea Dutymen. After hours of heavy rain the *Ark Royal* berthed alongside a modern container terminal in Hamburg at 7pm, and despite the bad weather and the fact

The *Ark* leaves Gibraltar for the last time on 2 October 1978 with her 450ft paying-off pennant flying proudly, held aloft by a weather balloon. *(Imperial War Museum HU 69122)*

The *Ark Royal* sails out of Kalkara Creek, Grand Harbour, for the last time on 16 November 1978. The former naval base HMS *St Angelo* lies directly behind the ship. *(Imperial War Museum MH 25108)*

that it was already dark, a German youth band had turned out to greet her. During her four-day spell in the city it seemed to rain continuously, but this did not prevent either the ship's company or the citizens of Hamburg making the most of the visit and, in fact, almost 11,000 Germans braved the elements to go and look round the ship. Members of the ship's company found various ways to enjoy the German hospitality; some spent time sightseeing in Berlin, others took advantage of places on various free tours of Hamburg which had been organized, while a few sought out the dubious delights of the Reeperbahn, even if only out of curiosity. On the morning of Wednesday 5 October it was back to work again as the time approached for the carrier to slip her berth at 8.30am. After a neat astern movement into one of the many dock inlets, she steamed ahead and began the long passage of the River Elbe back to the North Sea for the third phase of her work-up.

It was on a very wet and windy Friday 7 October that the *Ark Royal* arrived back off the Moray Firth where flying had to be restricted, but three days later the carrier's Operationl Readiness Inspection began. For four hectic days Admiral Staveley's staff toured the ship handing out small brown envelopes containing instructions for more evolutions, the final one of which was a towing exercise where the carrier successfully took the RFA *Resource* in tow. This accomplished, the *Ark Royal* could leave the Moray Firth, much to everyone's relief, and set course for the Bristol Channel via the north coast of Scotland, through the Hebrides to the west coast of Ireland, where gales and heavy seas turned a few faces green, for the large-scale NATO autumn exercise code-named 'Ocean Safari'. It was the *Ark Royal's* first operational task of the year, and she was flying the flag of Rear-Admiral Staveley, in his role as the NATO Commander of Carrier Striking Group Two. Although units from the USA, Canada, Netherlands, Portugal, West Gemany, France, Norway and the UK took part in the exercise, the *Ark Royal* was the only fixed-wing carrier present and after setting off from the coast of Cornwall she steamed south in a zigzag pattern across the Bay of Biscay. By Friday 21 October she was off Lisbon where the Sea Kings of 824 Squadron provided an ASW screen and the Phantoms carried out combat air patrols and medium-level intercepts against 'enemy' aircraft sent to test the carrier's defences. 849B Flight's Gannets provided AEW cover and during 21 October the Buccaneers staged attacks on the Portuguese military range at Alonichele just outside Lisbon. With the *Ark Royal* having steamed north back into the Bay of Biscay, the Buccaneers were in action again, this time delivering 'attacks' on the Stuttgart region of Germany. The exercise finished at midnight on 28 October with the *Ark Royal* in the Channel and, after disembarking Admiral Staveley and his staff, she set course for Gibraltar.

The passage south was far more relaxed than on the previous occasion and despite strong winds, flight deck sports were organized or, for the less energetic, there was a conker contest, the 'tools' for which had mostly been collected by the PT staff in Hamburg. As the ship neared the Mediterranean the chefs commenced mixing the Christmas pudding, assisted by Captain Anson and JMEM David Grieve, the youngest member of the ship's company, who added the rum. On the last day of October a most enjoyable concert was held on the quarterdeck and at 5.30pm the next day the ship berthed alongside Gibraltar's South Mole.

After a month at sea it was the first run ashore since Hamburg, but it was only brief and 24 hours later the *Ark Royal* was at sea again, steaming east across the Mediterranean for Malta and now it was the hot sun and lack of wind which restricted the flying operations. In the early hours of Saturday 5 November the carrier was off the north-west tip of the Maltese group of islands, and at 10am she made a full ceremonial entry into Grand Harbour, watched by the President of Malta and the Flag Officer Malta, together with a number of European Ambassadors, before being moored in Kalkara Creek. During the seven-day self-maintenance period in Malta, when the local dockyard offered their assistance in repainting the ship, the warm and sunny weather meant that everyone was able to relax and get ashore, usually with the help of the local dghaisamen. Upon her departure from Grand Harbour on Saturday 12 November the *Ark Royal* set course for Toulon, but in the early hours of 14 November she ran into gale force winds and high seas as the mistral hit the southern French coast. Instead of putting into Toulon the carrier rode out the storm and then went on to join 'Exercise Isle d'Or', a French-sponsored multi-national exercise which included the USS *Saratoga* and ships from Italy, Holland, Greece and Canada. During the first phase the *Ark Royal* operated off the west coast of Corsica before moving to an area south-east of the Balearic Islands. However, throughout manoeuvres the mistral had constantly disrupted the flying operations and finally, with each ship battling against the elements, the exercise was brought to a premature end.

However, once the carrier had set course for Naples, the weather improved and apart from some light rain which marred the entry into the Italian port, it remained calm. During the stopover large numbers of the ship's company took the opportunity to visit places of interest such as Pompeii, Herculaneum, Vesuvius and even Rome where Christmas shopping could be indulged in in earnest. There was even a deck hockey match between the ship's team and the Wrens based at the NATO Headquarters, which ended in a draw. After leaving Naples on the morning of Monday 5 December, the lucky crews of two Sea Kings flew home to Culdrose on a navigational exercise, while during the passage to Gibraltar the PMO performed the 100th operation since leaving Devonport in September, the

The last fixed-wing launch on 27 November 1978, performed by a Phantom F4K flown by Flt-Lt M. Macleod RAF and Lt D. McCallum RN.

(Imperial War Museum FL5573)

problems ranging from a depressed fracture to a case of an ingrowing toenail. The final evolution before reaching Gibraltar was a 'Towex' in which the frigate *Ariadne* took the giant carrier in tow.

The call at Gibraltar lasted only 48 hours, which nevertheless was long enough for some last-minute Christmas shopping. To the dismay of some, the 'Top of the Rock' race was cancelled because of bad weather, but everyone was delighted to be setting course for Devonport on 10 December. Two days later all serviceable aircraft were flown off and on Thursday 15 December the carrier arrived in Plymouth Sound. Much to everyone's frustration, fog prevented her from steaming up harbour that day and although some families were brought out to the ship, it was the morning of Friday 16 December before the *Ark Royal* was able to berth alongside at Devonport, and leave and the maintenance period could begin.

In the last few weeks of 1977 strikes had affected all manner of trades, from undertakers to shipyard workers, as the country was beset by industrial troubles and on 14 November 1977 the nation's firemen had gone on strike over a 10 per cent pay claim. This industrial action had a direct effect on some members of the *Ark Royal's* ship's company in that they were temporarily drafted to different locations in the country to man the emergency 'Green Goddess' fire engines which had been brought out of storage. Fortunately, on 16 January 1978 the strike was settled and the 'volunteers' were able to return to the ship.

On the day after the strike ended Captain Anson unveiled British Rail's diesel-electric locomotive which they had christened *Ark Royal,* and at the same time he presented two ship's crests in gunmetal, which would be mounted on either side of the locomotive. On Thursday 26 January 1978 the ship's last Executive Officer, Commander J. L. Weatherall RN, took up his appointment for the *Ark Royal's* final year of operational service, although seven years later he would, in fact, be the first commanding officer of the fifth *Ark Royal.*

By the weekend of 18 February 1978 the *Ark Royal's* maintenance period was coming to an end, and on Tuesday 21 February she sailed for her short period of trials and work-up, passing the forlorn sight of her older sister *Eagle,* laid up and awaiting her summons from the shipbreaker's yard, which would come before the *Ark* arrived at Devonport for the last time. The first night back at sea was spent in Lyme Bay, where four Gannets and seven Phantoms were safely embarked, although the Buccaneers remained fogbound at their RAF Honington base. Having landed on the aircraft the carrier set course for the North Sea by way of the Strait of Dover, where the Buccaneers were able to join her. During the trials and work-up, fog and bad weather plagued operations, but nevertheless Rear-Admiral Staveley was able to carry out the Sea Inspection on Saturday 4 March, after which he commented on the happy spirit on board and the pride which everyone felt for the ship. Following the departure of Admiral Staveley and

The *Ark Royal* arrives at Devonport for the last time to pay off and decommission. She is flying her paying-off pennant while her flight deck is manned for the last time.

(R. W. Shopland & Fleet Air Arm Museum)

The farewell dinner for the former commanding officers of the fourth *Ark Royal*.　　　　(*L. Fleming*)

most of the aircraft on 5 March, on the next day ground crews were disembarked to RAF Leuchars and the *Ark Royal* steamed south for the Channel. After disembarking the Sea Kings to RNAS Culdrose, the ship returned to Plymouth Sound to spend the night at C buoy ready for an early morning start and 'Families Day'. The guests began arriving on board at 6am on Thursday 9 March and at 9am, after they had eaten breakfast, the ship slipped her moorings with approximately 1,500 extra passengers on board. Once in the Channel they were able to watch the launch and recovery of the remaining Gannets, Buccaneers and Phantoms, but unfortunately fog in the afternoon curtailed flying and prevented a display which had been planned, and it was left to the Royal Marines Band to entertain the guests. Fortunately the music, the splendid food and guided tours of the carrier made for a most enjoyable day. As the carrier approached Plymouth Sound

in the late afternoon, weather conditions improved and Captain Anson decided to steam up harbour. That evening, as the ship berthed alongside at Devonport, the fog closed in again, as a lot of tired but contented passengers disembarked.

During the four weeks alongside, the ship's company were kept busy with frequent visits to the carrier by individuals and groups, and during the weekend of 18/19 March there was a nostalgic reunion on board of 170 former officers and ratings who had served in the third *Ark Royal*. The guests included Admiral Sir Hector MacLean, the former Navigating Officer, and Captain H. Traill, a former Commander (Air). After a tour of the ship the visitors watched a film and then attended a performance by the Royal Marines Band. The evening ended with a dinner at a hotel ashore, and on the following day there was a commemorative church service in the upper hangar.

All too soon the leave period had passed and at 4.45pm on Wednesday 5 April 1978 the *Ark Royal* slipped her moorings and steamed out of Plymouth Sound at the start of her final deployment. As she steamed into the choppy waters of the Channel, a signal was received from HMS *Fearless* which echoed the thoughts of the whole country. It read: 'Farewell big sister, you will be sorely missed, very best wishes for your final deployment.' That same evening the four Gannets of 849B Flight were recovered and after a night spent cruising off the coast of Cornwall, the Buccaneers and Phantoms of 809 and 892 Squadrons were safely recovered the next day. At 6pm that evening, in company with the destroyer *Devonshire* and the RFAs *Olmeda* and *Resource,* the *Ark Royal* set course for her last WESTLANT deployment in the Caribbean and the USA. As she steamed south-west the weather became warmer, and by Monday 10 April she was off the Azores. That afternoon an SOS message was received from the 39,000-ton Liberian-registered oil tanker *Tarseus III*, which was on fire 185 miles from the carrier's position. The tanker had reported that she was on fire in the engine room and that she had a number of casualties who required immediate medical assistance. Two Sea Kings of 824 Squadron, with a medical team, were soon on their way to the stricken tanker, but by the time they reached the *Tarseus III* the fire had been brought under control and repair work was in hand. Three of her crew were returned to the carrier for medical treatment to their burns and once it was clear that all was well with the oil tanker, the *Ark Royal* and her group were able to continue their transatlantic passage. On Wednesday 12 April the ship's company changed into tropical rig and soon afterwards there were some very red, sore, sunburned limbs in evidence. During the afternoon of Sunday 16 April some of the fixed-wing aircraft disembarked to Roosevelt Roads, Puerto Rico, and on the following morning the *Ark Royal* herself berthed at the US Navy's base.

For most of the ship's company the three days spent alongside presented the opportunity for rest and relaxation either at the naval base itself, or further afield on the island, where some even got as far as the city of San Juan 50 miles away. On leaving Puerto Rico the ship steamed south, and after recovering the aircraft she passed through the area between Culebra and St Thomas to take up station in the US Navy's exercise areas to the north of the islands. Once again full use was made of the weapon ranges in the area, and on 29 April Rear-Admiral Staveley visited the ship, inspecting full Ceremonial Divisions the following day which were conducted in full tropical rig within sight of the Puerto Rican coast. During his visit the Admiral flew in all the different aircraft and on 1 May he carried out Rounds of the ship. As always he was well pleased with everything he witnessed and everyone he met on board, and by the time he left on Monday 8 May there was little he had not experienced in the ship. At 10am the next day

the carrier anchored off Charlotte Amalie, the main town of St Thomas, where shore leave was granted, and although it was boats routine once again, at least the weather was congenial. For many, the most popular activities were the organized banyans to Magers Bay Beach which, before the days of mass tourism, was beautifully unspoilt.

After leaving St Thomas in company with HM Ships *Devonshire* and *Antelope* and three RFAs, the *Ark Royal* headed north to the Jacksonville area for more flying exercises. The passage was enlivened by a fancy dress fair which raised a total of £585 for charity, and by the afternoon of Thursday 18 May the carrier had arrived off Jacksonville where once again the flight deck was operating as a busy and dangerous airfield. Despite the fact that flying was disrupted by a lack of wind and boiler problems which also caused water rationing, on 23/24 May the *Ark* took part in the US Navy's annual 'Exercise Solid Shield', where she found herself operating 'against' the USS *John F. Kennedy*. After the exercise there was flying of a totally different kind from the flight deck when 'Hands to Kite Flying Stations' was piped to announce the Grand Kite Flying Competition, an event which attracted over 70 home-made kites, some of which made swift suicidal dives straight into the sea. Two days later the squadrons and air department gave an awesome demonstration of their fire power before, on Monday 29 May, the ship set course for Port Everglades. Next afternoon the *Ark Royal* made what turned out to be a quiet entry into the port where, during the 14-day maintenance period, everyone enjoyed Florida's hospitality. As always, the nightclubs, discotheques, bars, restaurants and other places of entertainment catered for everyone's tastes, and in turn about 10,000 local people toured the *Ark Royal*.

After leaving Port Everglades during the afternoon of Tuesday 13 June, the ship replenished both fuel and stores before the engineers showed that the ship could still wind on a good turn of speed when they subjected her to a full-power trial which achieved 29 knots. Next day saw the 1,000th fixed-wing recovery of the year, followed by the 1,000th launch. Unfortunately the day also saw problems with the fresh water evaporators and the introduction of periodic water rationing. On Monday 19 June the *Ark Royal* began four days of exercises with the US Navy in air defence and air strike operations with US Navy destroyers acting as planeguard escorts. The problems with the evaporators continued to make life difficult for everyone on board and there was relief all round when, on Friday 23 June, the carrier steamed into Mayport, Florida, with full ceremony to undergo a 15-day maintenance period. Once again the ship's stay was dominated by the magnificent hospitality shown to the ship's company, and the fact that a tropical routine was worked ensured that everyone got the opportunity to relax. There were many sad faces in evidence when, on the morning of Tuesday 8 August, the

Ark Royal sailed out into the Atlantic Ocean to recover the squadrons from the Naval Air Station at Cecil Fields. Unfortunately, despite the maintenance period, there was a recurrence of the mechanical faults in the evaporators as well as a new problem with the main engine condensers in Y unit, and water rationing had to be reintroduced.

On 11 August the new FOCAS, Rear-Admiral P. G. M. Herbert OBE, embarked and hoisted his flag in the *Ark Royal* and three days later, with full ceremony and accompanied by numerous gun salutes, the *Ark* entered the dockyard at Norfolk, Virginia, and secured near to her host ship, the giant nuclear-powered carrier, USS *Nimitz*. The main purpose of the visit was a final briefing session before the start of the major NATO exercise 'Northern Wedding', and few complaints were heard from the ship's company who took full advantage of their last seven-day visit to the USA. It was during the forenoon of Monday 21 August 1978 that the *Ark Royal* took her final departure from the United States as the tune 'Sailing' drifted over the naval base, and some of the emotions surrounding the ship's imminent demise were expressed by our NATO allies who had hung a banner ashore declaring, 'Keep The *Ark* Afloat, The Rain May Be Coming.' In the event the 'rain' did come, in the spring of 1982.

After leaving the North American coastline behind, the squadrons were recovered and the *Ark Royal* rendezvoused with HM Ships *Ajax, London, Charybdis, Active, Fife* and *Plymouth,* together with three RFAs for 'Exercise Common Effort', a combined British and American exercise designed to reinforce US Forces in Europe. A fleet of American amphibious ships sailing east had a screen of nuclear-powered submarines for protection, with the *Ark Royal* providing air defence. In the event, rough weather conditions disrupted the fixed-wing flying, but a helicopter of 824 Squadron evacuated a sick rating from the submarine USS *Sculpin* to the carrier's own sickbay, after which the *Ark Royal* and the USS *Montgomery* left the exercise to make a fast passage to the Azores in the hope of finding better weather for flying operations. From the Azores area course was set for the cold waters of the Arctic Circle and on Sunday 3 September, when the carrier was in the latitude of Newcastle upon Tyne, the ship's company changed into blue uniforms. Noon next day saw the start of 'Exercise Northern Wedding' which involved over 200 surface ships from the NATO countries operating in the Norwegian and North Seas in exercises to test the various plans for the defence of northern Europe. The only two fixed-wing carriers present were the *Ark Royal* and the USS *Forrestal* and during the course of the manoeuvres the *Ark Royal* steamed to a northerly point of 64° - 38', before returning to the Moray Firth. The Phantoms provided air cover for the ship and the Gannets carried out surveillance duties, while the Buccaneers were probing radar contacts and carrying out necessary air strikes. The Sea Kings of 824

Squadron flew round-the-clock anti-submarine patrols, and once off the Moray Firth the Buccaneers flew sorties into Norwegian airspace to provide cover for a landing by the amphibious forces from the US, Britain and the Netherlands. As always the NATO exercise was attended by real-life hostile observers in the form of Russian 'Bear' surveillance aircraft, Kresta-class cruisers, and Kashin and Krivak-class destroyers, who were all in close company at various times. Inevitably in northern latitudes the weather also played a major role and on the weekend of 16/17 September, as the exercise drew towards its close, the remnants of Hurricane Flossie moved north-easterly through the area. With gusts of wind in excess of 70 knots and mountainous seas, the *Ark Royal* sustained some structural damage, particularly on the quarterdeck which took the full brunt of the huge waves. There were sighs of relief on Tuesday 19 September when, in the calmer waters of the Moray Firth, the exercise ended, FOCAS and his staff disembarked and preparations were put in hand to greet the ship's royal sponsor.

The Queen Mother had expressed a wish to pay a farewell visit to 'her' ship and at 11.30am on Wednesday 20 September, while the *Ark Royal* was in the Moray Firth, she flew on board in a helicopter of the Queen's Flight to be met by Captain Anson. During her four-hour visit she met a number of the officers and men personally and informally, watched the launch and recovery of some of the ship's aircraft, together with a mini flying display, and toured the Operations Room and Aircraft Direction Room. After lunch with the Captain and Heads of Department, she went to the upper hangar where, in the presence of about 1,000 members of the ship's company, Captain Anson presented her with a small silver replica of the ship's bell mounted in a miniature wooden tabernacle. Addressing her audience the Queen Mother remarked, 'It might seem strange to some people that a man-made floating construction of steel and weaponry should evoke the intensity of feeling, and indeed emotion, which I am sure we are all feeling.' The speech brought a tear to many an eye and when she had concluded, the hangar resounded to the sound of three hearty cheers. At 3.30pm the Queen Mother left her ship after what had been her saddest visit, and on the following day Captain Anson received the following signal from Her Majesty: 'I greatly enjoyed my visit to *Ark Royal* and I was thrilled by your excellent and very exciting flying display. I was deeply touched by your charming gift of the ship's bell with its beautifully constructed tabernacle, it will always remind me of a very happy day spent on board *Ark Royal*. Elizabeth R.'

As soon as the royal visit was over, the helicopters of 824 Squadron embarked stores and a number of passengers, including three Members of Parliament, the Chaplain of the Fleet, and a recording team from the BBC who were embarked for the passage to Gibraltar. The voyage south

The *Ark Royal* laid up in Cremyll Creek awaiting her final voyage to the shipbreaker's yard.

(Imperial War Museum FL 5582)

On 22 September 1980 the *Ark Royal* left Devonport for the last time, bound for Cairnryan and the shipbreaker's yard.

(M. Lennon)

During her slow voyage north, the Sea Harriers of 800 Squadron flew over the *Ark's* deserted flight deck, which had once reverberated to the roar of the jet engines. *(Fleet Air Arm Museum)*

took the ship by way of the north of Scotland and the west coast of Ireland where she fuelled from RFA *Olmeda*. On the evening of 23 September a Sods Opera was staged in the upper hangar, during which the BBC team recorded the ship's company's rendering of 'The Last Farewell', with 'You'll Never Walk Alone' and 'Land of Hope and Glory' on the B-side. In the event the record sold well over 100,000 copies. During the forenoon of Monday 25 September the carrier berthed alongside Gibraltar's South Mole for a seven-day visit and when she left the colony for the last time on Monday 2 October she was flying her 450ft paying-off pennant. After leaving the familiar sight of Gibraltar's Water Catchments behind, course was set for Sardinia where the *Ark* was to play her part in the NATO exercise 'Display Determination 1978', with units from the USA, Italy, Portugal, Greece and Turkey. The aims of the exercise were to test plans for the defence of various strategic areas of the Mediterranean, and the *Ark Royal* joined the manoeuvres on Wednesday 4 October. For seven days the carrier moved from one operating area to another, spending time off Sardinia, Sicily and Greece, with her aircraft performing with exemplary efficiency despite the fact that this was the *Ark's* final lap. For the last time she operated with her old friends, the US Navy's carriers *Forrestal* and *John F. Kennedy,* and on Tuesday 10 October the C-in-C Fleet, Admiral Sir Henry Leach, was embarked. One of his first tasks during his two-day visit was to help stir the final Christmas pudding mix and he was ably assisted by JS Neil Jackson. The *Ark Royal* left the exercise on 11 October and during Sunday 15 October the

Navigating Officer took a scenic route to Naples via the Strait of Messina and round the volcanic Aeolin Islands, which include Stromboli. Next morning, at just before 9am, the *Ark* berthed alongside the Molo Angioino to begin a five-day visit to Naples, the first of four visits during the last few weeks of the deployment. Although it rained on most days of the stay, at least it was warm and the bars, cafés and shops did a roaring trade. Before leaving the city, Admiral of the Fleet Sir Michael Pollock embarked for the passage to Athens, and at 11am on Saturday 21 October the *Ark Royal* bade farewell to Naples, which had always been a popular run ashore, and set course for the toe of Italy. For several days the carrier operated her aircraft to the south-east of Sicily and on Monday 23 October FOCAS, Rear-Admiral Herbert, flew his flag for the last time in the *Ark Royal*. Two days later, during the night of 25 October, the carrier set course for Phaleron Bay, Piraeus, and during the forenoon of Friday 27 October she anchored for a six-day visit to the Greek port.

During the morning of Thursday 2 November the carrier weighed anchor, and after exercising with the USS *Saratoga,* she arrived in Malta's Grand Harbour during the forenoon of Monday 6 November. Although most departments carried out routine maintenance tasks during the ten-day stay, the general atmosphere on board was one of relaxation and many members of the ship's company took station leave. Towards the end of the visit the ship was descended on by television crews, who were to film as much as they could of what was the end of an important period in the Royal Navy's history. Another prominent guest was the wildlife artist and conservationist, Mr David Shepherd, who came to photograph, sketch and generally get a 'feel' for the carrier, in preparation for his painting of the *Ark Royal* which had been commissioned for the Fleet Air Arm Museum. On Thursday 16 November an era came to an end when the Royal Navy's last conventional fleet aircraft carrier slipped her moorings and, watched by over 10,000 people who had lined the vantage points of Valletta to wave goodbye, the *Ark Royal* steamed out of harbour, her paying-off pennant flying in the breeze. It was a very poignant sight which the sightseers who lined the fortifications of the island's capital will never forget.

Soon after leaving Valletta, the First Sea Lord, Admiral Sir Terence Lewin, embarked to observe some of the last flying from the carrier and after spending 24 hours on board he left the ship, but the following signal which he sent caught something of the atmosphere on board: 'I have never seen the *Ark* looking smarter, and for everything from flying operations through to the evaporators to be at such a high pitch at this stage is a tribute to you all. Good luck to each one of you for the next few weeks and for the future, whatever it may hold.' That same afternoon there was a rather more light-hearted farewell when the faithful old wardroom piano was ceremoniously 'buried at sea' after being launched from the bow catapult by Captain Anson. During the forenoon of Saturday 18 November two Buccaneers and two Phantoms left the carrier for good and flew back to the UK. It was the last operational day for the Air Group and Lt Slade RN of 849B Flight had the honour of making the final arrested recovery in Gannet 044. That night course was set for the Balearic Islands and for the port city of Palma on the holiday island of Majorca. It was to be the *Ark's* last foreign visit.

The *Ark Royal* arrived off the island on the morning of Monday 20 November and after a full ceremonial 'Procedure Alpha' entry, including the 21-gun national salute, she secured alongside the Dique De Oeste, which was more accustomed to greeting cruise ships. For five days the ship's company were made welcome by both the local people and the British tourists, and the shops, cafés, nightclubs and hotels were popular venues. Unfortunately, the ship's departure at 10am on Saturday 25 November was marred by a torrential downpour, which precluded holding a full 'Alpha' ceremonial and prevented the ship's company from witnessing the departure. Once at sea all efforts turned towards the disembarkation of the Air Group, but high seas and gale force winds prevented the operation from going ahead on 26 November. Next day, despite continuing high winds and rough seas, all the aircraft were successfully launched for the UK. The honour of the final fixed-wing launch went, ironically, to an RAF officer, Flt-Lt M. Macleod, who, with Lt. D. McCallum RN, was sent down the waist catapult at 3.11pm. This marked the end of flying operations for the *Ark Royal*.

The final evolutions were completed on 28/29 November when, in cold and windy conditions, ammunition was transferred back to RFA *Regent* and Customs officials joined the ship to carry out their unpopular task. On Thursday 30 November there was a brief stop off Gibraltar to disembark the television crews, and that afternoon the ship passed through the Strait of Gibraltar into the Atlantic Ocean, where the swell seemed to push the carrier northwards. That day had also seen the announcement that the third 'through deck cruiser' would take the name *Ark Royal* instead of *Indomitable,* as had been originally intended, and so the name would live on. During the forenoon of Sunday 3 December, whilst the ship was in Mounts Bay, the helicopters of 824 Squadron ferried personnel and stores ashore, and later that day the final Christmas dinner was served. The carrier remained in the Channel that night and before dawn on Monday 4 December she set course for Plymouth breakwater for her final, and much publicized, homecoming. She was to receive a welcome in Plymouth the like of which had not been seen since the frigate *Amethyst* had returned after running the gauntlet of Communist guns in the River Yangtse. In the half-light of dawn, as the carrier moved slowly through Plymouth Sound, the ship's company began to man the flight deck, while the 450ft paying-off pennant, supported by weather balloons, flew from the mainmast. Daylight revealed huge crowds gathered on Plymouth Hoe and all other vantage points, and as the ship approached Drake's Island hundreds of small boats converged on her. As the *Ark Royal* passed the thousands of well-wishers on Plymouth Hoe, the ship's company were allowed to break with tradition and wave back to the crowds. As she passed the Royal William Victualling Yard, the ships berthed there blasted long salutes on their sirens, but as she entered the River Tamar, complete silence fell which was broken only by the shrill sound of the bosun's whistle sounding the 'still'. This was a signal for the officers and men to come to attention as the carrier steamed slowly past Admiralty House at Mount Wise and Flag Officer Plymouth was saluted. As the *Ark Royal* neared her berth, all the warships in the harbour saluted her with their sirens, drowning out the Royal Marines Band on the flight deck. They were joined by a second band ashore, and the cheers of 3,500 relatives who were waiting on the jetty. By 8.30am the first heaving lines were ashore and at 8.50am Captain Anson gave the order, 'Ring off main engines', and the reply came back, 'Engines rung off for the last time, Sir.' The *Ark Royal* would never go to sea under her own power again.

Even before the *Ark Royal* had completed her last deployment calls for her to be preserved were coming from every quarter but, as is often the case with ship preservation, the enormous cost of berthing and maintaining what is, in effect, a dead vessel was given little thought. One plan was put forward to turn her into a floating museum, while

The *Ark Royal* alongside the shipbreaker's yard at Cairnryan. Demolition has not yet started in earnest. *(R. W. Shopland)*

another suggested that she be turned into a floating prison, and the eventual fate of the carrier inevitably became a subject for debate in the letters page of *The Times* newspaper. Perhaps the wisest words were contributed by Admiral Anson, the last commanding officer, who commented: 'I have seen enthusiasts run out of enthusiasm in the past, then all you have is a very fine ship that is slowly allowed to rot to pieces. The public do not generally realize the expense and the difficulty of keeping a ship of that size as a museum or similar function.' Although the debate would continue well into 1979, preservation was never a feasible option and at Devonport work began to remove all remaining stores and the equipment which could be reused. As part of the forward planning for destoring, two Dockyard Inspecting Officers had joined the ship at Naples and returned to the UK with her. One of them had already assisted with destoring the *Ark Royal* in 1967 prior to her major refit, so the undertaking was not as daunting as it might have first appeared to be. The task started in earnest on 5 December 1978, when the carrier was still at 6 and 7 wharves, with the upper hangar being the major centre of activity as the main sorting and packing area. While all this was going on Captain Anson hosted a reunion dinner for eight of her former commanding officers on Wednesday 13 December 1978, and in keeping with the mood of nostalgia the menu started with 'Whyunit Consomme Royal' – named after the engine room which had given them all a

headache at one time or another, being the one which almost invariably caused problems.

Whilst alongside the sea wall all stores were loaded into lorries or trailers which were actually lifted onto and off the flight deck by cranes. On Tuesday 13 February 1979 the White Ensign was lowered for the last time, and eight days later, on Wednesday 21 February, the ship was moved into No 5 basin and moored against the East Wall, where a purpose-built Bailey bridge, constructed by the Royal Engineers, was set up between the jetty and the flight deck allowing vehicles to drive on and off, which saved a great deal of time. The destoring was finally completed in late May 1979, and on Friday 1 June responsibility for the ship was formally handed over to the Fleet Maintenance Staff. Three days later, at 11am on Monday 4 June, the *Ark Royal* made the short journey under the tow of dockyard tugs from No 5 basin to Cremyll, where she was secured to the same buoy which her sister *Eagle* had occupied until she had been towed to the shipbreaker's just eight months before.

For nine months the *Ark* lay rusting at her mooring, and she soon became a familar sight to the commuters using the Torpoint and Cremyll ferries. In March 1980 the Government announced that the ship was to be sold as scrap, thus ending months of indecision and speculation. In May that year she was still moored off Cremyll when the first of a new generation of light fleet aircraft carriers (the original title of through deck cruisers had been dropped),

HMS *Invincible,* visited Devonport for the first time. In July 1980 came the announcement that the *Ark Royal* had been sold for £750,000, with a 'no-resale' clause in the contract which effectively scotched all the last-minute attempts to save the carrier.

Originally it had been intended that the *Ark Royal* would leave Devonport for the breaking-up berth at Cairnryan on Friday 19 September, but she enjoyed a short reprieve when bad weather prevented the tow from getting under way. Three days later, however, her final voyage began when three large tugs shepherded the *Ark* from Devonport on the first stage of the passage north. Six days later, in the brilliant autumn sunshine of Sunday 28 September 1980 and watched by large crowds, she arrived at Cairnryan for demolition. A local journalist described her arrival thus: 'It was 12.45pm on Sunday afternoon. The swell of the sea lapped against the side of the *Ark Royal* as Captain Bill Simpson took his boat *Carstiona* alongside. The massive grey hull of the aircraft carrier curved out overhead and from halfway up her side a rope ladder was thrown. As I watched the pilot and riggers climb the ladder, I steadied myself on the deck of the *Carstiona* as the sea which looked calm from Cairnyan had a swell which became apparent only as we lay alongside the aircraft carrier. It was now the moment of truth and after momentarily considering staying where I was and forgetting the whole thing, I grasped the ladder with both arms and started to climb. For a few seconds I was pleased with my progress until the swell lifted *Carstiona,* which pushed against me. A moment of panic, and I began to climb furiously, holding the sides of the rope ladder like grim death. Forcing myself on I was ecstatic with relief to find arms reaching out and pulling me up the last few steps. On board at last and what a feeling of achievement as I marched off in line behind one of the *Ark Royal's* skeleton crew into the body of the carrier. There were no lights and the darkness grew until it was pitch black in the narrow passageways. A torch lit the way at the head of the expedition but I fell behind as I took smaller steps, not knowing what was in front of me. Soon we were moving up decks ladder by ladder and before long we were up past the bridge and standing on the superstructure. On the open bridge Commander Davies remembered a visit he had paid to *Ark Royal* during his naval service, when jets were roaring up the now deserted flight deck. Sunshine reflected and gleamed from the cars stretching solidly from Cairnryan past Finnants Bay as thousands watched the last few miles in the life of one of the world's best known ships.'

The demolition of the *Ark Royal* was more difficult than had been anticipated, and in 1982, the year that Argentina invaded the Falkland Islands and the British Government struggled to find sufficient maritime air power, the cut-down hulk eventually changed hands, and by 1984, as her successor was nearing completion, the last traces of the aircraft carrier disappeared forever.

A final view of the fourth *Ark Royal* in February 1981. Her island superstructure has gone and her flight deck is gradually disappearing too. *(Fleet Air Arm Museum)*

Commanding Offiicers:

Captain D. R. F. Cambell DSC RN	16 September 1954
Captain F. H. E. Hopkins DSC RN	24 September 1956
Captain P. J. Hill-Norton RN	1 October 1959
Captain D. C. E. F. Gibson DSC RN	14 August 1961
Captain M. P. Pollock MVO DSC RN	21 January 1962
Captain A. T. F. G. Griffin RN	24 January 1964
Captain M. F. Fell DSO RN	25 October 1965
Captain R. D. Lygo RN	17 July 1969
Captain J. O. Roberts RN	9 March 1971
Captain A. D. Cassidi RN	22 August 1973
Captain J. R. S. Gerard-Pearse RN	27 November 1973
Captain W. J. Graham RN	28 March 1975
Captain E. R. Anson RN	28 September 1976

Principal Particulars:

Length Overall:	808ft 3in
Beam:	188ft 5in
Draught:	35ft 7in
Main Propulsion Machinery:	Four shaft. Parsons geared turbines. Eight Admiralty three-drum boilers. 152,000 SHP: 30.5 knots.
Armament:	Eight twin 4.5-inch guns. 40 x 40mm Bofors guns.

Part Three

HMS *Ark Royal*
1985-1999

Chapter Eight

The Name Lives On

The late 1960s were traumatic years for the Fleet Air Arm and for a time following the cancellation of the proposed new fleet aircraft carrier, CVA 01, it appeared that there would be no more fixed-wing flying by the Royal Navy after the demise of *Eagle* and her sister *Ark Royal* in the late 1970s. There was a need for the Navy to re-examine its requirement for sea-based aircraft and, as a result, the small light fleet carriers of the Invincible class were born. Although the three ships of the class are not totally satisfactory in the role once undertaken by the powerful fleet carriers, within the restraints set by successive governments and their defence budgets, they are certainly preferable to the complete abandonment of strike aircraft at sea. However clever their design, the whole concept was only made possible by the successful development of the British Aerospace STOVL Sea Harrier FRS. Instead of catapults the new ships' short decks incorporate a ramp at the forward end to permit rolling take-offs at maximum weight. Initially in 1967, when the first plans were advanced for a 12,500-ton command cruiser designed to carry Sea King helicopters, the proposed vessels looked more like the French helicopter carrier *Jeanne d' Arc*, but by moving the superstructure to the

starboard side a greater area of deck space was achieved. However, the politicians of the day were vehemently opposed to what appeared to be a resurrection of the fleet aircraft carriers, and although the final design of the ships was that of an aircraft carrier, complete with flight deck, aircraft lifts forward and aft, a hangar and starboard island superstructure, they were referred to as 'through deck cruisers'. Three of the new vessels were proposed, with the names *Invincible, Illustrious* and *Indomitable,* which evoked memories of the wartime fleet aircraft carriers that played such an important part in the closing stages of the war against Japan, when they formed the backbone of the British Pacific Fleet. Originally only the *Invincible* was ordered and her keel was laid down at Vickers Shipbuilding & Engineering, at Barrow-in-Furness on 20 July 1973. Although she was designed to act as a command ship on anti-submarine duties at a time when the massive Soviet submarine fleet was perceived as the main threat to world peace, it was also intended that she should operate Sea Harriers in an air defence role. In May 1976 the second ship, *Illustrious,* was ordered and her keel was laid on 7 October that year at Swan Hunter Shipbuilders Ltd at Walker on Tyne. By this time it was also apparent that the

On 2 June 1981 the fifth *Ark Royal* was sent into the waters of the River Tyne by her royal sponsor, Her Majesty Queen Elizabeth The Queen Mother.

(Fleet Air Arm Museum)

third ship of the class would be built and that she would be named *Indomitable*. However, even before the third ship had been ordered, a flood of letters written to *Navy News* prompted second thoughts within the Ministry of Defence about this choice of name, and on Thursday 30 November 1978, as the fourth *Ark Royal* was steaming home at the end of her 23-year career, the Admiralty Board sent the following signal to Captain Anson: 'The return to rest of another Great and Royal *Ark* marks the end of a glorious period in our naval history, during which we have led the world in naval aviation techniques and efficiency. It also marks the beginning of a new and exciting epoch in which we can continue to demonstrate our determination and ability to remain in the forefront of maritime aviation matters. The Admiralty Board stand dedicated to the provision of organic air power at sea, in our ASW carriers and cruisers and in our destroyers and frigates. The aircraft in the fleet in the future, fixed- and rotary-wing, will play a vital part in our National and Alliance capability. It is particularly important therefore that the traditions, professionalism and dedication you have all demonstrated in the *Ark Royal*, ship's company and squadrons alike, are carried forward into this new era, so maintaining the high standards expected of us. To remind the fleet and future generations of these high standards, it is intended that CAH 03 shall be named *Ark Royal*. Well done and good luck to you all.' Two days later, following the launch of HMS *Illustrious* on the River Tyne, the Minister of Defence, Mr Fred Mulley, announced that the fifth *Ark Royal* would be built at a cost of more than £200 million by Swan Hunter Shipbuilders, Wallsend on Tyne, and that her keel would be laid just 13 days later, on 14 December. For the people of Tyneside it was very welcome news as work on the vessel would, at its peak, provide work for

about 30,000 people in the area. With the commissioning of HMS *Invincible* in July 1980, the pretence of the 'through deck cruiser' was dropped and the three ships were officially designated as aircraft carriers for ASW support.

Although the design of all three ships is very similar, the *Ark Royal* has an overall length of 680 feet (209.09m) and a beam of 114 feet (35m), while her official displacement is given as 20,000 tonnes, although her operational displacement is in the region of 21,500 tonnes. Like her two sisters she is powered by four Rolls-Royce Olympus TM3B gas turbines driving through reversing gearboxes onto twin shafts with fixed pitch propellers. At maximum power the main engines develop 100,000 SHP giving the ship a speed in excess of 30 knots; she is fitted with twin rudders and two sets of stabilizers to reduce rolling. One very positive advantage of this method of propulsion is the fact that the same fuel can be used for the main engines, the aircraft and, for that matter, the eight Paxman Valenta diesel generators (similar to the engines of an InterCity 125 High Speed Train), which supply enough electrical power to light a town the size of Gosport. Although her original complement was listed as 57 officers, 160 senior and 449 junior ratings which, with embarked squadrons, increased to 141 officers, 285 senior and 642 junior rates, she was often destined to carry more, which inevitably put a strain on the domestic facilities. As for armament, the ship is fitted with a single Sea Dart GWS 30 Sea-Air Missile launcher forward, with two fire control radars; three, 30mm Vulcan Phalanx radar-controlled air defence guns and two, 20mm visually aimed AA guns. The first two ships of the class were fitted with 7° ski jump take-off ramps which allowed for an increased payload of the Sea Harriers, whereas the *Ark Royal* was built with a 12° ski jump which makes for a marked improvement in aircraft

A very cluttered
flight deck during
the fitting out of
the new carrier.
*(Fleet Air Arm
Museum)*

operational capabilities. Following on from what had been learned from her sister ships' accommodation, the *Ark Royal* could be constructed to the latest specifications, including spacious dining facilities for all members of the ship's company. In addition to the large laundry, manned in keeping with tradition by contractors from Hong Kong, there is also a large and comprehensive sickbay with a well-equipped operating theatre. Like her predecessor, the ship has an excellent CCTV system and her radar fittings include a Type 1022 long-range air warning set, a Type 992 target indication radar, two high definition surface-warning Type 1006 radar, Type 2016 sonar and various types of electronic warfare equipment. All three ships of the class were designed to carry a combination of up to 22 Sea King helicopters and Sea Harrier aircraft.

In March 1981 it was announced that the *Ark Royal* would be launched by Her Majesty Queen Elizabeth The Queen Mother in June of that year, but controversy was already in the air with some critics saying that, among other things, the ships of the class were expensive for their size and that they would be vulnerable to enemy missiles. Some senior RAF officers even remarked that the only reason the vessels had been built was to '...feed the Navy's obsession with big ships and give admirals a chance to look important.' Within 12 months all these criticisms would be silenced and the shortcomings in the RAF's ability to provide strike power and air cover for the fleet would be clear for all to see when Britain went to war, not in northern waters, but in the South Atlantic. However, in the early summer of 1981, before she was even launched, the most serious threat to the *Ark Royal* came from the Government of Mrs Margaret Thatcher. Ministers were determined to cut government expenditure to a bare minimum and a Defence Review, whose conclusions were not published until several weeks after the *Ark's* launching ceremony, ultimately forced massive spending cuts on the Royal Navy, giving rise to speculation that the *Invincible,* the *Illustrious* (which was undergoing contractor's sea trials) and the *Ark Royal* would be mothballed, or worse, by the end of 1983. The Secretary of State for Defence, Mr John Nott, when asked specifically about the *Ark Royal's* future, openly admitted that the ship would never have been ordered in mid-1981 and he refused to give a commitment that she would actually enter service which, in its turn, fuelled speculation that the *Ark Royal* would go into reserve even before she was completed.

The controversy did not, however, spoil the launching which took place on Tuesday 2 June 1981, and 20,000 people cheered when the Queen Mother sent the new carrier stern first into the River Tyne. As the *Ark* entered the water, two Sea Harriers and two Sea Kings overflew the ship as the tugs began to tow her to the fitting-out berth. The only discordant note at the ceremony came from Mr John Nott who grudgingly acknowledged that the *Ark Royal* would

'proceed to completion', but he refused to say whether all three carriers would eventually enter service. Only two weeks after the launch the controversy surrounding the three new carriers erupted once again when it was reported in the press that the Government was prepared to sell the *Invincible* to the Australian Navy as a replacement for the ageing Majestic-class aircraft carrier HMAS *Melbourne* at a very modest price, which was reported to be well below the building cost. It was even rumoured that the US Navy was showing interest as a possible purchaser. There is no doubt that the great amount of media coverage, together with the Defence Minister's obvious feelings that the carriers were expensive luxuries, was being closely watched by the military leaders of Argentina, who had long-standing claims to the Falkland Islands.

As 1981 drew to a close, the controversy continued with rumours of the fate of the Invincible-class ships becoming rife. In December, in reply to a Parliamentary Question asking whether it was true that discussions had taken place between the British and Australian Governments about the sale of the *Invincible* to that country, a Government minister replied, 'I cannot deny that.' When asked, 'What aircraft are going to be available to fly from the *Ark Royal* when she comes into service? Has permission been given for the Royal Navy to order Sea Harriers and helicopters?' the Minister replied, 'There will be Sea Harriers and Sea Kings but there is no clearance for additional aircraft as yet.' The Government's Defence Review argued that Britain's only realistic wartime naval task was to be confined solely to anti-submarine warfare in the Eastern Atlantic Ocean, and that this could best be carried out by a combination of shore-based aircraft and nuclear submarines. It was clear that the Government, keen to save money, was willing to discard one, or even more, of the new aircraft carriers.

Salvation for the Invincible-class carriers came in early 1982, and from an unexpected quarter, when on 2 April that year, Argentine forces invaded the Falkland Islands and quickly overran the small Royal Marines garrison. The sense of national shock and outrage in Britain was instant and unparalleled, and the Defence Minister, John Nott, who was finalizing plans to sell off the *Invincible* and retire the *Hermes,* suddenly had to assemble a task force of up to 40 warships and troop transports, headed by these two ships. Three days after the Argentine invasion, the carriers and the assault ship HMS *Fearless* slid out of Portsmouth Harbour on the morning tide amidst scenes of emotion, the like of which had not been witnessed for many years. The politicians made great capital out of the sailings, mainly in order to divert attention from the government blunders which had allowed the invasion in the first place, but there is no doubt that the sight of the *Hermes* and *Invincible* steaming into the Solent awakened historic memories.

There are few ships, or types of aircraft, which have, on

An aerial view of the ship alongside her fitting-out berth. *(Fleet Air Arm Museum)*

Winter on the River Tyne as the ship nears completion. *(Fleet Air Arm Museum)*

their own, decided the outcome of a military campaign, but the *Invincible, Hermes* and the Sea Harrier did just that, and without them the successful mission by the Royal Navy Task Force to eject the invaders from the Falkland Islands would not have been possible. Politically, the effect of the campaign was to convince the British Government that they should cancel the proposed sale of HMS *Invincible* and end their short-term economies thus ensuring that the *Ark Royal* would be commissioned into operational service with the Royal Navy.

In June 1982 key members of the ship's company began to join the ship at Wallsend on Tyne, but it was over two years later, on Friday 19 October 1984, when the carrier left the Tyne for the first time to begin her contractor's sea trials. During this period the ship was under the command of Trials Master, Captain George Kitchen RN (Retd), and Swan Hunter's Shipyard Director, Mr Norman Gilchrist, was also on board. Although he had not yet taken up his appointment, the commanding officer designate, Captain James Weatherall RN, was also embarked. During almost

three weeks of trials in the North Sea, testing all aspects of the ship's machinery and equipment, and demonstrating to the Ministry of Defence that the requirements of the contract had been met, the *Ark Royal* met her older sister *Illustrious,* before returning alongside her fitting-out berth on the River Tyne on Friday 9 November.

In late March 1985 Captain Weatherall joined the ship, which was close to completion at Swan Hunter's Walker shipyard. Captain Weatherall had joined the Royal Navy in 1954 and he had gone on to specialize in navigation. The greater part of his career had been spent at sea, during which he had commanded the minesweeper *Soberton* on fishery protection duties, and the frigates *Ulster, Tartar* and *Andromeda.* Captain Weatherall had also been the last Executive Officer of the fourth *Ark Royal,* so he was no stranger to the ship's historic background. When Captain Weatherall joined the ship she was still far from complete, and on 12 April 1985 she left the River Tyne once again for two days of final machinery trials. On Wednesday 26 June the main body of the ship's company moved on board and forty-eight hours later she sailed from the Tyne bound for Portsmouth with 140 Swan Hunter employees still in attendance to finish off the cleaning up. Also on board for the voyage, parked at the forward end of the flight deck, was a Swordfish aircraft as a reminder of the third *Ark Royal.* Another reminder of this predecessor was the ship's silver bell which had been bought in 1945 with £598 from that ship's welfare fund. The bell had been hallmarked at Goldsmith's Hall, London, earlier in 1985 and its inscriptions contained the ship's crest, the names of commanding officers from November 1938 to November 1941, a summary of the principal operations during the Second World War and the dedication, 'From the company who sailed in the *Ark* in the years 1938 to 1941 to those who follow them.'

The *Ark Royal* at sea in April 1985, carrying out machinery trials. *(Fleet Air Arm Museum)*

Flying the Red Ensign, and with a Swordfish parked at the forward end of the flight deck, the *Ark Royal* steams south from the River Tyne to Portsmouth.
(Fleet Air Arm Museum)

Chapter Nine

The North Atlantic And The Caribbean
1985-1988

After leaving the River Tyne the *Ark Royal* inevitably attracted a great deal of interest from Soviet spy ships which followed her down the North Sea and into the Channel. It was clear that they were impressed by the reputation that the name generated. During the morning of Monday 1 July 1985 she arrived in the Solent, from where she was welcomed into Portsmouth Harbour with a fly-past by Sea Harriers of the Fleet Air Arm. As the *Ark Royal* approached the harbour mouth, thousands of people gathered on the beaches of Southsea and the ramparts of Old Portsmouth cheered her in. Drawn up on her flight deck were the Swordfish and a Sea Harrier, both of which were links with previous *Arks*. Although she had been completed ahead of schedule, at a cost of £320 million, the fleet's newest acquisition carried 250 Tynesiders who still had a great deal of painting and cleaning up to finish. It was said that as she carried out power trials and roll manoeuvres on the way down through the North Sea, a lone 'Mrs Mopp' was still doggedly swabbing the uppermost decks after all personnel had been ordered below. Although the workers remained on board for another two weeks, Captain Weatherall accepted the ship from the shipbuilders, and the ship's company underwent intensive training to prepare the carrier for her trials and for her commissioning ceremony which was set for November that year.

It was on Monday 15 July, with the builder's employees having finally left the ship, that the *Ark Royal* sailed for her acceptance sea trials with five Wessex helicopters of 845 Squadron embarked. On completion of these trials she returned to Portsmouth where personnel from Swan Hunter's were on hand to rectify defects which had arisen, and the ship herself took pride of place at the city's Navy Days during the Bank Holiday weekend. Next came even more trials, following which she was opened to the public at Portland where, despite strong winds, she was berthed alongside. Finally, on Friday 1 November 1985, the *Ark Royal* was commissioned at Portsmouth with Her Majesty Queen Elizabeth The Queen Mother in attendance and making it clear that she would take as much interest in the fifth *Ark Royal* as she had in the fourth. Three days later, on Monday 4 November, the carrier sailed for further sea trials with two Sea Harriers, setting course for the warmer waters of the Mediterranean Sea and a deployment which took her as far as Crete. On 9 November she was in Gibraltar, and after leaving the colony she carried out flying trials in waters

which had been so familiar to two of her predecessors. On Thursday 14 November 1985, exactly 44 years to the day since the torpedoing of the third *Ark Royal* in the Second World War, she stopped over the spot and a wreath was laid. Eleven days later, on Monday 25 November, she made the first 'foreign' visit of her career, to Marseilles, and a week later she had anchored in Crete's Suda Bay prior to carrying out exercises in the area. The passage home in early December was punctuated by exercises with the French helicopter carrier *Jeanne d'Arc* and Italian naval units, and on Monday 16 December she arrived back in Portsmouth from what had been a successful deployment, not least in consolidating the sense of team spirit among the ship's company. Three days after her arrival saw the transfer of 801 Squadron (Sea Harriers) and 820 Squadron (Sea Kings) from the *Invincible* which was about to start a long refit.

It was late January 1986 before the *Ark Royal* left Portsmouth again to continue with her sea trials, which included a visit to Amsterdam, and in February she started her work-up in the Portland area. Early April 1986 saw the carrier off Western Scotland for the second phase of her work-up, during which a Sea Harrier was lost, but fortunately the pilot was rescued. The ship's Operational Readiness Inspection took place on Wednesday 23 April and, having passed this successfully, she returned to Portsmouth the following day. During the stay alongside the installation of her weapons system was completed, and Tuesday 10 June 1986 marked the final acceptance of the ship from Swan Hunter Shipbuilders Ltd.

On Tuesday 17 June 1986 the *Ark Royal* left Portsmouth Harbour for her first full operational deployment, and once into the Channel she embarked her Air Group, together with three Sea King AEW helicopters of 849B Flight, with their ungainly looking radar suspended from the side. The first exercise of the deployment, code-named 'Liberty Train', took place in the North Atlantic during the ship's passage west to New York. On the morning of Saturday 28 June, together with the frigates *Sirius* and *Cleopatra*, the carrier arrived off the Sandy Hook Lightship and, flying the flag of Flag Officer Third Flotilla, Vice-Admiral Sir Julian Oswald, who was also responsible for aircraft carriers, she steamed into New York Harbor to berth alongside the Cunard liner *QE2* in Manhattan. The visit had been planned for almost a year so that the *Ark Royal* could take part in celebrations to mark the Statue of Liberty's 100th birthday, and also the reopening of the

On 1 July 1985, with a Sea Harrier and a Swordfish on deck, the *Ark Royal* arrived alongside Portsmouth's Middle Slip Jetty for the first time. In the background is HMS *Victory* and the covered dock housing the *Mary Rose*. *(Fleet Air Arm Museum)*

The *Ark Royal* leaves Portsmouth on 27 January 1986 for her sea trials. *(W. Sartori)*

newly refurbished monument to visitors. America's great symbol of hope had been delivered to the USA as a gift from France in 1886, and she had been sorely in need of a full facelift in order to restore her to her former glory, with appropriately, Monday 4 July being chosen for the opening ceremony. On the evening of 28 June Admiral Oswald hosted a dinner on board the *Ark Royal,* at which the American Secretary of State for Defence, Mr Caspar Weinberger, was the guest of honour. On 4 July the *Ark* joined 40 other warships from the US Navy and various other nations in the harbour, which President Ronald Reagan then reviewed from the battleship *Iowa.* Many people thought that the *Ark's* Harriers stole the show when they staged a remarkable display of hovering and 'bowing' to the Statue of Liberty. The visit to New York was concluded on Tuesday 8 July, when the carrier left the harbour to take part in 'Exercise ASWEX 1/86' along the USA's eastern seaboard, during which she commanded the anti-submarine strike force of the NATO Fleet.

On Wednesday 23 July the ship sailed into Port Everglades, Fort Lauderdale, Florida, for rest and recreation, as well as maintenance, during a seven-day visit to the port. Although it had been seven years since her predecessor had paid her last visit, there were many happy memories of the earlier ship and the newcomer received the same enthusiastic welcome. There then followed exercises in the Bahamas area, before she sailed north to Norfolk, Virginia, where Admiral Oswald rejoined the ship and

preparations were made for the carrier's participation in 'Northern Engagement' and 'Northern Wedding', two major NATO exercises. The first exercise was carried out as the fleet steamed north-east across the Atlantic, then they proceeded with 'Northern Wedding' on reaching the Northern Atlantic and the Norwegian and North Seas. On conclusion of the exercises the wash-up was held in Amsterdam on 22 September, and five days later, on Saturday 27 September, the *Ark Royal* arrived back in Portsmouth to undergo a 16-day self-maintenance period.

It was Monday 13 October 1986 when the *Ark Royal* left Portsmouth again, this time to take part in 'Exercise Autumn Train', a national exercise in which the participating ships rendezvoused in the Western Approaches before steaming south to Gibraltar. During the passage a Sea King of 820 Squadron was lost, but happily the crew were rescued, and on 23 October the *Ark* put into Gibraltar. Three days later, on a beautiful warm and sunny day, a major pop concert was recorded for television on the carrier's flight deck while the whole harbour rocked to the sounds of the pop star Bob Geldof and a full supporting cast; the programme was transmitted on ITV channels on Christmas Day. It took most of the evening and night to dismantle and unload all the staging and equipment, after which the ship sailed at 6.30am for Lisbon. Upon departure from the River Tagus at the end of her visit to the Portuguese capital, the *Ark Royal* sailed north and after disembarking 820 Squadron off the coast of Cornwall and

In January 1986, during her sea trials, the *Ark Royal* paid a short visit to Amsterdam. It was her first foreign visit.

(Fleet Air Arm Museum)

landing on the Sea Kings of 845 Squadron, she set course for the Firth of Forth. It was intended to exercise the ship in her alternative role of a commando carrier, and on 5 November she embarked the Commodore Amphibious Warfare and the First Dutch Amphibious Combat Group by helicopter off Gourock. The exercise which followed, code-named 'High Tide', was completed in the area off Arbroath near the Firth of Tay after which, in mid-November, the Dutch marines were disembarked to Valkenberg Air Force Base, near Maastricht. Although the exercise itself was a success, the ship's services had been strained to the limits. The *Ark Royal* then paid a short visit to Hamburg before returning to her home port for an assisted maintenance period and, more importantly for the ship's company, seasonal leave.

After leaving Portsmouth on Monday 12 January 1987 and embarking 821 Squadron on the following day, it had been intended to set course for the warmer waters of the Caribbean, but when the after lift broke down it was necessary to return to Portsmouth where repairs could be put in hand. The design of the aircraft lifts installed in the Invincible-class carriers, and the technology employed, was derived from what had been planned for the ill-fated CVA 01 and the 'scissors' arrangement allowed open hangar space on three sides. Once the ship was alongside, the helicopters of 820 Squadron and 849B Flight were embarked, and five days later the *Ark Royal* rejoined the main group which were

waiting in the South-Western Approaches. The scheduled transatlantic exercise was drastically reduced because of severe weather in the Atlantic Ocean and on 26 January, when the ship was in the vicinity of the Azores, a section of the bow plate was forced off by heavy seas. Although the resultant flooding was easily controlled, speed had to be reduced and the *Ark Royal* was diverted to Bridgetown, Barbados, where 10AZ compartment was filled with concrete as a temporary repair.

The carrier remained alongside in Bridgetown for six days between Monday 2 February and Sunday 8 February, and during this time her second commanding officer, Captain M. G. T. Harris RN, relieved Captain Weatherall and took over command of the ship. Captain Harris had spent a great part of his career in submarines, during which time he commanded the *Osiris*, the *Sovereign* and the 3rd Submarine Squadron. Between 1980 and 1982 he commanded the Type 42 destroyer HMS *Cardiff*, which saw service in the South Atlantic in the Falklands campaign. He took the *Ark Royal* to sea on 9 February for 'Exercise ASWEX 1/87' with the US Navy, when the Harriers of 801 Squadron gave an awesome demonstration of their effectiveness on the US Navy's bombing range at Vieques Island, off the main island of Puerto Rico. As a break from the exercise the carrier anchored off Tortola Island, which forms part of the British Virgin Islands, just west of Puerto Rico. This spell enabled a large number of

Sea Harriers of 801 Squadron on deck.
(Fleet Air Arm Museum)

A Sea Harrier takes off from the ramp
of the *Ark Royal*.
(Fleet Air Arm Museum)

The *Ark Royal* enters Port Everglades on
Wednesday 23 July 1986 during her first
exercises in US waters.
(Fleet Air Arm Museum)

people to get ashore onto remote beaches for rest, recreation and magnificent barbeques. An official visit was also arranged to San Juan, the capital of Puerto Rico, designed to help promote trade between the island and the UK, and in the first week of March the *Ark* put into the US Naval Base at Mayport, in northern Florida, for maintenance. This was followed by exercises off the south Florida coast, code-named 'Punish', a title which, on Wednesday 18 March, turned out to be rather appropriate when the ship's port-outer Olympus gas turbine suffered a catastrophic failure and smashed turbine blades were sent flying like bullets through the uptakes and onto the flight deck. Such was the versatility of the vessel's method of propulsion and such the skill of her engineers that they were able to replace the crippled turbine whilst the ship was at sea, and on Monday 23 March she paid a visit to Charleston, South Carolina. On Thursday 9 April 1987 the *Ark Royal* returned to Portsmouth for leave and maintenance, although there was not enough time to complete repairs to the hull damage sustained during her outward transatlantic passage.

During the first week of May 1987 the *Ark Royal* left Portsmouth again, flying the flag of the newly appointed Flag Officer Third Flotilla, Rear-Admiral H. White, for 'Exercise ASWEX 2/87', which entailed two weeks of anti-submarine exercises in the North-Western Approaches. These manoeuvres were followed in early June by Staff College Sea Days, which saw the *Ark Royal* navigate the River Thames and the Thames Barrier on 4 June to moor to buoys in the river opposite Greenwich Pier. She was the largest warship ever to pass through the Thames Barrier, and afterwards when describing the experience, Captain Harris remarked that it had left him feeling like the driver of a car who had just survived a foolishly narrow scrape. The visit to London celebrated the 400th Anniversary in the previous year of the launching of the first *Ark Royal* at Deptford on 12 June 1586. The main event of the stay was a formal banquet which had been organized by the White Ensign Association, for which a huge marquee was erected on the flight deck and tables were laid for 800 in the hangar. The guest of honour was HRH Princess Alexandra and other guests included Admiral of the Fleet Lord Lewin, the tennis star Virginia Wade, and several politicians who were taking time out from campaigning for the General Election which was being held three days later. The evening ended with a fly-past and a fireworks display, and next day the carrier's royal sponsor, Her Majesty Queen Elizabeth The Queen Mother, visited 'her' ship.

After leaving the River Thames on Wednesday 10 June, the *Ark Royal* set course north for the Firth of Forth and Rosyth, where she took part in Navy Days at the port which was then still a naval base. Two days later she participated in Joint Maritime Course (JMC) 872, the aim of which was to exercise ships and aircraft of different nations in combined operations. During the first phase of the exercise, pilots of the RAF's No 1 Squadron and their Harriers were embarked, and the ship also worked closely with the RAF's new Tornado F3 fighter-bombers from RAF Coningsby in Suffolk. At the end of the exercise the *Ark Royal* was off the Orkneys on a lovely summer's evening and she was preparing to leave the area when a signal was received from the Coastguard to the effect that a German fishing trawler, the *Hessen,* was sinking in a position not far from the carrier. Helicopters with damage control teams took off at once, with the ship following at her best speed, and in the event the Sea Kings rescued the trawler's crew as their vessel sank beneath them.

The *Ark Royal's* next commitment, 'Exercise Hadrian's Wall', involved landing Special Forces on Scotland's east coast, for which the carrier spent a great deal of time anchored off St Andrews. This completed, she set course south for Portsmouth, where she arrived on Friday 3 July for maintenance. Ten days after her arrival at Portsmouth the *Ark Royal* went into D Lock dry dock, but she was out again in time for Navy Days at the end of August. As soon as these were over, she put to sea again on Tuesday 1 September for three days of post-refit trials followed by a Royal Navy Equipment Exhibition at Portsmouth. On Tuesday 22 September hard work started again in earnest when a sea training programme began at Portland, during which the ship took on a full load of ammunition from the RFA *Fort Austin,* an operation which saved a great deal of time on transfers from lighters. At this time the carrier also conducted live Sea Dart missile firings in order to test new equipment which had been installed during the refit. The aviation work-up started on Wednesday 14 October off the coast of Scotland, and on the next day a Sea Harrier was lost after a collision with a bird, but fortunately the pilot ejected safely and he was rescued by a Sea King of 820 Squadron. This was a time of intense pressure involving long periods of flying operations and defence watches, but finally, on Friday 23 October, came the Operational Readiness Inspection. In his report, Admiral White commented on the ship's company and their 'most creditable all-round standards' and their 'positive attitude and good humour amongst a well-led and happy ship's company.' Following the inspection the ship returned to Portsmouth to carry out maintenance, before sailing on Tuesday 3 November to take part in a major fleet exercise code-named 'Purple Warrior'. This was the biggest single national exercise since the Falklands War, and it was designed to test the abilities of a task group to evacuate British nationals from a distant and hostile shore. Also present was HMS *Illustrious* with 40 Commando Royal Marines embarked and the helicopters of 845 and 846 Squadrons. The *Ark Royal* meanwhile, with 800 and 801 Sea Harrier Squadrons, 849B Flight, part of 826 Sea King (anti-submarine) Squadron and No 1 RAF Squadron of

The *Ark Royal* (RO7), and her sister ship *Illustrious* at sea together.

(Fleet Air Arm Museum & C. Minett)

On 29 January 1988 the *Ark Royal* paid her first visit to the River Tyne since her departure from the builder's yard in June 1985.

(A. Sparrow)

Harriers embarked, acted as both command ship, air defence and strike carrier. She flew the flag of Flag Officer Third Flotilla and also had on board the staff from the Joint Forces Headquarters, which pushed her complement up to almost 1,500 so that temporary accommodation had to be arranged in passageways and any other spaces which could be utilized for this purpose. Clearly, the Navy was feeling the loss of the fleet carriers and these much smaller ships were being required to perform a role for which they had not been designed. The commando landings were carried out along the south coast and once these had been completed the Harriers had to engage 'hostlile' Buccaneers and Jaguars, and intercept shadowing Nimrod aircraft. On 12 November the RAF Harriers and the Joint Staff disembarked, which eased the pressure on the ship's services, and on 16 November the Sea Harriers of 800 and 801 Squadrons flew over 50 sorties. On Tuesday 17 November, the final day of manoeuvres, the *Ark* went into Loch Linnhe in the Firth of Lorn to carry out coastal air defence exercises. Next day, having steamed south again, most of the Air Group was disembarked to Yeovilton, before the *Ark Royal* made a short visit to the French port of Cherbourg prior to returning to Portsmouth on Tuesday 24 November for seasonal leave. The carrier had played a vital role throughout the exercise, despite having lost the use of her port-inner gas turbine on 8 November which limited her speed to 25 knots, and the C-in-C Fleet congratulated the ship's company on having risen to the challenge, thereby contributing greatly to the success of the exercise.

The *Ark Royal's* operations got under way again on Tuesday 26 January 1988 when she left Portsmouth to embark 801 and 820 Squadrons and 849B Flight for two days of exercises before heading north on Friday 29 January to navigate the River Tyne for the first time since June 1985. This was followed by air defence exercises in the North Sea where the Air Group operated with RAF Tornadoes and Phantoms and the US Air Force's F111s from their bases in East Anglia. On Monday 8 February, the 25th Anniversary of the first STOVL landing on an aircraft carrier, the occasion was marked by the landing of a Harrier carrying the original test pilot, the late A. W. (Bill) Bedford. After a short stay at Rosyth the *Ark Royal* then took part in JMC 881, which was hampered by an outbreak of influenza on board, then the first two days of March were taken up with exercises with the *Illustrious,* before the *Ark* sailed up the River Elbe, flying the flag of the C-in-C Fleet, for a visit to Hamburg. Sadly this was marred by the death of a member of the ship's company for whom a memorial service was held on the first day out at sea. From Hamburg the *Ark Royal* went straight into 'Exercise Mallet Hammer', an air defence and interception exercise, during which the carrier acted as a command centre for the United Kingdom's air defences. Although foul weather inhibited flying, on 17 March 801 Squadron's Harriers executed 104 interceptions in the course of 25 sorties. The end of the exercise saw the *Ark* pay a short visit to Rotterdam before returning to Portsmouth on Wednesday 23 March 1988 to carry out maintenance and for the ship's company to take leave before the most important deployment of the year.

Chapter Ten

East Of Suez And Into Reserve
1988-1998

When Britain withdrew from her military bases east of Suez in late 1971, and linked her future to Europe by joining the EEC shortly afterwards, it was generally thought that the Royal Navy would be confined to operations in the Mediterranean and the North Atlantic. However, Britain still had military links with countries in South-East Asia, and 1988 had been chosen for a very special deployment east of Suez. That year marked Australia's bicentenary and it had been decided to send a naval task group to the Far East and Australia to take part in the celebrations. Leading the task group would be the *Ark Royal,* flying the flag of Rear-Admiral A. P. Woodhead (FOF2), the Type 42 destroyer HMS *Edinburgh,* the Leander-class frigate HMS *Sirius* and the RFAs *Orangeleaf* and *Fort Grange.* In operational terms the deployment, code-named 'Outback 88', was a demonstration to friendly countries in the area that Britain was willing, and still able, to send a force to the Far East

should political circumstances require it.

However, before she left for the deployment, the refit had to be completed, and this entailed two gas turbines and one of the diesel generators being replaced. On Wednesday 1 June ammunition was embarked and two days later a 'Families Day' was held, when 2,500 guests were taken to sea for the day. This was followed on 6 June by a shakedown cruise during which the Air Group was embarked, and on Monday 13 June the *Ark Royal* sailed out of Portsmouth Harbour accompanied by her escorts and the RFAs with course set for the Mediterranean. On board the *Ark* was a detachment of Royal Marines and 22 aircraft, made up of eight Sea Harriers, nine anti-submarine Sea Kings, three AEW Sea Kings and two helicopters of 845 Squadron's Commando Flight. Once again the accommodation on board was stretched to the limits and the ship's gymnasium had been converted into a mess deck. In addition, with no bases east of Suez,

On 16 June 1988 there was an unusual rendezvous off the coast of Portugal when the *Ark Royal* met the P&O liner *Canberra* which was nearing the end of a luxury cruise to the Mediterranean. *(Fleet Air Arm Museum)*

In June 1988, with anti-nuclear protesters having blocked the entrance to Grand Harbour, the *Ark Royal* anchored in St Paul's Bay, Malta. The statue of St Paul can be seen in the background.

(M. Cassar)

The *Ark Royal* berths astern of the battleship USS *New Jersey* at Subic Bay in the Philippines. For many it would be their first visit to the never-to-be-forgotten town of Olongapo.

(Fleet Air Arm Museum)

The *Ark Royal* berths alongside the old naval base HMS *Tamar* during her visit to Hong Kong on 23 August 1988.

(Fleet Air Arm Museum)

Exercises with the USS *New Jersey*, during which the battleship demonstrated her firepower. *(Fleet Air Arm Museum)*

enormous quantities of spares had to be carried in case of emergencies. After leaving the security of Portsmouth Harbour the group took part in 'Exercise Jolly Roger' in the Bay of Biscay with the RAF and the French Navy. During the morning of Thursday 16 June there was an unusual rendezvous when the carrier met the elderly P&O liner SS *Canberra,* which was nearing the end of a 14-day Mediterranean cruise. The *Canberra's* master, Captain Michael Bradford, had announced to his passengers that they were approaching the task group and that if weather conditions permitted, the carrier would put on a flying display. The story is taken up by one of the *Canberra's* passengers: 'Everyone was up on deck early the next day, but it was cloudy and overcast. At 9am a lone Harrier appeared to check the weather and we were told that a fly-past was on. Later, however, we were told that the weather over the carrier was not good enough, but that the *Ark Royal* herself, some 64 miles away, intended to come over for a visit. We were all ready, with cameras poised, as two Sea Harriers flew over, and then we spotted the *Ark Royal* approaching us. She finally came within 200 yards of us, sailing alongside and exchanging courtesies. One signal read: "Lovely to see you again. I still remember the smoked salmon from six years ago this month. You are, as ever, a credit to the Blue Ensign. Bon voyage to yourself, your passengers and ship's company." We continued to cruise alongside each other for ten minutes with all of us taking photographs, and before breaking away, *Ark Royal* signalled, "I wish you a pleasant voyage." *Canberra* replied, "Thank you very much. I wish you a pleasant voyage." We exchanged blasts on our sirens and the *Ark Royal* turned at speed, heeling over dramatically, and sped off into the distance, soon disappearing from our sight.' Two days later the *Canberra's* cruise ended at Southampton, while the *Ark Royal* and her group continued on their way to the Mediterranean as they set course for Malta. However, there was soon to be a discordant note to the proceedings.

In the Mediterranean the task group met with an Italian naval force led by the aircraft carrier *Guiseppe Garibaldi,* a very similar ship to the *Ark Royal,* and a few days later she met the Soviet Navy's Kirov-class aircraft carrier *Baku* (now called *Admiral Gorshkov*). The meeting took place off the Golfe de Hammamet, Tunisia, and the Russian CO seemed keen to show off the 'Forger' VTOL aircraft which the vessel carried. It is generally widely known, although never officially admitted, that certain Royal Navy warships carry nuclear weapons and, in anticipation of the *Ark Royal's* imminent visit to Malta's Grand Harbour, anti-nuclear protesters blocked the harbour entrance by anchoring a large oil tanker, the MV *Copper Mountain,* just inside the breakwater. Although this ship was removed, the protesters were undeterred and on Saturday 25 June, the day scheduled for the task group's arrival, they again blocked the harbour, this time with the tanker MV *Olympic*

Rainbow. In the event, the visiting ships put into St Paul's Bay, just as generations of naval vessels had done before, where they were greeted by a flotilla of small boats and enthusiastic well-wishers. During the stay liberty men were landed at Bugibba, and the island's Prime Minister and his officials were guests at formal dinners on board. When the *Ark Royal* left on Wednesday 29 June, bound for Port Said, she and the other ships of the group were given a warm send-off. After exercising with RAF aircraft from Cyprus and the US Navy's submarine *Cincinnati,* and evacuating an injured seaman from a US auxiliary, on Saturday 2 July the *Ark Royal* made her first southbound transit of the Suez Canal, passing the former colony of Aden on 14 July, where she received no welcome. Two days later, in the Indian Ocean, a major storing exercise was undertaken by two of the *Ark's* Sea Kings, flying between Colombo and RFA *Fort Grange.* This operation was followed by 'Exercise Starfish', in company with forces from Australia, New Zealand, Malaysia and Singapore, which was part of a programme under the agreement signed with these countries at the time of the British withdrawal from the region in 1971. The Sea Harriers operated from the Malaysian air base at Kuantan, the scene of that disaster for the Royal Navy 47 years earlier when the capital ships *Prince of Wales* and *Repulse* were lost to superior air power. On Saturday 23 July the *Ark Royal* berthed at the Sembawang Dockyard, the former base for the Royal Navy, which for many proved a nostalgic event. During the visit a Fleet Maintenance Unit flew out to assist the ship's company with work on the vessel's machinery, and on Sunday 31 July the Prime Minister, Mrs Margaret Thatcher, and Singapore's Defence Minister were guests at a dinner on board. In the meantime the Sea Harriers stayed at Singapore's old civil airport at Paya Lebar, where they were able to carry out a training programme. On 5 August, 100 special guests enjoyed a Defence Equipment Sales Day, followed three days later by a Defence Export Sea Day, before the *Ark Royal* and her group sailed for the Philippines and the US Naval Base at Subic Bay, where she docked astern of the battleship USS *New Jersey.* After four days sampling the dubious delights of Olongapo which, to many old hands, did not seem to have changed much since the 1960s, the group sailed for exercises with the US Navy, during which the *New Jersey* gave a demonstration of 'old-fashioned' fire power with her 16-inch guns. Impressive though it looked, it was clear that it was not going to hail the start of a new age of supremacy for these levathians. On Tuesday 23 August the task group put into Hong Kong for five days, and back at sea on 29 August one of the *Ark's* Sea Kings spotted a small boat, drifting helplessly, which turned out to be full of Vietnamese refugees trying desperately to escape from their country. In the event, they were rescued by HMS *Edinburgh* and taken to Singapore on board one of the RFAs. In early September the units participated in

Ark Royal alongside Sydney's prestigious Overseas Passenger Terminal for her 11-day visit to the city in September/October 1988. (*Fleet Air Arm Museum*)

On 15 December 1988 the *Ark Royal* arrived back in Portsmouth from her 'Outback 88' deployment. (*W. Sartori*)

'Exercise Setia Kewan', designed to assist the Brunei Armed Forces, during which the Sultan visited the ship. There then followed a joint exercise with Malaysian and Singaporean forces, with the defence equipment sales receiving a boost from a visit to the ship by the Minister of Defence who had flown out from London. On 11 September there was even a Defence Sea Day for Indonesian naval staff, and on Saturday 17 September, after mock attacks by the RAAF, the *Ark* negotiated the northern Barrier Reef to anchor off the rocky island of Cape York, Queensland, now known as Possession Island, where on 22 August 1770, after hoisting a Union Flag, Captain Cook claimed the whole coast of Australia from that point to 38°, which was close to his original landfall at what is now Cape Everard, Victoria, for King George III. After anchoring, Captain Harris went ashore from the *Ark Royal* with a ceremonial guard to unveil a plaque rededicating a memorial to the event 218 years before. This small ceremony heralded the start of the visit to

Australia and after further exercises with Australian forces some of the aircraft were flown ashore, then on Wednesday 21 September the *Ark Royal* berthed at Hamilton Wharf, Brisbane, for a four-day visit. With the city hosting Expo 88 and extending lavish hospitality, there was plenty to occupy the ship's company, who also participated in a bicentennial march past through the city centre. On Sunday 25 September, surrounded by an enormous amount of press publicity, the *Ark* left the Brisbane River and set course for Sydney where she arrived to a warm reception, although there were a few anti-nuclear protesters in evidence again. After dodging a flotilla of small boats, the carrier berthed alongside the prestigious Overseas Passenger Terminal, in the shadow of the famous Harbour Bridge. The social programme during the carrier's 11-day visit was almost overwhelming and on 29 September her ship's company took part in a march past in the city. On the following day she was moved out into the harbour and on Saturday 1

October came the highlight of the visit, the Bicentennial International Fleet Review by HRH The Duke of York in HMAS *Cook*. Among the ships that day were the USS *New Jersey* and the FS *Colbert* which, with the *Ark Royal,* were the largest ships present. To round off the occasion, four Sea Harriers and three Sea Kings from the *Ark* took part in a fly-past. Six days later, after a memorable visit, the carrier left Sydney for exercises in Jervis Bay, during which the Sea Harriers sank the Attack-class fast patrol boat HMAS *Buccaneer* with 1,000lb bombs.

After leaving the area the task group set course for Melbourne where the *Ark Royal* had been scheduled to berth alongside Princes Pier in the city but, once again, anti-nuclear protests by the Seamen's Union, whose members manned the tugs, prevented her from getting into the harbour. Even in perfect conditions the entry into the port is a difficult manoeuvre, but at the time high winds were blowing and to try to enter the harbour without assistance was out of the question. For three days the *Ark Royal* waited outside in Port Phillip Bay before, on 16 October, she eventually set course across the Great Australian Bight for Fremantle. On 22 October the task group arrived off the west coast of Australia where some of the aircraft were flown ashore, and the next day the *Ark* prepared to enter harbour. However, yet again her attempts were frustrated by anti-nuclear demonstrations and this time the Crane Drivers' Union also boycotted the ship, which meant that for two days personnel had to go ashore by boat. Fortunately the boycott was lifted for the visit of the Australian Defence Minister and despite the difficulties the antipodean sojourn was enjoyed by all.

After leaving Fremantle the *Ark Royal* and her task group set course across the Indian Ocean for Bombay, carrying out exercises en route, and on Tuesday 15 November they reached the Indian port where, once again, Defence Export Days were held, both in harbour and at sea. By 19 November the group had left Indian waters and while crossing the Arabian Sea exercises were carried out with the USS *Nimitz* which was in the area to keep an eye on developments in the Iran-Iraq War. On 2 December the *Ark* made her northbound transit of the Suez Canal and after operating with the USS *John F. Kennedy* and FS *Clemenceau* in the Mediterranean, and making a short stop at Gibraltar, she set course for home. Whilst crossing the Bay of Biscay she joined manoeuvres with her sister ship *Illustrious* and over the next two days the squadrons were flown off. As she sailed along the Dorset coast she met *Illustrious* again and also *Invincible,* in their first meeting at sea. On the evening of Wednesday 14 December she anchored at Spithead and next day she sailed up harbour to berth alongside South Railway Jetty after an absence of six months. Captain Harris was able to report that the deployment had been an unqualified success and now it was time for seasonal leave and maintenance.

As far as the *Ark Royal* was concerned 'Outback 88' had been a 'one-off' and when she left Portsmouth for the first time in 1989, on Tuesday 7 February, it was for a more routine shakedown cruise in home waters. Ten days later she returned to Portsmouth for conversion to an LPH (Landing Platform Helicopter), or commando carrier role for 'Exercise Cold Winter' which, as its name suggests, was held in the northern hemisphere off Norway. In readiness for the exercise she embarked the helicopters of 845 and 846 Squadrons, together with the Royal Marines of 42 and 45 Commando and a detachment of Dutch marines, who were landed in the Tromso area of Norway, after which the *Ark* returned to Portsmouth. For her next exercise, 'Springtrain', in April, the carrier again embarked the Sea Harriers of 801 Squadron, and on conclusion of these manoeuvres on 21 April she put into Gibraltar, returning to Portsmouth six days later.

During her three-day stay in her home base there was a change of command, with Captain J. P. Brigstocke RN taking over from Captain Harris. Captain Brigstocke had joined the Royal Navy as a cadet at Britannia Royal Naval College, Dartmouth, and had specialized in gunnery. He had commanded HM Ships *Upton, Bacchante* and *York,* as Captain (D) 3rd Destroyer Squadron. However, he had very little time to settle in before, on Monday 1 May 1989, the *Ark Royal* sailed for 'Exercise Minibus' and a visit from Admiral of the Fleet HRH The Duke of Edinburgh. Next came 'Exercise Square Nut' in company with Dutch and Belgian forces, which ended with a call at Hamburg. Once again the welcome was overshadowed by an anti-nuclear protest and after leaving the Elbe, Flag Officer Third Flotilla, Vice-Admiral A. Grose, hoisted his flag in the carrier for exercises with the RAF off Scotland's east coast. During the summer of 1989 it seemed to the ship's company that one exercise followed another without a break, starting with 'Vendetta' in late May and ending with 'Sharp Shear' in mid-September. There were also Staff College Sea Days and JMC operations as well as Navy Days at Rosyth in June, and at one stage in July the carrier operated Sea Harriers of the Spanish Navy. On 4 October, when she was in Lyme Bay carrying out flying operations for NATO officials, a Sea Harrier struck one of the ship's radar aerials and crashed, but fortunately the pilot ejected safely. The ship paid a visit to Brest and in mid-October she was the subject of unwelcome publicity in Lisbon when some members of the ship's company unwittingly became involved in rioting by visiting US Navy personnel, which resulted in an early return to Portsmouth. After a 'Families Day' on Friday 20 October and the cancellation of a scheduled exercise, the carrier began an assisted maintenance period in Portsmouth Dockyard on 23 October.

It was in the third week of January 1990 that the *Ark Royal* emerged from Portsmouth Dockyard once more and sailed for a shakedown cruise, followed by a short break and then 17 days of sea training, with a visit to

The *Ark Royal* on exercises with HMS *Norfolk* and other units.

Copenhagen. The first two weeks of March saw her carrying out her aviation work-up and her Operational Readiness Inspection, in severe weather, which caused some structural damage and washed a deck tractor overboard. On 17 March she returned to Portsmouth to prepare for a Western Atlantic deployment, 'WESTLANT 90', during which she would lead a task group consisting of the destroyer *Glasgow,* the frigates *Brave* and *Cumberland* and the RFAs *Fort Grange* and *Olna.* For the *Ark* and the two frigates the deployment started on Wednesday 18 April, when they sailed for the anti-submarine exercise 'Jolly Roger' and on 1 May they joined manoeuvres with the US and French naval units, during which Sea Harriers operated from the FS *Foch.* During the first week of May the *Glasgow* joined the group and Admiral Hill-Norton hoisted his flag in the *Ark Royal* for a four-day visit to New York starting on Wednesday 9 May. After leaving the 'Big Apple' she sailed south with the *Olna* for a maintenance period at Mayport, Florida, which lasted until the end of May. Then on Wednesday 30 May she left the ever-popular Florida

base to rendezvous with the task group for 'Exercise Marcot' in the Atlantic between Bermuda and Halifax, Novia Scotia, commanded by a Canadian force. It was rounded off on 15 June by a visit to fogbound Halifax where, once again, anti-nuclear demonstrators tried to disrupt her arrival, but the ship's company still enjoyed a warm welcome from the local people. After Halifax the ship moved on to Boston for a few days and during the short passage south-west the port-outer gas turbine had to be changed as the bearings were showing signs of wear. Upon her departure from Boston the *Ark* set course eastward for the transatlantic passage back to the UK and on Wednesday 4 July, after an eight-day voyage, she arrived at Portsmouth to begin an assisted maintenance period.

During the refit the first modifications to prepare the ship for female personnel were implemented, with the accommodation for both officers and ratings being increased. Some essential maintenance was also undertaken in the machinery spaces, including repairs to the vessel's auxiliary boilers. It was Tuesday 21 August when she put to sea again

The *Ark Royal* closing to fuel from RFA *Appleleaf* during 'JMC' exercises off the north coast of Scotland.

(G. Mortimore/Action Photos)

for two days of trials, after which she was back alongside at Portsmouth to 'star' in a local television programme and to participate in Navy Days at the port. Work started again in earnest when, in early September, she took part in the NATO exercise 'Teamwork 90', which, like many of the organization's exercises, was held in the Norwegian Sea and was designed to show that the participating nations were able to conduct naval operations in the area against a hostile shore. However, by the summer of 1990 the threat from Eastern Europe and the Warsaw Pact was decreasing as the countries which had been dominated by the Soviet Union since 1945 began to shake off their Communist Governments, with even the Russians gradually freeing themselves from the political system which had dominated them for over 70 years and had brought them to the brink of economic ruin. But in its place a new danger had emerged, this time in the volatile politics of the Middle East where Saddam Hussein, the brutal and ruthless leader of Iraq, had carried out a threat which had been voiced by his country's dictators since 1961, when his army invaded the small, oil-rich state of Kuwait on 2 August 1990. The immediate reaction to

the brutal invasion was a worldwide freezing of Kuwaiti assets and the formation of an international coalition under the auspices of the United Nations, following which the armed forces of 30 nations, led by the United States, prepared to re-establish the independence of Kuwait – by force if necessary. The Iraqi claim to Kuwait was based on the fact that, under the old Ottoman Empire, it had been a province of Basrah – which was indisputedly Iraqi territory, but with Saddam Hussein threatening the security and stability of the whole area, and oil supplies to the West, this cut no ice with the Western leaders. With many US forces being diverted to the Persian Gulf, the *Ark Royal* and *Invincible* assumed a major role in 'Exercise Teamwork 90', which was followed by a visit to Oslo before returning to Portsmouth on Wednesday 26 September.

With the rapid expansion of the British complement to the international force assembling in Saudi Arabia, the *Ark Royal* was kept at 30 days' notice for a deployment to the Persian Gulf. When she left Portsmouth on 15 October for Gibraltar she had a full Air Group embarked, and flying exercises and training were carried out en route to the

The carrier leaves Portsmouth with Sea Kings and Harriers on deck.   *(W. Sartori)*

The *Ark* at Malta in June 1994, carrying out maintenance. Unlike her two predecessors she is able to berth alongside. *(M. Cassar)*

The *Ark* operating with the Italian aircraft carrier *Giuseppe Garibaldi* and other units in June 1994.

(Fleet Air Arm Museum)

colony, where she arrived on Friday 19 October. Four days later there was another change of command when Captain N. E. Rankin RN took over from Captain Brigstocke. Captain Rankin had joined the Royal Navy in 1958, and five years later he was awarded his pilot's wings. He had commanded HMS *Bacchante* and had served as Commander (Air) in HMS *Invincible.* He had also, as Captain of the 8th Frigate Squadron, commanded HMS *Andromeda.*

In the short term it was decided that an aircraft carrier was not required in the Persian Gulf, and so on Thursday 25 October the *Ark Royal* left Gibraltar to return to Portsmouth. During November 1990, as the build-up of coalition forces in Saudi Arabia continued, and the diplomatic pressure on Iraq was intensified, the *Ark* remained in home waters but on notice to sail east if required. In early November she carried out trials in the Western Approaches with the new FRS2 Sea Harrier, while the embarked Air Group also exercised for a possible deployment to the Persian Gulf. During Christmas 1990 the coalition planned for the liberation of Kuwait in the first week of the new year and at the start of January 1991 scheduled exercises for that month were cancelled,

whereupon the *Ark Royal* sailed for the Mediterranean on 10 January 1991 as the flagship of Task Group 323.2 which also included the destroyer *Sheffield,* the frigate *Charybdis* and the RFAs *Olmeda* and *Regent.* Three days later the group rendezvoused with the destroyers *Manchester* and *Exeter* to carry out weapons training, and the *Manchester* joined the *Ark's* group for the passage east. When they were off Gibraltar Rear-Admiral Brigstocke arrived to hoist his flag in his former command, and the force continued its way eastwards. On Thursday 17 January 'Operation Desert Storm' was launched by the coalition forces in Saudi Arabia and the task group went to defence watches. On 22 January the force arrived off Cyprus but only the *Manchester* sailed south through the Suez Canal; the *Ark Royal* and the remainder of the group had the onerous and frustrating task of maintaining surveillance on the coaltion's lines of communication in the Eastern Mediterranean, operating closely with the US Sixth Fleet's USS *Virginia, Philippine Sea* and *Spruance.*

Fortunately, hostilities were confined to the northern sector of the Persian Gulf, with the land campaign taking place in Kuwait and Iraq itself. During the days that followed, the *Ark* and her group operated with the American ships as well as units from the Greek and German Navies, and by the end of February defence watches had been stood down. On 1 March, after 51 days at sea, the carrier navigated the Strait of Messina and berthed at Naples for a well-earned break. With the international tension having eased somewhat, the Italian visit was followed by a five-day call at Athens and, whilst on passage back to Portsmouth, the *Ark* put into Palma, Majorca, for a week. Finally, in the second week of April, the carrier arrived back in her home port for leave and to undergo an assisted maintenance period.

During the summer of 1991 the *Ark Royal* took part in training exercises and a NATO exercise in the North Sea and the Atlantic. She was one of the star attractions at Plymouth's Navy Days, and in September she participated in a WESTLANT deployment with the destroyer *Gloucester* and the frigate *London,* during which she visited Bermuda, Port Everglades and Mayport. Unfortunately, during the voyage between the latter two ports there was an outbreak of salmonella food poisoning on board which affected 200 members of the ship's company. After leaving Mayport on 22 October she set course for Gibraltar, where she arrived on 4 November to embark a television camera team who were there to record a Frankie Howerd show. From Gibraltar the carrier set course for the UK and embarked a giant Chinook helicopter for trials which, during its time on board, made 400 deck landings. It was Monday 18 November when the *Ark Royal* finally arrived home, and next day she was visited by her royal sponsor, Her Majesty Queen Elizabeth The Queen Mother, to celebrate the 10th anniversary of the ship's launching. During her time on board the royal visitor met officers and men of the ship's company and their families. Five days later there was another landmark in the ship's career when the first draft of 73 Wrens embarked and, despite the organized chaos of the refit and the fact that the ship was about to go into dry dock, they appeared to settle in well. It was Wednesday 12 February 1992 when the carrier sailed for her post-refit trials, and just over two weeks later, on Friday 28 February, the Chief Commandant of the WRNS, the Princess Royal, paid a visit to the ship to meet the Wrens and learn how they were integrating into the ship's company.

After completing repairs to the main gearbox the *Ark Royal* sailed again on Wednesday 4 March for her work-up, which kept her at sea for ten days. On Monday 20 April there was a serious accident during the flying operations of the aviation work-up. The Sea Harriers were carrying out bombing practice with small 28lb bombs onto a splash target which was being towed astern, when one of the bombs landed on the flight deck and exploded. The detonation penetrated into 2J2 mess deck immediately below where five men were injured, one of them suffering serious burns and stomach injuries. As the casualties were being attended to by the PMO and his staff, another member of the ship's company was taken ill with acute appendicitis, which also necessitated an emergency operation. Next day the casualties from the bomb explosion were evacuated to RNH Haslar at Gosport and, having worked through the Easter weekend, the ship headed north for a five-day visit to Greenock. Following this she returned to Portsmouth where the damage to the flight deck and 2J2 mess was repaired, and other essential maintenance was carried out. June saw the ship flying the flag of the C-in-C Fleet while she carried out a 'Shop Window' display off the Isle of Wight, which she went on to repeat in the Bristol Channel, off Liverpool, the Firth of Forth, Newcastle upon Tyne and Hull, with the aim of giving the public an opportunity to meet the Navy. After a visit to Copenhagen later that month the ship returned to Portsmouth, and at the end of the month she sailed south to Gibraltar where Captain J. J. Blackham RN took over command from Captain Rankin, with his first duty being to bring the carrier back to Portsmouth. During the summer she received a visit from Marshal Grachev, the Russian Federation's Defence Minister, indicating the change in the political situation in Europe following the end of the Cold War.

On Wednesday 2 September the *Ark Royal* sailed west for what was to be her final WESTLANT deployment. Accompanying her was the destroyer *Exeter,* the submarine *Triumph* and two RFAs, and during her time in US waters she exercised with the USS *John F. Kennedy,* visited Norfolk, Virginia, Mayport, Florida, and Nassau in the Bahamas. On her return to Portsmouth on Friday 6 November preparations were put in hand for the final and most important event of the year. This was a dinner hosted on board by the Admiralty Board on Monday 16 November to commemorate the 40th Anniversary of Her Majesty The Queen's accession to the throne. The First Sea Lord, Admiral Sir Julian Oswold, presided, with the Queen and other members of the Royal Family being the guests of honour, and all available commanding officers of HM Ships attending. The end of the year saw her annual assisted maintenance period, and 1993 would bring duties for the *Ark Royal* in a different part of the world.

Following the end of the First World War and the complete collapse of Habsburg power, it was possible to construct a sizeable Serbo-Croat-Slovene state, Yugoslavia, but right from the start this new country was torn by rival nationalistic ambitions of the Serbs, Croats and Slovenes. After the trauma of German occupation in the Second World War a Croatian communist, Josip Broz Tito, who had led a partisan resistance movement against the occupying Germans, became the country's leader and he took a very independent line from Moscow, organizing a federal constitution which recognized the different nationalities within the country. When he died in May

HMS *Ark Royal* assumes responsibility from HMS *Invincible* for the Adriatic Patrol in February 1994.

(Fleet Air Arm Museum)

1980 he was succeeded by a collective leadership of representatives from the different nationalities. This coalition lasted until December 1988 and upon its collapse the dominant Serbians began to exert their military grip on the other areas of the country which led, in mid-1991, to Croatia and Slovenia declaring their independence from Yugoslavia; it was clear that the long-feared disintegration of the country was imminent and civil war loomed. In January 1992 the inevitable hostilities became even more intense and bitter when Bosnian Serbs declared a republic and soon afterwards the world learned of atrocities on a scale which had not been seen in Europe since 1945, as the different nationalities slaughtered civilians and internees, mainly in Serb-run prison camps in Bosnia. That same month a UN-sponsored ceasefire came into effect and a few weeks later a UN peacekeeping force was placed in disputed lands occupied by Serbs. Then in early 1993 it was decided to send a naval task group into the Adriatic to

support British troops who were deployed to protect the UN aid workers, and the *Ark Royal* was assigned to lead Task Group 612.02, which also included the frigates *Coventry* and *Brilliant* and the RFAs *Olwen* and *Argus*. In readiness for this role the carrier embarked eight Sea Harriers, three AEW Sea Kings and eight commando carrying Sea Kings. On Thursday 14 January 1993 she sailed for a short work-up, and 13 days later she arrived in the Adriatic and took up position within five hours' sailing time of the Croatian port of Split. Soon after the *Ark's* arrival in the area the USA and France deployed their own carrier task groups, with the USS *John F. Kennedy* and the FS *Clemenceau* leading them, and the three forces co-operated closely over the following weeks as tensions ebbed and flowed round the gunlines in what was formerly a popular holiday destination for Britons, among others.

In late February, with tension having eased somewhat, the *Ark Royal* called at Trieste, after which she exercised with the Italian Navy and paid a visit to Piraeus. With the carrier full to overflowing with personnel again, in March 279 members of the ship's company were flown home for a period of leave. On 13 April the *Ark* was able to visit Naples for nine days where there was another change of command and Captain T. W. Loughran RN relieved Captain Blackham and in doing so assumed responsibility for the naval group. Captain Loughran was bringing to bear his earlier experience in the carriers *Centaur* and *Victorious* as well as his rotary-wing flying career which had included 824 Squadron, the first Sea King squadron embarked in the fourth *Ark Royal*. In addition to command of the Exocet Leander-class frigate HMS *Phoebe* and Executive Officer of HM Ships *Intrepid* and *Bristol,* he had commanded the 'stretched' Type 42 destroyer HMS *Gloucester* and her attendant Task Groups on two deployments of the Armilla Patrol in the Persian Gulf, spanning the most intense period of the tanker war.

Soon after the *Ark Royal* left Naples on 22 April, tension heightened in the Bosnian town of Srebrenica when Canadian troops interposed themselves between the warring factions in the area, and TG 612.02 were put at 24 hours' notice for intervention, with the *Ark Royal* being declared capable of using laser-guided bombs. A few days later the United Nations tightened the sanctions in force against Serbia and Montenegro, which increased the risk of retaliation from the former Yugoslav Navy, and in May, TG 612.02 were authorized to support the naval forces which were enforcing the blockade. On 18 May Rear-Admiral Brigstocke hoisted his flag in the *Ark Royal* and six days later, on Monday 24 May, the *Ark* arrived in Corfu for a four-day visit. During the stay Captain Loughran laid a wreath at the grave of 44 Royal Navy personnel who were killed in the largely forgotten 'Corfu Incident' of 22 October 1946, when the destroyers HMS *Saumarez* and HMS *Volage,* which were making a goodwill visit to Corfu, were severely damaged by mines which had been deliberately placed in the Corfu Channel by the Albanian Government. Upon her departure from Corfu the *Ark* returned to her station in the Adriatic, before docking in Malta's Grand Harbour on Tuesday 8 June for a nine-day self-maintenance period. It was the first visit to Valletta by a British aircraft carrier since the visit of the previous *Ark Royal* in November 1978, and she was opened to an enthusiastic public from 11am to 5pm on Saturday 12 and Sunday 13 June, with a notice at the foot of the gangway announcing, 'We would like to be open longer but we regret that we have important maintenance work going on that prevents us from doing so.' The Royal Navy was as popular as ever on the George Cross island.

On Thursday 17 June the *Ark Royal* left Malta to a rousing send-off from the people of Valletta in a demonstration of the mutual affection between Malta and the Royal Navy. Next day she was back on station and cross-operating with the Italian aircraft carrier *Giuseppe Garibaldi,* when she received visits from the Italian Defence Minister and senior naval officers. The first day of July saw the *Ark* at anchor in Suda Bay, Crete, for a five-day break, and two days after returning to her station in the Adriatic the Ministry of Defence announced that the *Ark Royal's* Sea Harriers would be made available to NATO forces to carry out air strikes in Bosnia should they be required, and 801 Squadron undertook the necessary training in Italy. On 12 July Admiral Brigstocke was relieved by Rear-Admiral M. P. Gretton MA, a former commanding officer of HMS *Invincible.* The *Ark Royal's* last visit of the deployment was at the end of July when she called at Palermo, then a few days later she handed over to the *Invincible,* to which Admiral Gretton transferred his flag. Over the next few days the serviceable aircraft were flown off from the *Ark* and on 3 August the carrier arrived back in Portsmouth, having been away for over six months.

Over the next three months the *Ark Royal* underwent base assisted maintenance, and it was November 1993 before she put to sea again for trials and work-up, during which she operated with French naval units, and carried out further trials with two Harrier FRS2s. Christmas was spent alongside in Portsmouth, but in the early weeks of 1994 it was clear that she would have to undertake another deployment to the Adriatic, and on Friday 28 January 1994 she left Portsmouth, again at the head of Task Group 612.02, for exercises and the Mediterranean. Seven days after leaving the Solent she arrived at Gibraltar where, after a few days alongside, she rendezvoused with the *Invincible* and assumed responsibility for the Adriatic deployment, code-named 'Operation Hamden', from her. The situation in the former republic of Yugoslavia had changed little and Serb separatists had now mounted an armed siege of the ancient Ottoman city of Sarajevo; soon after the *Ark* left Gibraltar artillery fire caused heavy loss of life in Sarajevo, which renewed and reinforced calls for NATO air strikes against the offenders. The *Ark Royal* took up her station on 13 February and consequently air operations were flown to prevent any side from using their air power in the war. The Harriers also made a vital contribution to NATO's eyes over the war-wracked region of the Balkans as they flew photo-reconnaissance missions over the area. Throughout the Sarajevo crisis the Harriers of 801 Squadron flew up to 14 sorties a day and provided invaluable information to NATO and the UN on the position and movement of tanks and guns in the exclusion zone around the beleaguered city. On Tuesday 22 February, Swedish soldiers came under mortar attack while escorting a convoy between Tuzla and Sarajevo and as a result two Sea Harriers which were in the area were diverted from a reconnaissance mission to investigate the incident. They quickly identified the convoy which was moving towards Tuzla, but they were unable to identify the aggressors. As the two aircraft

A Sea Harrier on patrol over a snowbound city of Sarajevo. The former Olympic Stadium, which was used for the 1984 Winter Games, can be clearly seen.
(Rear-Admiral T. W. Loughran)

returned to refuel, other Harriers were launched to keep an eye on the situation and eventually the convoy reached its destination. Captain Loughran remarked of the incident, 'While air strikes themselves were not required, the noise of the jets alone reminded those on the ground of the resolve of NATO and the UN to bring about a ceasefire.' The crisis in Bosnia led to the cancellation of planned visits to Naples and Toulon, but on 31 March the carrier did go to Piraeus where she stayed for 11 days to carry out maintenance. However, during the stay a caller claiming to represent a left-wing terrorist group, 'November 17', rang a local radio station claiming that it was responsible for a failed attack on the carrier. A subsequent police search found two home-made rocket launchers loaded with 3.5-inch rockets close to where the carrier was moored, and it seemed that rain and damp weather had prevented their detonation. Fortunately, it was an undamaged *Ark Royal* which left the Greek port on Monday 11 April, to return to the Adriatic, where more drama was to follow.

Whilst the *Ark Royal* was at Piraeus, Serb forces in Bosnia had been attacking the town of Gorazde, despite threats of a NATO air strike, and the UN Commander had subsequently ordered strikes to go ahead. These were initiated by F-18 fighters of the USAF and by Saturday 16 April the helicopters of 845 Squadron were evacuating badly wounded civilians from the area. During this mission they were being covered by Sea Harriers of 801 Squadron, two of which, flown by Lt N. Richardson and Lt O. Phillips, were on patrol when they were directed to the besieged town to clear a tank which had been firing into the area close to the UN forces. In order to avoid collateral damage and to positively identify the target it was necessary to fly three passes over the target area and on the first pass they were engaged by an SA7 missile which they were able to avoid. Because of the desperate situation which the UN troops were in they heroically pressed ahead with their attack, and the aircraft piloted by Lt Richardson was then hit by a misssile, but fortunately he managed to eject safely, suffering only cuts and bruises. After being looked after by UN personnel he was returned to the ship. In the words of Commander John Jacob on board the *Ark Royal,* 'The pilots of both aircraft displayed commendable courage and professionalism in their continued attempts to carry out their mission, despite having come so close to being shot down on the first attempt.'

Following this period of high tension and activity the carrier took another break at Corfu in May and participated in a major NATO exercise 'Dynamic Impact 94' in the Western Mediterranean, the largest exercise the organization had carried out since the end of the Cold War, and this was followed by a popular ten-day visit to Palma. In Geneva on 10 June, the three sides involved in the Bosnian conflict accepted a cessation of hostilities, and before she finally returned home the carrier was able to visit Istanbul, Crete and Malta. At last, after seven months in the Mediterranean, on Friday 2 September 1994 the *Ark Royal* returned to Portsmouth and a rapturous welcome from relations, friends and well-wishers.

Following her return from the Adriatic the carrier hosted a 'Families Day' at sea off the Isle of Wight, during which three brightly painted experimental Buccaneers from Boscombe Down flew over the ship, providing a unique display for the guests who crowded onto the flight deck. Then, on Wednesday 21 September, the *Ark* made a visit to her birthplace at Newcastle upon Tyne, from where her ship's company visited her affiliated city of Leeds. Whilst she was alongside, a number of *Ark Royal* veterans were entertained on board and, headed by the Band of the Royal Marines, her ship's company exercised their privilege of the Freedom of the City of Leeds and marched through the streets with bayonets fixed. It was a fitting end to the ship's operational service for the time being for, upon her return to Portsmouth, she paid off for a long refit before being placed into reserve. Today the carrier lies at Portsmouth awaiting the refit that will take the Fleet Air Arm, and the most famous name in the Royal Navy and that special '*Ark Royal* Spirit', which she has done so much to enhance, into the 21st century.

The fifth *Ark Royal's* commanding officers at a reunion dinner hosted by Captain Loughran. They are, left to right: Vice-Admiral Blackham, Vice-Admiral Weatherall, Captain Loughran, Rear-Admiral Rankin, Rear-Admiral Harris and Admiral Brigstocke.
(Rear-Admiral T. W. Loughran)

Commanding Officers:

Captain J. L. Weatherall RN	1985-1987
Captain M. G. T. Harris RN	1987-1989
Captain J. R. Brigstocke RN	1989-1990
Captain N. E. Rankin RN	1990-1992
Captain J. J. Blackham RN	1992-1993
Captain T. W. Loughran RN	1993-1994

Principal Particulars:

Length Overall:	677ft 9in
Beam:	104ft 6in
Draught:	29ft
Main Propulsion Machinery:	Twin shaft. Four Rolls-Royce TMB3 Olympus gas turbines. 112,000 SHP: 28 knots.
Armament:	Single Sea Dart SAM Missile launcher Three 20mm Vulcan Phalanx weapons systems

HMS *Ark Royal*
Battle Honours

Armada 1588	Spartivento 1940
Cadiz 1596	Mediterranean 1940-41
Dardanelles 1915	*Bismarck* 1941
Norway 1940	Malta Convoys 1941

Appendix Two:

The First Two *Ark Royals*

The first *Ark Royal* was ordered by Sir Walter Raleigh and was built at Deptford on the River Thames. She was launched on 12 June 1586, by which time she had been sold to the Crown. Originally it had been intended that she be named *Ark Raleigh,* but after the sale this was changed to *Ark Royal.* She had an overall length of 100 feet, a beam of 37 feet and she was rated at 692 tons. She was armed with 38 brass muzzle loading guns, eight short-barrelled heavy shotted demi-cannon, 12 long-barrelled 18-pdr culverins and 12, 9-pdr demi-culverins which, in those days, made her a powerful ship. Admiral Lord Howard of Effingham flew his flag in the *Ark Royal,* when he led the entire fleet against the Spanish Armada in 1588, and he also used her in 1596 when he successfully attacked and occupied Cadiz. In 1608 she was completely refitted and rebuilt and in 1625 she took part in the ill-fated expedition against Cadiz. In 1636 the old ship ran aground in the River Thames and was damaged beyond repair, thus ending her career very close to where she had started it 50 years before.

It was 277 years later that the name *Ark Royal* was used again, and this time it was given to a 7,400-ton collier which was purchased by the Admiralty in 1913 whilst it was on the stocks. This rather incongruous looking warship was commissioned on 9 December 1914 as a seaplane carrier and she served in the Mediterranean, where she supported operations in the Dardanelles and the withdrawal of Allied forces from Gallipoli. After the war she remained in the Mediterranean, but returned home in 1923. After a period in reserve during the 1920s, she then became a catapult trials ship but, in 1934, she was renamed *Pegasus* in order to make the name *Ark Royal* available for the Royal Navy's magnificent new aircraft carrier which had been ordered from Cammell Laird's at Birkenhead. After serving through the Second World War she was sold in 1946 for conversion to a merchant ship, when she was renamed *Anita I.* However, the conversion was never completed and after being sold to a succession of owners she was broken up in 1950.

Acknowledgements:

My thanks to: Rear-Admiral Terry Loughran CB, the last operational commanding officer of the present *Ark Royal,* for kindly writing the foreword to this book: Mr Brian Conroy for his watercolour paintings used on the dust jacket: Mr John S. Morris for his pen and ink sketches.

I must also thank the following for their help and, in many cases, for the loan of very valuable photographs:-
Jim Allaway, Editor, *Navy News*: C. L. Asher, Dunfermline, Fife: E. Baker, Rochester, Kent: Roger Beacham, Cheltenham Reference Library: Michael Bennett, Plymouth, Devon: Ian Carter, Department of Photographs, Imperial War Museum, London: Michael Cassar, Valletta, Malta: Michael Elliott, Bolsover, Derbyshire: Lee Fleming, Hayes, Middlesex: F. George, Lowestoft, Suffolk: Peter Harris, Wath-upon-Dearne, Sth Yorkshire: Charles Heath, Waterlooville, Hampshire: Andy Hernandez, Miami, Florida, USA: Vic Hocking, Solihull, West Midlands: Vic Jefferey, Royal Australian Navy Public Affairs, Rockingham, Western Australia: Robert Lakey, Darwen, Lancashire: Michael Lennon, Waterlooville, Hampshire: Steven Mathis, Birmingham: Charles Morgan, Gosport, Hampshire: George Mortimore, Action Photos, Isle of Wight: James Newman, Verwood, Dorset: Anthony J. Perrett, Gosport, Hampshire: Walter Sartori, Portsmouth, Hampshire: Robert Shopland, *Ships Monthly,* Burton-on-Trent, Staffs: Jerry Shore and Debbie Stockford, Fleet Air Arm Museum, RNAS Yeovilton, Ilchester, Somerset: Ron Skinner, Dursley, Gloucestershire: Don Smith, Selby, Nth Yorkshire: Kenneth Smith, Angus, Scotland: Alan Sparrow, Billingham, Cleveland: Frank S. Stockton, Wrexham: Adrian Vicary, Maritime Photo Library, Cromer, Norfolk: Mrs M. D. Walden, Gloucester: Vice-Admiral D. B. H. Wildish CB, Petersfield, Hampshire: Finally to my wife Freda and my two daughters Caroline and Louise for their invaluable help.

Also In The Series

HMS *Centaur* 1943-1972   £16.95
(Plus £2.00 p&p in UK/EU or £4.00 airmail to all other countries)

HMS *Victorious* 1937-1969   £21
(Plus £2.00 p&p in UK/EU or £4.00 airmail to all other countries)

Other Titles From FAN PUBLICATIONS
SS *Canberra* 1957-1997   £21
(Plus £2.00 p&p in UK/EU or £4.00 airmail to all other countries)

For current list write to:
FAN PUBLICATIONS
17 Wymans Lane
Cheltenham, Glos GL51 9QA
England
Tel/Fax: 01242 580290